T5-ASQ-673

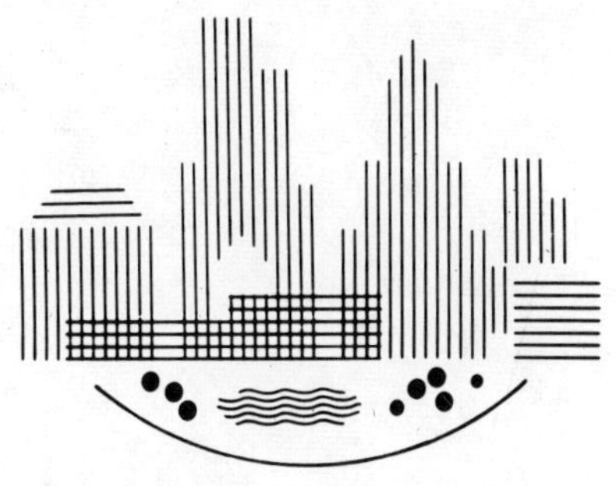

THE RISE OF URBAN AMERICA

THE CHILD IN THE CITY

Sophonisba P. Breckinridge, editor

ARNO PRESS
&
The New York Times
NEW YORK · 1970

Reprint Edition 1970 by Arno Press Inc.

Reprinted from a copy in The University of Illinois Library

LC# 77-112541
ISBN 0-405-02437-1

The Rise of Urban America
ISBN for complete set 0-405-02430-4

Manufactured in the United States of America

The Child in the City

A Series of Papers Presented at the Conferences
Held During The Chicago Child
Welfare Exhibit

Published by
The Department of Social Investigation
Chicago School of Civics and Philanthropy
1912

Elizabeth McCormick

1892-1905

EDITOR'S PREFACE

The papers presented in this volume were read at the conferences held during the Chicago Child Welfare Exhibit, May 11-25, 1911. These conferences varied in form and purpose. Some of them were organized in order that the needs of the less fortunate groups of city children might be presented in popular form by those who had given years of expert service in behalf of neglected childhood. Opportunity was always given for questioning, but the purpose of these meetings was to inform and instruct, or, perhaps, to persuade and arouse, the mothers, the voters, the men and the women with leisure and talents for service, and the other interested persons who attended the sessions.

The other meetings were genuine conferences among those who were already actively engaged in some form of child-caring work and who assembled to discuss among themselves some of the problems of the task to which their hands were set. These conferences were often specialized and technical, and, although the public was admitted, it was understood that the discussions were not only by experts but primarily for experts.

Because of these differences in purpose, there will appear in the following papers marked differences in form and in method of presentation. It is believed, however, that their common topic, the unfulfilled demands of childhood today, sufficiently unifies them to allow of their being grouped in a single volume; and they are also believed to be sufficiently serious and careful in preparation and statement to justify presenting them in this permanent form. It is in fact hoped that they may prove to be a real contribution to the discussion of the unsatisfied claims of childhood upon the modern community. Not all the papers read at these conferences are published here. Some have been published elsewhere and some have been utilized in special cases by societies especially interested in the subject discussed. Nor has it been possible to preserve the discussions which followed the reading of these papers, many of which were valuable and constructive and had effective, definite, and concrete results.

Certain acknowledgments of obligations are permitted. To those who gave their time and strength to make this contribution to the better understandings of the needs of the city child today, all who would serve children better will give thanks. To those who made possible this great co-operative undertaking, who have permanently associated the name of a beloved child with the work in behalf of the most needy children, words of acknowledgment are superfluous. The final paper voices the hope of one whose generosity has made possible the publication of this volume. She is, however, repaid in full wherever better service is rendered "unto the least."

SOPHONISBA P. BRECKINRIDGE.

CONTENTS

PAGE

PART FOUR

SPECIAL GROUPS OF CHILDREN

PART FIVE

THE WORKING CHILD

Contents

PAGE

PART SIX

THE LAW AND THE CHILD

PART SEVEN

LIBRARIES AND MUSEUMS

ILLUSTRATIONS

INTRODUCTORY REMARKS

CYRUS H. McCORMICK

A great educator has said, "There is nothing in all the world so important as children—nothing so interesting."

If mankind is to be reformed or improved, we must begin with the child. This Exhibit has been organized to show what has already been done for children, and to demonstrate the importance and the necessity of doing much more along this line.

In my capacity of assistant to your Honorary President, I have been asked to preside at this meeting, and in so doing let me first thank Miss Addams, Mr. Kingsley, and all the committees for their devoted and enthusiastic labors which have brought this undertaking, in so short a time, to this splendid fulfillment. It is inspiring to see one thousand people giving their time and strength to the work of these committees and spreading the message of welfare to the helpless and undeveloped child.

Chicago is now to be given an opportunity to study child life in all its various phases. Here will be seen the latest steps in progressive educational efforts for children, as well as the vitally important needs of sanitation and of housing conditions to protect the child's life and health. The needs of children are being intelligently considered today as never before by parents, doctors and scientists; and this Exhibit will show that this investigation is not merely the work of the doctrinaire and the visionary, but that it is rational and practical.

The city tenement robs the child of his birthright of pure air, of pleasant and wholesome play, and of appropriate work. What advantages in return does the community afford for instructing the child as he grows up, and training him for a useful life-work? Do the laws sufficiently provide for the protection of the inherent and essential rights of childhood? The wise care of its children is one of the highest duties of the State. Those who enjoy the benefits and share the responsibilities of our cities must plan for the children, for, although they are our youngest citizens, they are potentially the most important. The city that cares most for its children will be the greatest city.

Human life is sacred because the individual lives it but once, and society has but one chance to benefit from it. We are told that three hundred thousand children die annually in this country. A large proportion of these deaths, perhaps one-half, are due, not to unavoidable conditions, but to ignorance. Physicians and philanthropists, after careful observation, agree that the prevention of infant mortality depends upon the earnest, united and continued effort of intelligent and capable men and women.

The child carries the burdens of heredity, environment, parental influence, lack of play, insufficient food; of poverty, sorrow, sin, and all the economic and social influences which have affected his parents. We shall see in this Exhibit—as perhaps we have never realized before—the sadness of child life, and if we ask ourselves the question, "What can be done about it," we shall learn that wise men and women have given us the answer and are showing us how we can meet these needs; how we can lift the burden from the backs of the little children, and receive our reward in their smiling faces.

This Child Welfare Exhibit will surely lead to definite things, and when, in future years, we can realize our hopes, and the child of the congested districts shall have better hygienic surroundings;

when the efforts of humanity shall have overcome the "White Plague"; when school life and home life shall conduce to better and more normal development of our children, then may we realize a new era for the community of "children of a larger growth." The march of progress will begin with those who bring betterment into the lives of children, and "a little child shall lead them."

OPENING OF THE EXHIBIT

JANE ADDAMS

I am sure, fellow citizens, that you will all agree with me that this is the time and place in which a woman should "keep quiet in meeting," for I fear that, try as I may to make myself heard, it will be utterly impossible to raise my voice above this cheerful din. I am therefore only going to put on record the statement that the committee responsible for presenting this Exhibit, which has been made possible through the generosity of Mrs. McCormick, ardently hopes that the opening of this great Exhibit will prove to be the opening of a new era for the children of Chicago. (Applause.)

It is most fitting that the Exhibit should have been opened with a chorus of school children; and every voice in that chorus called out, "I am the spirit of youth; with me all things are possible." And it is because all things are possible to youth, that it has seemed worth the greatest effort that Chicago could put forth, to assemble under one roof those things that will teach us how best to develop the children. May I draw your attention to the fact that the most valuable things being done for the children of Chicago at present are done by the city itself?

As you go around this Exhibit you will find the activities of philanthropic associations displayed on one side and the activities of the city on the other. You will see that the city with its schools, its libraries, its health department, its playgrounds, is taking over and absorbing into itself the manifold activities which were formerly under philanthropic management. These are gradually being recognized as civic obligations, and just as soon as the voters are ready, the philanthropists will be only too eager to hand over to the city all the rest of the things which they are now carrying on.

There is one thing to which I should especially like to draw your attention; that is that the youth of Chicago have been brought together from all parts of the world into one splendid cosmopolitan community, into one melting pot, as it were. And if I may end this speech which is not yet begun, because my voice is giving out, I would like if possible to quote those beautiful lines of Swinburne's, as appropriate to Chicago's youth. Let us imagine their young voices chanting together

"We mix from many lands,
    We march for very far;
  In hearts, and lips and hands
    Our staffs and weapons are;
    The light we walk in darkens sun and moon and
        star."

When this wondrous light, which ever surrounds the swift feet of youth, shall at last be shed over this great ugly community of ours, it will be ugly no more but transfigured into comeliness; when their faculties, free and trained, take hold of our vexed civic problems, then may we secure social order as well as beauty and find ourselves living within a new city.

WELCOMING ADDRESS: THE DAY OF THE CHILD

JULIAN W. MACK

Judge, United States Commerce Court

Two years ago, during the discussion of the great Children's Charter in the House of Commons in England, one of the members, aroused to an enthusiasm seldom witnessed in that body, said: "We want to say to the child that, if the world or the world's law has not been his friend in the past, it will be now. We say that it is the duty of this Parliament, and that this Parliament is determined to lift the child if possible and rescue him; to shut the prison door and to open the door of hope." And that represents the spirit of these meetings which are going to be an essential part of this Child Welfare Exhibit.

The day of the child has come; and it is fitting that we in Chicago particularly should celebrate it, for here in Chicago was founded under the auspices of Judge Tuthill, that court now so ably presided over by Judge Pinckney, the first juvenile court in the world. And the aim of that court has been to carry out the spirit of those words; to shut the prison door before the child shall enter, and to lift up the child so that he may never be in danger of entering it. And all of the forces that have gathered together for this celebration are aiming towards that end. We begin with the infant, and in the work of such organizations as the Infant Welfare Society we endeavor to preserve the infants of Chicago so that they may not be numbered among that tremendous percentage that die yearly in this and in all other countries. And here again the municipality and private philanthropy work hand in hand;

for nothing can be accomplished of any lasting good unless the people as a whole, the nation, the state, and the municipality, recognize their duty towards the children and earnestly and zealously endeavor to fulfil it. The babies cannot thrive unless the milk supply of the community is pure. It helps but little that private organizations secure pure milk for a few poor sick babies. All of the citizens in this community are entitled to have pure milk for their children; and it is the duty of the municipality to see to it that the supply is made pure, and is received pure in their homes; and so with the question of water and all other questions connected with the work of the health department.

And then, as the child grows older, come the problems of the school. Private philanthropy again sets the pace and the standard. The physician and the nurse, first placed in the private schools of the best class, are now recognized in all civilized communities as an absolute essential to the public-school system. We in Chicago are following in the footsteps of the leaders, although we are not following so fast as many of us would wish. When we send the child to school and by our laws make education compulsory, it is our duty to make that compulsory education real and to fit that child for his future tasks. It is our duty, and it is a public duty, to see to it that the child, compelled to go to school, compelled to study and to learn, is in a fit physical and mental condition to absorb the knowledge that is to be gained there. And when we recognize that it is our duty to the school child to see that he is properly nourished so that he can study, we realize at once that our duty goes far beyond this; that the school child is but one member of the entire family and that upon the foundation of the family our civilization is built. We must go beyond the child, into the home; and the municipality must see to it that the home is a proper home for the child; and there comes in again the work of the juvenile court. The child is entitled to a home. The dependent child is entitled to the individualized love and care that it is impossible to secure even in the best orphan asylum. The aim of the municipality must be, particularly in the case of the decent but poverty-stricken widow, not to take her children away from her, not to wreck the home, which is the foundation of our civilization, but to keep mother and child together for the good of the child and for the salvation of many a young mother. Private philanthropy is leading the way along these lines, and public organizations must follow. This is real conservation. Let us do the thing that presents itself as our duty. If we take a child away from the mother, we willingly pay an asylum to care for him; the public funds pay for his support. Why should not the public funds pay it to the mother herself and keep the family together?

But mere suport, mere life, mere education, is not all that the child needs. He needs recreation and pleasure and happiness and joy, and the opportunity to satisfy these natural cravings. And here again it is for the community for its own sake, in its own self-defense, in rearing the future citizens of the country, to see to it that they have the opportunity to which every child is entitled.

We in Chicago have nothing in all our history of which we can be more justly proud than the great system of small parks and recreation centers, in which we lead the world. We have recognized that it is the duty of the public not to force the children to become delinquents and criminals. What can the boys do if they have no place for play but the streets? If they play in the streets to the torment of the neighbors and the torture of the policemen, many are sure to come into conflict with the law and to get into the courts. And how are we going to keep them out? Grand as is the work of the juvenile court, finer still is the work of the people that saves the children from coming into any court. The public recreation centers, supervised play, is doing this. But we are not doing all that we should do. We are providing in a measure for the younger children; we are providing in a measure for the older children; but there are some terrible problems still unsolved that confront a great city like Chicago. There is the problem of the working-girls, toiling all day long, some in the sweat shops, some in the stores, some in the factories, coming home at night many of them into those slums that we still tolerate in this civilized community to our everlasting shame and degradation, coming home into those dark corners, but, like your daughters, filled with that never-to-be-stilled cry for happiness. Where are they going to get happiness? How are they going to satisfy their demand for innocent, decent recreation? If they live near some of the settlements, if they live near some of the small parks, if they have been drawn into contact with the churches, which today more than ever in their history are recognizing their social duties, many of them will be saved. But if they do not get into contact with these forces, if they are driven into the dance halls connected with the saloons, they go to their downfall night after night.

And what is the help? It is not by destroying the dance halls, and then being satisfied with your work. Destructive help is but half help. Constructive help is the real thing. Destroy the evil, but do not destroy the half good, until you are ready to substitute in its place the real good. Give us in place of the saloon dance hall, what the Juvenile Protective League has been demanding—municipal recreation halls under proper supervision, where the young people of the city can find innocent pleasures; and they will not go to their downfall. For theirs is not a cry of lust; it is the cry for happiness that leads so many girls astray. And then give us education, education along the lines in which we are going to have conferences during the next week, education to guard the innocent children from the dangers besetting them on all sides.

I can only conclude by saying that if we realize in these great gatherings all that we hope for, we shall surely speed the day when all Chicago, when all America can cry out with the poet: "God's in His heaven, all's right with the world."

PART ONE

PERSONAL SERVICE

"God's possible is known through this world's loving"

BODY AND SOUL IN WORK FOR CHILDREN

RICHARD C. CABOT, M. D.

Massachusetts General Hospital and Harvard Medical School

In speaking on this subject in a city where I know nothing of the local conditions, it seems to me inevitable that I should deal with what are sometimes called "glittering generalities." What the audience thinks of as glittering generalities, however, the speaker usually thinks of as fundamental principles. And it is of one of these fundamental principles that I mean to try to speak this morning; and so far as I can give it a name, I shall speak of it as the unity of the body and the soul of social work for children.

Among theoretic discussions and philosophic problems, there are few, it seems to me, more nearly settled than the old problem between the materialists and spiritualists. There are today, I believe, very few theoretic materialists or spiritualists. But there are a great many practical materialists, a great many men and women who try to nourish the souls of human beings without reference to their bodies and some who try to nourish the souls of their philanthropic undertakings without reference to what I should call the bodies of those undertakings. But it seems to me that any closehand knowledge of work such as you are all undertaking cuts across this whole distinction of body and soul.

When a man sings, does he sing with his body or with his soul? If he sings so that you or I care to listen to him for a minute, he sings with both all the time. There are, of course, people who sing only with their bodies, "without expression" as we say, and with exclusive attention to technique and vocalization. There are also those who think that if you have an idea you are ready at once to speak, without any attention to the clothing of that idea, its body, the technique of its presentation. But it is clear beyond dispute that if a person is to speak or sing we want him to do it with his body and his soul inseparably combined. The more perfectly combined they are, the more perfectly he does his work.

When a man paints, does he paint with his body and his hand, or with his brain and his soul? You remember the answer of one of the great painters of the Renaissance when asked, "How do you mix your colors?" "With brains," he said; and he meant the things that I am trying to say, that he painted with an inseparable union of body and soul.

Now I see in most communities that I have anything to do with, examples of disaster, of failure of one kind and another, due to the attempt to separate the body from the soul of social work in one or another direction. I see people, for example, going on the principle that man can live not precisely by bread alone, but by eggs and milk alone, in the treatment of tuberculosis; and not succeeding even in curing his body because they have neglected his soul, because they have allowed him to become either so fearfully bored that he does not care to get well, or so blissfully lazy that he never will work again. That is an example of what happens when we assume that man lives not quite but nearly by bread alone.

There are many other examples that I shall come to in detail in the body of my address. Here I shall speak of just one or two points, one or two institutions that exemplify the opposite error—the more or less disastrous attempt to present soul without body. The Christian church in its great day never made this fatal separation of soul and body. It ministered to the bodies of men as well as to their souls. It kept the temporal activities abreast of the spiritual. I think the greatest accusation against the Protestant church today is that it is attempting to present the soul of its idea without the body. The Protestant church is today a pathetic soul seeking a body and trying to find it in various "institutional" departments, with various degrees of success. On the positive side the thing that I am trying to express seems to me the essence of Christianity, the essence of the Gospels; Christ's sayings are full of it; and it is only in so far as the modern church has strayed from this idea that I have anything to say against it.

For the same reason modern collegiate education is today a thousand times weaker than it should be because it is trying to present to the young man the soul without the body of life. And if we were to try to state what it is that distinguishes what is "academic" in the bad sense, what we mean when we say of a thing it is "merely academic," I think we should conclude that we mean an attempt to express the soul of history, politics, or what not, without any body to it.

Coming back to the characteristics which distinguish the most successful parts of social work for children, I should say that they are all notably marked by the union of body and soul in their undertakings.

Prenatal Work

To exemplify that statement I shall begin at the beginning of child life, with what is called prenatal work for children. I do not know how much of it you have here in Chicago; I know that you have some of it, done through the District Nursing Association; and we are beginning to have some of it in Boston. This prenatal work, in so far as it is good, deals with the mother not merely as a physical machine, and yet never forgets that she is, in part, a physical machine. It always starts from the physical facts but it never stays there. It is always busy with such teaching and nursing as will do what is best for the physical conditions, but it always tries also to make the coming mother know something of what maternity is to be, of what a child might mean to her. Any one who has had to do with women in the period of gestation, knows that their physical and mental troubles are inexplicably mixed up with each other so that if you do not minister to their souls you never can minister to their bodies. If you do not make them feel something of the majesty and the greatness and the dignity of child-bearing, and if you do not calm some of their unnecessary fears, you will not be able to do your duty by them in relation to the physical side of their troubles. In so far as any of you may have to do with prenatal work, I hope with all my heart you will hold before yourselves this idea of never ministering to a woman without attention to the physical side and never ministering to the physical side without attention to the spiritual side.

Placing Out

In the great variety of activities that center around what is called "placing out" of children all the way from the placing out of young infants from asylums—those death-dealing institutions—up to the placing out of girls and boys of the adolescent period, we are dealing with essentially the same problem. We must see that the children are physically cared for; we must see that they get enough to eat; we must see that their sleep is uninterrupted and that they have some time for proper recreation and exercise. But after all, any one who knows anything about placing out, knows that the essential thing is the character of the people with whom the child is placed. If the foster-parents are people of the right sort, then in ninety-nine cases out of a hundred they will see to it that the child is properly fed, properly clothed, properly schooled, given a proper chance for play and recreation.

I believe that we cannot account satisfactorily for the extraordinary difference between the mortality of infants in infant asylums and the mortality of children placed out, unless we allow for the fact that children are not merely better fed and nursed in private homes but that they get that personal maternal care, which I believe is one of the prime needs and rights of every child. It is not merely because the asylum is huge and impersonal but chiefly because there is no mother for the child that the children do not survive.

Vacations for Children

The same is true of the various movements called summer outings, country week vacations and so on. Those who have been in close touch with those undertakings know that they can be a curse as well as a blessing to a child; that every opportunity given is an opportunity for evil as well as for good; and that at every turn, in making your selection and in your supervision of the children in these summer outings, summer camps, country weeks and so on, you have to look out for the character, the personality of those with whom the child is in contact.

Home and School Visitors

We are developing in Boston an institution which Chicago may have carried on as far or farther; we call it the "Home and School Visitors." The home and school visitors in Boston supplement the work of the probation officers, truant officers, and attendance officers, and as it seems to me carry out the particularly synthetic function on which I am insisting this morning.

The public-school teachers cannot possibly carry all the burdens that are being put upon them today; they are the hardest worked people and the poorest paid that I know; and they do magnificent work in proportion to what we ask them to do; but they cannot possibly do all the things that we ask of them. More and more are we tending to load burdens on them that they cannot bear and ought not to be asked to bear. Many of these burdens concern the physical welfare of the child and the relation of the child to his home and to his parents. A child does not come to school; why doesn't he come? He is sick; why is he sick? He falls asleep in school; why does he fall asleep? He looks ill nourished; why? He is backward; why?

The teacher is bound to her teaching and to her school and ought to be. She cannot follow up all these tracks. And yet unless someone follows them up, she is attempting to present the soul without the body of education; she is trying to train half the child and has necessarily neglected the other half. No one is more alive to this than the teachers themselves. I have very often heard teachers express the desire that they could know more about the home, that they could have more co-operation with the parents; and often express the bitter regret that their efforts are utterly undone because the child unlearns at home and on the street what he learns at school.

The home and school visitor, it seems to me, has one of these ideal positions that deals with physical necessities but does not stop there. She does her

BURDENED CHILDHOOD

The Little Mother

The Heavy Task

Oh little feet
that ache and bleed
beneath your load

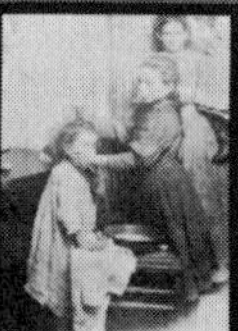

Hunting for fuel.

Foraging in Chicago's garbage.

Heavy burdens upon children in the years when their strength should be fostered and trades that waste their latent abilities and deform their character.

Many children gather old iron, rags, bags, and bottles, and sell them to the junk men.

part in looking after the physical necessities as a basis and as one element of the whole growth of the child. Here she has, I think, the ideal point of approach to the child. Later I shall speak more fully on this matter; the ideal approach to deeper spiritual problems given us by a knowledge of the physical side.

Play and Athletics

Athletics and indeed all forms of out-door play illustrate in a slightly different way the same point. We all know something of the blessings of playgrounds; and I suppose all of us who have had much to do with them know also how far they may be a curse. Some playgrounds furnish opportunities to develop all that is worst in children, others all that is best. What makes the difference? It is wholly a question of the human element in the control of that playground. Give a child a playground; and he may be able to make no use of it; he may not know how to play, or he may play so silly a game that it is no real fun to him and no real use to him. His play has to be supervised from start to finish if it is going to be any fun to him or any good to him in the long run. If you are to hold the boys on the playground and have them use it, you have to have supervised play; you have to have not merely the body on the playground, not merely the legs and arms, you have to have the soul of play there also. If you are to use athletics, as you must and ought to use it, as one of the most valuable outlets for creative, vital, and sexual energy, you also must have not merely decent, but far more than that, really exceptional instructors in athletics. The greatest power in the life of an adolescent boy to keep him straight in matters of sex, is the influence of the right kind of athletic instructor; the kind of athletic instructor who may never say a word about sex hygiene but who is known by the boys as a man who keeps straight; whom they worship as boys will worship their athletic instructors; and from whose behavior they catch an ideal, which is implanted in them, as I believe, all the more deeply because so little is said about it.

I was talking not long ago with Dr. Gulick of New York, formerly director of physical training in the New York public schools, on this much-discussed topic of sex hygiene; and he told me that his years of experience with boys in the schools of New York had convinced him that there was no single power so great for good or for evil in relation to the sexual morality of boys as the influence of their athletic instructors.

That we should have, then, upon our playgrounds experienced athletic instructors, not merely of average character, but of very much more than average character, may mean, as it seems to me, absolutely everything to the souls and the bodies of the children who use the playgrounds.

The Boy Scout Movement

I have welcomed, as I suppose every one of you has welcomed, the boy scout movement as an ideal example of something that stimulates the best activities of the boy, the activities that use both body and soul; the activities that cut across this false old distinction of body and soul, that use the whole boy and appeal to the whole boy. I believe the boy scout movement has a great future. I am not going to speak at length on it; many of you probably know more about it than I do. I bring it into this list simply because I believe that it has appealed to us all, in this country and other countries, so swiftly and so poignantly, for the very reason on which I am trying to insist on the different points of view.

Juvenile Court

The Juvenile Court, which was developed in Chicago earlier than in Boston, I suppose we all recognize as exemplifying among its other beneficent activities, the point that I am trying to make. All the better juvenile courts take account of the physical status of the boy because his physical condition bears upon the reasons for his crime and its prevention in the future. His physical condition and his mental condition must be studied by an intelligent judge, independently as well as through the experts whom he calls to his aid. But any intelligent judge, of course, in a juvenile court, more and more outgrows the idea of being a judge and becomes an educator.

In every one of the activities that I have been speaking of the "man at the wheel" is coming to think of himself as an educator. We think of a nurse as some one who cares for physical disease, but every one who knows the district nurse knows that she is primarily an educator. We think of the superintendent of a playground as a person who is a gymnast and knows the technique of athletics, but if he is of any use on a playground he must be an educator. The scout masters obviously enough are the best kind of educators, approaching the type of education that we get in the English public schools, where masters are with the boys out-doors as well as in-doors. And with the juvenile court we have reached, it seems to me, that great turning point in the conception of justice and law in its relation to children that the law is essentially a form of education and that all that we have been thinking of as punishment we must think of as education.

Social Service in Hospitals

Finally I wish to speak of the field with which I am more personally identified, hospital social service work. Social service work in hospitals is not in the least different from social work outside a hospital, except that it has one great point of advantage over many other kinds of social work: its method of approach. The method of approach from the physical side is, it seems to me, unequaled as an opportunity for getting the confidence of the child as well as of the adult, for getting information as you cannot otherwise get it, and for giving in return anything good that you have to give. We have heard so many times that we have already forgotten its significance the old proverb that "a touch of nature makes all the world akin." Some of you, I suppose, have friends who went through the San Francisco earthquake and fire a few years ago. I had some intimate friends there, and as I talked it over with them afterwards, the thing that impressed me was not so much the terrible accumulation of suffering and sorrow as what they told me about the human relationships of the first forty-eight hours after the fire when no one knew whether he had any property or not, when all, rich and poor alike, were standing in line waiting for the bread and milk to be dealt out to them, when everything that superficially divides man from man was taken away, and when there was—and this was the point of it—such a miraculous sense of human brotherhood as they had never seen in their lives and have never felt before or since. Of course it died away after a few days; and they got back into the old, busy, grasping ways; but for the first forty-eight hours after the San Francisco fire, so the survivors will tell you, that fearful touch, that fearful blow of nature did make all the world akin; did make a real brotherhood of man.

If there is anything we want as the first principle and foundation of our social work, it is human brotherhood. We know that it cannot be cheaply bought; we know that we cannot acquire friends and brothers at a dozen a week; we know that those great words, "friendship" and "brotherhood," are too sacred to be lightly used or won. But there does seem to me something actually supernatural, something miraculous, in this touch of what we call "nature," through disease in a hospital. The physical pain or weakness provides with almost miraculous swiftness the spiritual meeting-ground for the person who needs help and the person who has help to give—a meeting-ground such as nothing else can furnish. The hospital social service worker deals, as does every other kind of worker that I have spoken of, with the physical wants and needs of the patient, but he never stops there. He has to do with whatever in the family, in the work, in the school and in the recreation of those children has prevented their keeping their health or has brought them into a diseased condition. The hospital social worker does not deal with people simply because they are poor or simply because they are sick, but he deals with those whose sickness is due to their poverty, due to their housing conditions, due to their inheritance, due to the lack of fresh air and play, due to some of the other innumerable conditions with which they cannot themselves deal effectively.

Summary

The one thing to be said, the only thing I believe I ever shall have to say to any body of people as long as I live, is that personality is the essence of all good work. In modern social work we are trying to accomplish things mechanically and by wholesale and we are just as sure to fail as the Day of Judgment is to come. We never can do anything that is important for human beings except individually and personally; and all the rest of our technique, all the machinery of prevention and of public health, in which I am engaged from morning to night, has no worth except as the body of this soul, except as the medium for the contagion of personality. Personality cannot go without a body; that is why we have bodies, to convey personalities one to another. Social work also has its body, its machinery, of relief, its splendid scheme of investigation and co-operation, all of which exist simply to convey from one human being to another the essence of personality. But those of us who reverence personality know that after a very little while our personalities are drained dry unless they have access to some far greater source than ourselves. A person who thinks of personality primarily as finite and of his own personality primarily as finite, can never have any enthusiasm; can never have any spirit of joy in the work of which I am speaking. It is only when we believe that our personalities are part of an Infinite Personality, bearing the same relation to that Infinite Personality that one of our own thoughts does to our whole self; it is only so far as our work asks perpetually for the blessing of God upon it that it is going to survive or be of any use.

It has been said that this is consecrated work; to that, I say amen with all my heart. I do not believe any sort of social work is going to be worth the labor or the money that is put into it if it is not consecrated work, and I believe as we face the gigantic problems in any one of these fields, we are worse than foolish—we are insane—if we do not call to our aid the greatest of all powers, the power of religion.

SOCIAL WORK AND NURSING

RICHARD C. CABOT, M. D.

Massachusetts General Hospital and Harvard Medical School

I shall assume that I am talking to nurses, and therefore share with you the common bond of medical service which unites medical men and nurses. As you are nurses you do not need to be told that hospital work as it now exists is vastly incomplete; you do not need to be told this because you have seen it many times. My only doubt is whether you have not seen it so many times that you have become dangerously accustomed to it, nay, almost reconciled to it. We spend our days as physicians or as nurses amid fragments, fragments of lives, and we get so used to dealing with them as fragments that I am afraid that we are often apt to settle down and become content to accept them as the proper thing to deal with.

I remember once how the presence of an outsider in one of my teaching-clinics made me aware of my own shortcomings in this respect. I had just come in ready to teach and I had asked my assistant what we had in the way of "material," when the outsider said: "What do you mean by that?" I suppose that most of you know what I meant by "material." "Material" was a certain motley assemblage of human souls and bodies for the most part conjoined, each of whom had an immortal destination, each of whom, of course, thought himself as the center of the universe. But I remember the answer of my assistant, which shocked the outsider, and which through him shocked me. "Well," he said, "we have a pretty good lot this morning; we have a couple of good hearts, a pernicious anaemia, two or three big livers, and a flat foot.'' In most of us that sort of slang does not arouse any sense of disquietude, any sense of incompleteness, any sense of discontent with our work as it is. More shame to us!

Or, again, you know the way that a surgeon in an out-clinic, sitting at his desk, will perhaps strike his bell for the next patient. Some one will come in, a hand is held up before him, a septic hand, and he will at once commence work upon it. He does not have time to notice that the hand is hitched to a body. He attends to that hand, and by the time he is through with it, perhaps a foot is put at him or a shoulder or a knee, and so on. With such fragments as these he spends his life.

But it is not merely that we spend our lives with disembodied organs and fragments; still more we are content to spend our lives with fragments of the human story, even of the disease itself. The patient is under our observation but a few days, and, if someone asks us afterwards what happened to him, we have to confess, ''I do not know; he was discharged that day and I never saw him again.'' I suppose in your hospitals as in ours you write at the end of each record some little phrase that expresses that state of things up to date and is supposed to round off the full and complete duty of the hospital as usually conceived—''discharged relieved,'' ''discharged worse,'' ''discharged dead,'' but in all cases ''discharged.'' That is, the hospital has cut its connection with that individual; and so far as it is concerned does not see that it has any further business with him.

I do not mean to say that the hospital ought to do everything that is concerned with the individual for the rest of his life; for the hospital must draw the line somewhere. But I do say that the hospital ought in common-sense either to do enough for that individual to finish up the job that is begun or to see that others finish it. I can conceive of nothing more irrational than to spend one's time or one's money, as we hospital physicians and nurses do to a considerable extent, in beginning jobs that are never finished. If there is anything irrational in this world it is an unfinished job, and all the more irrational if it is a good job.

For the most part our work is good work and our jobs are good jobs; but I think that we are guilty in being content as we are with the scrappiness of our work merely because this state of things has gone on so many years. We allow our patients to go out of our sight without knowing even whether they have got far enough along to have made worth while the labor that we put into them. I have told many times of a baby brought to the Massachusetts General Hospital for the ordinary stomach and bowel trouble of which we see so much in summer. The amount of hospital care given to that baby, which for several reasons I took care afterwards to look up, cost about thirty dollars. The hospital spent thirty dollars on that baby and discharged it well. To all intents and purposes that baby was dumped on the sidewalk—that was the end of it; I do not mean materially, for materially it was dumped into its mother's arms; but the hospital knew nothing whatever about the competence of that pair of mother's arms for the care of that baby. Of course the mother had no reason to suppose that there was anything wrong with her mode of dealing with the baby hitherto. She therefore continued the same plan of feeding the baby that she had been accustomed to in the past. It was a four months' baby. She was a good, kind-hearted mother, and, of course, wanted to give the baby everything that was good to eat; she did not want to be stingy with the baby; so she used to give it a little of everything on the table. You know what results when this sort of large-hearted woman gets hold of a baby, which is not quite able to stand the full terrors of adult diet. Of course the baby again appeared in the hospital not very many weeks after it was "discharged." The point which I am making here is that, although we cannot expect that hospitals can follow all of their patients for all of their lives, we can expect that, if they are going to take thirty dollars of the money contributed by the state or the community or private individuals and put it into the care of that baby's illness, they shall follow that baby to its home and to its mother, sufficiently to know that those efforts and that money are not wholly wasted as they were in this case. The baby had it all to suffer over again, the hospital had it all to pay over again, and the mother had not begun to learn.

I have not the least doubt that this tragic little comedy is happening in thousands of cases in your city, as it is happening in my city all the time. It is bound to happen in most hospitals because we are used to cutting off these cases at the moment they step out of the front door of our institution.

This is one of the types of incompleteness from which we suffer, and yet with which we are content. It is perhaps the easiest sort of incompleteness to battle against and to reform, for it simply means that we are responsible for the convalescence of our patients. It is not worth while to nurse patients through the acute stages of their illness, to give them all the benefit of expert diagnosis and expert treatment, such as we give in a modern hospital, if the convalescence is such a disaster that it undoes all or a considerable portion of the good done by the treatment.

I suppose that most of you have at some time taken a personal interest in a hospital patient, enough to follow of your own initiative what has happened to that patient outside, and thus you have come to know that without your help outside the hospital, almost all the good work that has been begun would be undone. The patient has had, we will say, some pelvic operation, and has gone home as soon as the stitches would hold, and then has gone to work. Perhaps hernia or cystocele has resulted in such a way that half the good of that operation has been undone.

I know perfectly well that you, as nurses most of you, cannot correct this evil. You are doing the best you can. But I think that it cannot do any harm to have as many people as possible in the community vividly aware of how irrational a step it is for us to give as much as we give in the way of care in the hospitals and not to give any more. Either do not start the job—or finish it.

But the incompleteness, the fragmentary way in which we treat this matter is not always incompleteness stretched out in time; it is often an incompleteness at one given moment. I heard only today of a patient who could not sleep and could not eat because he had no knowledge of what was going on at his home; and his wound therefore could not heal properly. It was an accident case; he had been brought suddenly to the hospital; he had had no proper or satisfactory connection with his home and what was going on there since he left; the social worker made the connection between the hospital and the home, found out what was going on in the home; rectified what was wrong; brought the charities in to help, and was thus able to assure the man that things were going on right at home while he was cut off from his family. The patient began to sleep and eat only when the social worker took up the case. Parts of the treatment of that case were disastrously incomplete, untouched by the hospital, simply because they involved matters invisible to the hospital—I mean the life of the patient's family at home. In the end these matters were treated by the social worker, with the result that the hospital was able to finish its unfinished job, to make a good piece of work out of it instead of a poor one.

We may think that this cutting off of the circulation between husband or wife and the home is not after all such a terrible thing; people can "scratch along," we say. Very recently from a public health official, I heard a story that drove home to me more poignantly and more pathetically than anything ever had done, the truth of what I am now trying to say to you. It was a story of a woman who had both smallpox and gonorrhoea, a rather unusual combination. Her husband was taken with smallpox and removed to the smallpox hospital as quickly as possible in the hope that he might be isolated before any contagion could result from the case; but before long his wife was also brought in with smallpox, and it was noticed that she came from a different lodging from that of her husband. On inquiry as to the gonorrhoea, she said, "You took my husband to the hospital; there was no money and I had to eat."

I do not believe that there is one of us who can swear that a similar thing may not have happened in some of the cases we have as nurses or physicians been caring for, and I say that we are responsible. We are responsible for finding out that somebody else is looking after the families of our patients in case we cannot do it ourselves. We cannot do all the jobs in the world—nobody knows that better than I; but, when we cannot do some job which obviously needs to be done, we ought, it seems to me, to do everything in our power to see that somebody else does it. I am a medical man; I am not competent to do surgery; but if a boy comes to me on the Fourth of July with a toy pistol wound in his hand, I do not send him home with sticking plaster covering his cut, merely because I cannot do surgery. I consider myself responsible for seeing him delivered at the door of a surgeon who is competent to prevent him from getting lockjaw. So it seems to me with these other jobs; we cannot ourselves do many of them, but we are responsible for seeing that there is not such terrible miscarriage of justice as I have just quoted to you from the records of the health department.

I do not see how we can take our medical work seriously and keep at it long, either as nurses or as physicians, without asking ourselves whether after all it is worth while to be doing so much as we are doing unless we do something more in the way of prevention. Is it worth while to keep stopping up all the leaks that we find, if we cannot do something to prevent these leaks from occurring? So much more disease is being produced every day than you and I can cure that we can surely not be content to go on in our work unless we have a hand somewhere in the work of prevention. And that is another of the things which it is part of the business of the hospital and of the doctors and nurses connected with the hospital to see followed up.

A Chicago physician, Dr. Alice Hamilton, has recently made the most thorough study of poisoning in the lead trades that has been made in this country. If a case of lead poisoning comes to us, we are not doing our duty, it seems to me, if we merely cure that case, even if we also look after the family of the man while he is being cured. If there is one case of lead poisoning, it is certain that more cases will be developed from the same source from which that one came. We ought every time such a case occurs to act just as we should do if we found a case of smallpox. I do not suppose that there is one of us who, if he came in contact with a case of smallpox, would not do what he could to see that that case did not spread, to see where it was caused, to see whether serious contagion was not going on spreading to other cases. We have learned that lesson in relation to such things as smallpox, but we have not learned it in many other directions. We certainly have not learned it in relation to industrial diseases. And I do not see how we can have a good conscience or feel that we have made any sort of a reasonable job out of the work that comes before us unless we do something towards prevention. I do not say how much, I do not say all that could be done; but surely something could be done in each case. When such a thing as lead poisoning comes before us, we should run down the source of that trouble and prevent, so far as we can, or see that somebody else prevents, so far as the community is organized to prevent, the further spread of that mischief.

We are doing more and more all the time in America about public health; public-health movements are springing up everywhere. But I think that all of us who have to do with public health, and especially you nurses, have far more to do with private health. It is often said that, if we could carry through such and such public-health measures, if we could have perfect water supplies, if our milk was all pure, if we had the windows of our schools open and proper ventilation in them, if we could carry through a dozen or two such measures, then we should stamp tuberculosis, scarlet fever, pneumonia and typhoid out of the community. I do not believe it for a moment. I believe that the private causes of disease are far more potent than the public; that private health, personal hygiene, is the biggest thing to be sought for, and private disease the greatest obstacle. Let me give you an example of the way this immediately impinges upon my own work just now. I spoke of the investigation of the trades that give lead poisoning, undertaken by Dr. Alice Hamilton. There have been many other investigations of trades from the point of view of seeing whether we could not so modify the conditions of work that the trade would not be so death-dealing. I remember an investigation, for example, of laundry-work, and of the supposed injuries that come from laundry-work. The way such investigations are ordinarily made is to take from the records of the hospital so many cases of disease and trace out the patients' occupations until you put together perhaps a hundred cases of disease arising in laundry-workers; then say that such and such diseases are caused by laundry-work. You see, of course, the fallacy of that. The laundry-work is a factor, but how much of a factor no one can tell unless he knows also the private conditions, that is, the ordinary habits and home conditions of that girl. We have begun such an investigation as that at the Massachusetts General Hospital as a part of our Social Service Department. We are taking all of the young girls from fifteen to twenty-five years who come to our out-patient department for what the doctors are apt to call general debility —run down, tired out, no appetite, can't sleep, constipated, and so on—cases where we can find no organic disease. We may suspect tuberculosis, but we cannot prove it. We have been following up these cases both in relation to their industrial troubles and in relation to their personal habits.

That is, we have had a visitor go to the home or boarding-place of every girl and, without catechising her in any disagreeable way, find out the essentials of how she lives and also the conditions of her work. We have not finished that investigation, and I am not prepared to say how it is coming out, but as I read the careful records of the cases studied so far, the thing that strikes me is how much more potent are the private factors than the public. The way a girl eats or does not eat; the way she sleeps or does not sleep, and the various things that she does from morning to night, are more important, many of them, than what happens to her in her workroom.

All of this, it seems to me, is essential to our records if we are to accomplish any preventive work with our patients. A girl breaks down. We will do what we can to cure her and look out for her convalescence and look out for her people while she is ill; but she will drop down again, in all probability, and we cannot find out why she has dropped down unless we get acquainted with her habits and her home life.

It was the need of such investigations as I have been suggesting to you here that made us start what we call "social service" at the Massachusetts General Hospital. Many people have asked many times: "What is this 'social service,' anyway?" The word "social" is one of the vaguest words in the language, and the word "service" is just about as vague. I should say that social service in hospital work is the completion of all that is left criminally incomplete. Our hospital work is the work of specialists; this is necessary and right. But the work of the specialist is always and necessarily incomplete; it always needs to be rounded out and finished by somebody who goes after him and looks out for what has been forgotten. I am not blaming the specialists; I am not blaming the doctors or the nurses or anybody. It is not the fault of any individual; it is the fault of our long-established system of being content with fragments. All specialism necessarily involves narrowness, forgetfulness and one-sidedness. Symbolic of this necessary and rightful narrowness of specialism is the way we all use a microscope. When an inexperienced person uses a microscope—as you know, since probably you have tried it—he puts one eye to the microscope while the other eye is covered or closed by wrinkling up the face. When anybody who knows anything about a microscope uses it, he keeps both eyes open all the time, but only one eye sees. The eye at the microscope is fixed upon the bright and very narrow world contained within the microscope, the other eye is open but perfectly blind; it sees nothing. And that is exactly right; it is what ought to be. But it symbolizes exactly the strength and the weakness of specialism, medical specialism, nursing specialism, and every other kind the world over. We must provide that the evils which result from that good and rightful specialism are in some way neutralized. That is the task of social service in a hospital, to neutralize the necessary evils of medical specialism; to pick up all the dropped stitches that I have suggested and many others that I have not tried to suggest.

I remember once in my old stamping ground, the Massachusetts General Hospital, at one of the steep, narrow flights of stairs near the main entrance I saw ahead of me, clinging to the bannisters, unable to get up or down, a man who was breathing so fast and so hard that I had no doubt he had cardiac disease. He wore a dressing gown and carpet slippers, as most of our ward patients do; he had got downstairs in some manner and he could not get up. Just before I reached him, two nurses coming from their luncheon passed me, chatting and laughing pleasantly, passed right by him and went upstairs; they did not see him at all. Should we blame them? I do not think that they are really much more to blame than any specialist is to blame for his blind eye while he looks with the other eye into the microscope. But if we are to train our nurses as we do now train them, so that they shall be blind to most that goes on in a hospital, in order that they shall be technically efficient in certain things, then we must provide somebody else, the person whom I call a social worker, who shall have the ordinary human eye, able to see and act when he sees such sights as that man gasping on the stairs, sights that most of us do not see at all because we have seen them so many times.

When we started social work in the Massachusetts General Hospital, as I think I have hinted to you, my first motive was a sense of inefficiency, my own inefficiency. It was not that I was not doing anything worth while, but that I could not follow my cases, because I could touch only such a small fragment of them. Joined to that was the consciousness, coming from having worked with social workers for a considerable number of years, that there was close beside us in the community help for my patients, and that nobody was securing that help for them. We in the hospitals were so circumscribed, so narrow, that we did not know of all the charities, all the convalescent homes, all the fresh air funds, and the various other agencies that were ready, willing and anxious to help our patients. We did not know about them because we never had been taught about them; and I venture to say that there are not many nurses or doctors in the hospitals of Chicago today who know enough to make use of all the resources of the city waiting and wanting to be used for just such purposes. A social worker should know all the resources of the city which can be used for the benefit of his patient, with which the doctors and the nurses of the hospital cannot ordinarily be familiar. He must be enough out of the hospital, enough free from hospital routine and its dulling influence to be able to see freshly; and that means, I think, that he should not be in the hospital all the time; he should be somebody who is familiar with the great sources of the refreshment of human souls and who is not content to treat people as if they were walking automata.

I do not say that nurses and doctors generally treat patients as machines, but I do say that their training tends to make them do so. If it were not for the good in nurses that even training cannot spoil, they would treat patients, even more than they sometimes do, as if they were bodies without souls. If we are to do anything for chronic illness, for the debilitated and nervous patient, for the chronic dyspeptic who turns up in such numbers in our out-patient departments, we must raise the whole tone of his personality and increase his vitality. We cannot do this without tonics. We cannot do it without appealing to the great sources of happiness and vitality that are in human nature. I think chiefly of three—satisfactory work, recreation, and affection. A human being has a right to work, to recreation, and to affection. If, in spite of our best efforts, we fail to get proper work, proper recreation, and decent friendships and family ties for people, we ought to know that we cannot expect to cure their bodies. We ought to realize that their nutrition, the workings and the secretions of their stomachs, the way their hearts pump, and the way their livers work depend in part upon these three great spiritual factors. And as in case of the man who could not sleep or eat until he knew what was going on in his family, so we cannot make many of our patients sleep or eat or perform their physical functions until we attend to everything else that is of vital concern in their lives.

You see that I am laying out a fairly large order, and I am doing so intentionally. I think that the social worker who has to work in a hospital should be the highest type of woman that exists in the community; sometimes she is. I can show her to you in my own hospital, and I think that you would acknowledge that there is not any higher type either intellectually, morally or spiritually than we have there. You can get such women here just as well. You can get them, because this work calls out the very best and deepest portion of a woman, as nothing else that I ever saw does; because it rests with its feet right on the ground but with its head in the sky. It rests upon the firm foundation of physical usefulness, of direct personal service, but it does not stop there. It is ready to do whatsoever the patient needs in order to get well, and to allow for all the great factors that are part of a human being as well as those that are taught in medical schools and training schools for nurses.

Coming back to the words with which I started, I am conscious that I am speaking mainly to nurses, and I want to end with a few words about what seems to be the permanent, durable sources of satisfaction in your work and in mine. What is there that is certain? What is there that we can build on? Certainly not the success of our present medical hopes in public or private health. When I look, for example, over the changes—some of them advances and some of them hardly to be so classed—in the tuberculosis movement of the last five years—and I have been very closely associated with that movement for ten years—when I look back over the last five years I cannot say that I feel confident that the future will show that we were right in what we have been doing. Tuberculosis is looming up as a much bigger problem than we knew it to be five years ago. The future may show that a large part of our work was wasted, in so far as we prescribed milk and eggs, or put people on their roofs, or did the various things we are doing now and must continue to do until we see something better to do. But there is a certain part of that work that I know is not wasted, that I know is good. That is the personal relation established between the nurses and doctors and visitors on the one hand and the patients on the other—the good to the visitors and to the nurses and doctors that came of knowing the patients, and the good to the patients that came of knowing the nurses and the doctors. That good is certain, and there is nothing else that is certain in our work.

One of the best things, it seems to me, about our profession is that the public has come to expect more of us than of anybody else. They expect us to be really superhuman, to be almost supernatural, in our relations to patients. Other people can sometimes be bored and act as though they were bored; but we cannot, of course. Other people can lose their tempers; for a nurse or doctor to lose his temper is unprofessional, is against our code of ethics, and is not expected of us. We are not to be human in these respects.

I remember the case of a nurse who was discharged from a case of typhoid because she was human. The nurse wrote upon her night record while the patient was delirious: "Gave milk and medicine at twelve and at two; patient insulting." That does not at first sound like much of a crime. Why should the patient not have been reported as "insulting?" Any ordinary human being would have had the right to consider the patient insulting; but the nurse has not, and was rightly discharged because of that record. And I am grateful that we are held up to such a standard, not fully, of course, but far more than we should be if the public did not expect of us this superhuman, this almost supernatural strength. People do not give us gratitude, as you know, and they do not always get well when we have done our best. None of the ordinary satisfactions, certainly not pecuniary ones, come into our profession. But this one thing we do have—we have opportunities for human relationships such as I think no other profession has, opportunities for giving more than other people give, and I believe that no human being can ask for anything better than that, the chance to put out the last ounce that there is in him for somebody else, with the possibility of believing that it will do solid good.

HUMANIZING THE HOSPITALS

RICHARD C. CABOT, M. D.

Massachusetts General Hospital and Harvard Medical School

Ever since I have had anything to do with hospital work, I have noticed the difficulty of breathing the spiritual atmosphere in hospitals. We think often of the fearful tragedy of a group of entombed miners, and of the wonderful happiness of those who have a chance to let in some air upon men who have been trying to breathe poisonous gases. It seems to me often that the spiritual atmosphere of a hospital is about as hard to breathe as the poisonous gases of a mine. A hospital is a grim place, and the people who find themselves there often pass through the most terrible experience of their lives. They hear sounds that they only in part understand and that they are fairly sure to interpret in some worse sense than they need. They see for the first time an accumulation of misery that they did not suppose existed upon the earth. We who as physicians and nurses are constantly in the presence of these things, forget that first impression of the newcomer, who sees so many sick people together and so much suffering that he forgets for the time being the normal world outside and is crushed by the sense that everything and everybody is diseased.

With regard to our great public institutions, public hospitals, public asylums for the insane, and public almshouses, we undergo every now and then spasms of doubt and skepticism that lead to investigations. We suddenly discover that this or that prison, this or that hospital, this or that asylum, has in it examples of indifference and callousness, or even of brutality and cruelty on the part of the attendants. We blame the superintendent, perhaps, or we blame the particular individuals who have acted in this way, but almost never do we recognize whose the fault really is. We fail to realize that the fault is ours, in that we allow these officials to be placed in a position that no human being can stand permanently without being brutalized.

The subject on which I am to speak is the humanization of our public institutions. I might have said the superhumanization of them, because what we need in these institutions, so long as they are conducted as they are, is something superhuman rather than human. The ordinary man meets misery, of course; he meets suffering; he meets all sorts of things that are disgusting; but he does not meet them constantly; he does not meet them every day and every hour of the day; he does not meet them to the exclusion of everything else. We must realize this psychological aspect of the matter, which Miss Jane Addams has so often insisted upon in other fields. Miss Addams has studied the question of just how it feels to be an immigrant coming into this country, contrasting what one would expect to feel with what one actually does. Many of the attendants in those places are men; in most of them, I am happy to say, there are a large number of women. It still remains the unfortunate prerogative of the national government in its army and navy service to keep women nurses out of many fields where they belong.

When last I had anything to do with our national government in relation to its medical work, at the time of the Spanish War, I had an experience that I never shall forget and one that I wish everyone else who is thinking of these subjects might have. In Porto Rico I saw to what a depth of degradation, to how foul a spiritual atmosphere you could get when you had only men nurses in a hospital—men nurses picked out at random as they pick them out in the army by drafting them as "orderlies" from the ranks. You cannot realize the superhuman value of women nurses until you see what the natural human reaction is of men in the presence of the duties of the nurse. The natural reaction is to be disgusted with the duties, to hate the sick man for being sick, and to act accordingly.

That is the result of putting the "natural man" face to face with the duties of public institutions. Yet we are surprised when now and then he is cruel and brutal. He is perfectly sure to be cruel and brutal in all the institutions of the country for most of the time so long as we manage those institutions as we now manage them, and just as surely will there be various other evils that we have not yet faced. For example, I have had a good deal to do with nurses and the training of nurses, and I suppose that there is no criticism of them that I have so often heard as that, after they leave the hospital and go into private nursing, they entertain their patients with exciting stories of the beautiful operations which they have witnessed in the hospital. The nurses are blamed for this, when it is we who run the hospitals who should be blamed for it. We give the nurses no possible chance to think of anything, to see anything but the hospital routine; and just so surely as when we put water into a pitcher and lift the pitcher to pour, water and nothing else will come out, when for eighteen months or two years you put one thing and only one thing into nurses' minds and then give the minds a chance to pour, they will pour out the one thing that has been put in. We who have managed training-schools for nurses have forced nurses to tell their patients the exciting stories about operations, which are the worst things they can tell. Why is this? Because we have forced them to face a monotony of experience that makes it psychologically impossible for them to tell their patients anything else.

The Illusion of Routine

The particular evils that are sure to arise in connection with the large public hospitals, asylums, and almshouses can perhaps be summed up under two headings, the first of which I shall call "the illusion of routine." In many public institutions there is some official whose business it is to do a simple piece of service, such as to direct the strangers in the building to Ward 31. After he has answered the questions that have to do with that particular piece of service a certain number of times, he is fairly sure to come to what I call the illusion of routine. When a hundred people have asked you the same question, irritating you a little each time, you are fairly sure to have the illusion that the hundredth man who asks you has asked the same question a hundred times and that he is as stupid as a person would be who had asked the question a hundred times and received the answer and still asked it again. You act accordingly! Physicians and nurses who have to do with the examination of patients in hospitals are in the habit, in the beginning of the examination, of asking the patient if he will please lie perfectly flat on the middle of his back in bed. In ninety-nine cases out of a hundred the patient, when told to do this, turns over upon his stomach. The first time the patient does that, one is amused and not especially irritated; the second and the third time one bears it fairly well; but when the hundredth patient does that, one succumbs to the "illusion of routine" and expresses himself in a way more forcible than humane, as though the same person had made that stupid mistake a hundred times. It is very common to point out these facts and to blame the individual for rudeness or brutality, but it seems to me that here again we are putting the blame in the wrong place. We ought to blame those who manage the institution that make it psychologically impossible for the individual unless he is superhuman to be other than callous or cross.

I wish that some of you who have to do with matters of routine would watch and see if this does not apply to hundreds of other matters; and if the reason we behave so badly is not due in a considerable degree to the illusion just described.

The Blindness of the Specialist

Another psychological law that leads, it seems to me, necessarily and naturally to the brutalization and the inhumanity which we want to stamp out is the law of specialization. The division of labor and the specialization of function, which all our modern institutions exemplify, has come, I suppose, to stay; no one in his senses thinks that we can get away from it. But those of us who believe in it, as I do, must face the fact that it has dreadful by-products and that something must be done to prevent those by-products from vitiating all the good that comes out of specialization. The specialist is perfectly sure to be narrow; we might as well admit it from the start; there is no chance of his not being narrow; he cannot be as keen and as expert as he must be unless he is narrow. But if we admit this, then we certainly must have something to supplement his narrowness, because his narrowness is sure to do harm in those matters of common humanity which are most precious and the loss of which makes our institutions no better than they are.

Let us, then, first of all realize that the conditions of our public institutions, which we discuss and rediscuss periodically through investigating committees and newspaper scandals, are perpetual, natural, and necessary conditions just so long as we manage our institutions as we do. There is nothing new about them, and there is little or no blame to any individual concerned. You or I would behave no better if we were put in the same place and forced to face these irritations, these disgusting things, these horrors, miseries, complaints, day in and day out. Let us face it as a general problem; let us recognize that it is no one's fault, and then let us see what we can do about it.

It seems to me that the lines of reform are indicated by what has already been said. The situation, as I have tried to draw it tonight, is one of very special strain, of particularly difficult and deteriorating atmosphere; one might speak of it as a climate deteriorating for both body and soul, but especially for soul. Since 1898 we have had in the Philippines an efficient public service, military and civil. We recognize the climate there as especially trying, and fairly sure, sooner or later, to cause the deterioration of individuals stationed there. With the knowledge of this fact and with the experience of European nations, especially of England, before us, we made provision that no individual should be kept indefinitely in that trying climate, having all that is good in him worked and baked out. The Government provides that once in so often he shall have a furlough which is not merely a short vacation but is long enough to enable him to catch up with his normal life, and to take back with him, if he goes back, a fresh lease of vitality.

Everything that we have recognized in relation to the Philippine service, we have systematically failed to recognize in relation to what is essentially the same situation in our great public institutions.

Every insane asylum, every almshouse, every prison, every public hospital, presents a situation of altogether unnatural concentration of temptation—temptation to become brutalized. We can resist these temptations when they hit us now and then; we cannot resist them when they are forced upon us all the time. The managers of public institutions ought to make provision for their workers exactly as we make provision to safeguard the public servant in the Philippine service. We ought to give long furloughs, not necessarily with total idleness, but with a very sharp change of occupation, so that the individual would get a total vacation from the work which otherwise is sure to crush his soul. We ought also, I think, to offer special educational opportunities. I was told yesterday that through Miss Julia Lathrop of this city the attendants in some of the public insane asylums of this state are to have just such special educational facilities away from their institutions throughout the summer of 1911. I was delighted to know that Miss Lathrop has carried out the idea that I have had in mind. She saw that those attendants were sure to become brutalized unless something was brought into their lives which would show them the higher possibilities of their work. So an attempt is made to show them what those insanities, those diseases they are treating, really mean. Such teaching should help them to greater insight into their work aside from its manual offices and thus tend to prevent the evil of which I am speaking.

Moreover, I think we ought to provide much more systematically for the recreation of our nurses, our attendants, and all who have to do with these abnormal conditions. It is only fair that they should have a chance to breathe freely now and then and to forget for the time being that they are cogs in this very terrible piece of machinery.

Besides providing for these educational outings and respites for the attendants and the nurses, I believe that we ought to have a different body of people going into these institutions. I mean not at all such a body of people as we have when the newspapers bruit abroad the occasional, sporadic, and more or less sensational investigations of a committee. When a committee of the city government, for example, is appointed to investigate an institution few of its members know how to conduct such an investigation. It is a very difficult thing even for one who has given his life to such work. Any committee going into an institution in that way is fairly sure to find conditions different from what they are ordinarily. We do not want, then, these occasional spasmodic investigations. We want people who see as freshly as an average outsider would and yet who will not be ignorant of ordinary conditions in institutions. Such people are sure to see and condemn something that does not deserve condemnation, and the superintendents and managers of institutions, knowing this, dread their visits. They know that, for example, if the visitors went into a surgical ward and happened to hear fearful shrieks from a patient, they would be apt to think he must be ill treated, when in fact he was merely in the process of being etherized and perfectly unconscious of the noise he was making. It is rather hard to explain this to a person who has not seen other patients etherized and who does not know from his own experience that there is no suffering really going on.

We want, then, someone who has the humane point of view, who does not forget the simple rights and desires of humanity, and yet who is not unacquainted with the conditions and the work of the institutions. We need that person in attendance, not occasionally, but every day. This, it seems to me, defines the office of the social worker in relation to the public institutions. The social worker should not be there merely to criticize; he ought to be there like everyone else in the institution primarily to serve, to fill a definite place and to be of definite use.

Any one who goes into a hospital, an asylum, or any such institution and stays there a few hours, will find many things undone that need to be done, things perhaps that could not be done, by the nurses and physicians. One of the first things that any patient in the hospital wants is to be brought into touch with his home and his family. He will fail to get well as he should—even the healing of his tissues and the knitting of his bones will not go on as they should—if he is in misery of anxiety about what is going on at home. But keeping a patient in touch with his home is only one of the things such a worker can do. He is concerned with any little service that he can get a chance to do as an entering wedge at the start, but he is concerned far more with what happens to the patient ultimately. He is concerned with his convalescence; he is concerned with whatever is worrying the patient at that time; he is concerned with whatever help he can give to the physicians. For example, there are a great many patients in a hospital who ought to have an operation but who are terrified—naturally, as most of us would be—at the thought, and either for good reasons or for bad have come to think that the surgeon is perhaps an interested party who does not look upon the question of an operation in a really disinterested way. Such patients want the advice of some disinterested person as to whether this operation would better be done, and very often the social worker can do a most useful act in persuading the patient to have the operation, which otherwise he would be incompetent either to accept or refuse without any information that seemed to him at once expert and impartial.

Again, such a social worker can do a great deal in giving the patient that confidence in his physician and in the institution which otherwise he could not get. The social worker, if she believes in the institution, as she ought to if she is to work there, can reassure patients as to the kind of things that are being done and are going to be done with them. There is no one else who explains; there is no other person in the hospital whose chief business it is to explain things. It is the strong point of doctors that they get to work and accomplish things; it is the weak point of most doctors that they do not explain but think that the patient will understand all that is good for him as he gets well. But I have heard it again and again from patients after they come from a hospital, "Well, he didn't tell me anything; he didn't explain; I don't know what it is all about." And very often the explanation would have been worth fully as much as the medicine or whatever was given without it.

The doctor is generally, as I stated, a man of action; he does not like talk and talkers; people who are very glib he generally distrusts. A social worker usually has had a great deal of training in this matter of explanation. After all, the social worker is fundamentally an educator, and the work of the educator is explanation. Therefore she is a fitting person to supplement the rather abrupt and inarticulate activity of the doctor.

These are some of the ways in which a social worker gets her footing in a hospital, serving at first in any capacity in which she can find a chance to serve, running any errands perhaps for the doctors and the nurses, and then gradually winning them over. She always finds antagonism. She always finds that the nurses think that she is trying to do nursing without a nurse's training, while the doctors generally think that she has a way of getting indefinite amounts of money for anybody and can tap endless sources of revenue. When they find that she cannot, they are apt to say: "Well, what are you here for anyway?" She has, then, to live down a number of misunderstandings. But if she will go on the Christian principle of trying to accept any chance of service that she can find, she can often wear down this opposition; people find before long that they cannot get on without her.

I recently had something to do with the installation of a social worker in the Buffalo General Hospital. She had been trained in our department in Boston, and I talked to her upon this text of doing whatsoever she was asked to do until she had found her place. One of the doctors of the Buffalo hospital said to me four months later, "We notice an altogether different atmosphere in our hospital since she has been here; we notice that our patients are grateful to us and to the institution and to the nurses, as they never were before." The doctors did not expect that in the least, and their feeling toward her was changed from top to bottom.

It is, then, the chief mission of the hospital social worker to fill up all the numerous empty places left as a result of a concentrated, specialized care on the part of the doctors and nurses, which leaves so much of humanity untouched.

But while she is doing this, her main business, she is filling the need of which we have spoken in bringing humanity, general humanity, into the hospital. She will not be there primarily as a critic, but nevertheless she will be far better than the average critic because she will be part of the institution and will be criticism from the inside, which I think is always the most valuable kind. There will be no such feeling of hostility as there is toward investigating committees, and the criticism will be constant and steady instead of being spasmodic and occasional.

I want to see social workers in our almshouses, our prisons, our insane asylums, and our great hospitals. We never shall get away from chronic inhumanity, from steady callousness and cruelty on the part of a large number of those who work in all those four institutions, until we have social workers there. We are sure to take time to be converted to this idea; we are sure to continue to think that scandals in institutions are the fault of certain cruel individuals or of certain bad managers, and to fail to realize that it is simply our fault, since we have put upon the shoulders of people burdens that no human being can bear. Of course, this is all a return to the belief in the personal touch as opposed to pure machinery. We have realized the great blessing of machinery, as we should not fail to do. But I always call to mind that great saying of Lotza, the philosopher, "machinery, everywhere present, but everywhere subordinate."

PART TWO

PHYSICAL CARE

"It may be," the children say, "that we die before our time"

THE PREVENTION OF BLINDNESS

F. PARK LEWIS, M. D.

President, National Association for the Prevention of Blindness and the Conservation of Vision

The subject of conservation of vision and the prevention of blindness is a subject so broad and one which it is possible to treat from such varied aspects, that I shall content myself in this paper with the endeavor to present but one aspect of it—the value of good vision as an economic asset.

In answer to the question recently put to a well-known statesman as to the meaning of the new nationalism, the reply was: "It is the application of common-sense in the administration of public affairs." It would, indeed, seem as if within a comparatively few years a new spirit has come to dominate the thought of the world. It is by no means wholly political in manifestation; it is animating every phase of human activity; it extends from the government of the nation and the state and the city to the control of corporations and the direction of our individual and private affairs; it is dependent upon a hitherto only partially realized sense of the power of combined forces, the enormously augmented value of united and co-ordinated effort toward a given end, and upon a truer sense of proportion concerning the things of real worth in life.

Our captains of industry first made the discovery in the world of business. They found that by uniting the resources of a group of small owners, the combined purchasing power of their money was disproportionately increased, and we had the beginnings of the great syndicates and the department stores with their cheapened products and increased profits. Gradually those who were interested in humanitarian projects began to realize that the policies which were good for business were good for charities; for with the highest aims and the best intentions, efforts were being duplicated, and the results in lessening human suffering were not proportionate to the time and labor and money expended upon the poor.

Then came a closer study of the causes of the misery of mankind, and the question was seriously debated whether poverty and disease and crime were the necessary accompaniments of our modern civilization. So men and women of trained minds began to investigate these social questions and they applied the same scientific methods that they would have used in the determination of any physical problem. Intensive studies were made, not by armchair philosophers, but by active field workers, of the conditions which obtained where crime was rampant and where poverty and disease held sway. Then came a great illumination, for all of the conditions that seemed to be undermining our social fabric were found to be interrelated and interwoven. Poverty was the result of crime, as well as its cause, and each was not infrequently both cause and effect each in relation to the other. The poor were crowded in insanitary tenements, where with lowered vitality they were made the ready victims of tuberculosis and of degenerating social infections. These in turn lessened the earning powers of those whose utmost exertions were barely sufficient to keep them alive, and they became not only the victims of demoralizing social conditions but the perpetuating causes of like conditions. Foci having thus been established, all ranks of society in time became invaded, and it became evident that if we would better the conditions under which we were living, if we would improve our own social status, we must begin by recognizing even the selfish truth of the fact that I am my brother's keeper.

When men lived in scattered communities, the force of this was less apparent, but as they gathered together in large cities, where there were necessarily common sources of supply and common interests, where the relationships became closer between office and workshop, parlor and kitchen, and where the worker from the tenement might be handling the source of supply of the family of the millionaire—we came to know, what most of us had before vaguely felt as a remote and abstract expression of socialistic philosophy, that the health and the prosperity and the happiness of each was contingent upon, and essential to, the welfare of all.

A community is simply a group of individuals. The power and effectiveness of that group depends upon the sum total of physical energy and force which it represents. Each member contributes as definitely to that aggregate sum, and in like proportionate degree, as does his horse or his cow. His financial value to the group is measured, as is that of the animal, by his productive powers. If for any reason that power is destroyed, the community loses an asset equal in value to a sum capable of producing an annual interest equal in amount to his yearly wage.

For instance, let us take an ordinary day laborer as a common example. He earns perhaps $2 a day in digging our sewers or in cleaning our streets. This is surely a minimum wage for a working-man. Omitting holidays, he would work three hundred days, earning thereby $600 in the course of the year. With this he supports his wife and several small children. An unforeseen accident happens, we shall say an explosion, and his sight is suddenly and irreparably destroyed. Instantly his earning power is absolutely taken from him, and to give him and his family a like sum for their maintenance would require an amount that put out at interest would produce $600 a year. That sum at 5 per cent is exactly $12,000. But our friend who has been able by his own exertions to meet this demand, is now not only not able to do so, but he, if not his family, must become dependent upon outside aid for food and clothes. This may come from friends or from public charity. In any event, it is diverted from other channels for his maintenance, and amounts to not less than $200 per year. This represents the earning power of $4,000. He, therefore, while not assuming an actual negative value of an additional $4,000, has diverted from its normal courses by reason of his misfortune a sum equal to the annual interest on that sum, and this would in part only represent the real loss to the community consequent upon his withdrawal from productive activity. I say in part, because we are not at all taking into account the important fact that he may be but one link in a chain; the boy must be taken from school and his future destroyed; the daughter through poor nutrition may become the victim of tubercular infection—no one can guess what evil may befall when the one supporting prop has been broken. It is enough to show that the individual financial loss to the community in the destruction of the productive value of even one of its least important elements is a fortune. The money loss is proportionately great as we ascend the social scale.

There are in the state of New York—which state I have taken because I am more familiar with the conditions there than elsewhere—somewhat more than six thousand blind people. It is the accepted conclusion of those who have carefully studied the question, that of these, had proper measures been taken in the way of prevention and of good care and correct treatment, one-third surely should never have lost their sight, and that the eyes in two-thirds of these cases might have been saved. The blindness in only one-third of the cases was considered absolutely inevitable, and, had the principles of eugenics—of which more will be said later—been practically applied, in even some of these cases blindness would not have occurred.

In this reckoning we are making no account whatever of the multitude who have lost one eye, who probably outnumber those who have lost both, and whose efficiency is materially lowered thereby. In one instance cited by the Minnesota Bureau of Labor, a skilled mechanic was reduced by such a loss to the position of a common day laborer. Neither are we considering the semiblind, who are able after a manner to struggle through the duties of life, although denied possibilities that would otherwise be theirs. Neither is it the intention in this presentation of the situation to make the slightest appeal to sympathy because of the sorrow and suffering and cruelty in permitting these our brothers to be robbed of a sense that would make life rich in added possibilities; but it is designed to endeavor to show as a purely business proposition the enormous financial loss that a community suffers in its failure to protect the eyes of its citizens from needless destruction, to demonstrate how prodigal is this waste of human eyes, to illustrate some of the ways in which eyes are needlessly lost, and to outline briefly some of the projects that are now under way for the conservation of vision and for its logical corollary, the prevention of blindness.

Let us suppose, in the consideration of the first of these propositions, that of the six thousand blind in the state of New York, the one-third whose eyes admittedly should never have been lost had proper preventive measures been employed, had received the adequate care necessary. What would have been the balance in our exchequer?

If, in accordance with our previous calculations, each man withdrawn from active participation in the world's work represents a loss to the community of the earning power of an invested sum of twelve thousand dollars, those two thousand blind people would represent a reduction in the capitalization of the state of the enormous sum of twenty-four millions of dollars. Even if we assume that half of these are women and children with a lower earning capacity, the sum would still be stupendous. And as these are added to by new accessions as the others die, it will be seen that, unless we stop this frightful sacrifice, the loss becomes a fixed charge against society.

The same facts that are found true in the state of New York apply equally to every other state in the Union. In Massachusetts and in Illinois there are about five thousand blind in each state, functionally blind, and the same proportion will be maintained from an economic standpoint in regard to the community.

It will be evident, moreover, that the earlier blindness occurs in the life of an individual, the greater the cost to the community. If the sight is lost before a child reaches school age, the training which he receives must be in a school specially provided for those having this disability. You have done somewhat better in Chicago, in placing some of your blind children in the public schools, where you are able in that way to lessen the economic loss to the community. In most of the states of the Union, however, the blind children are, as I have said, in schools specially designed for their instruction. The experiment is being made of educating blind children in schools for the seeing, but even there special teachers are required and the cost is proportionately increased. In the schools for the blind, the children are maintained at state expense, and the increased cost because of this, over the cost for the education of the seeing public-school child who lives at home, in the city of Buffalo, at least, is over $300 per year for each year of his school life. The added cost in Boston, where a large endowment supplements the state appropriation, making more adequate training possible, is, I believe, $100 more than this. The child enters the kindergarten at five years and remains until he is twenty. It does not require a high degree of mathematical skill, therefore, to determine that for each blind child the community during his school life pays $4,500 more than would have been required had normal conditions obtained.

And these conditions might have been very easily obtained. One of the commonest forms of blindness with which we have to deal is also the least justifiable, because it is one of those that are almost absolutely preventable. It is due to an infection that enters the baby's eyes at or shortly after its birth. It is present with the mother. It is an infection that she should never have received. It is usually—happily not always—an evidence of moral deflection on the part of the father. It is but one of a series of direful disasters that are consequent upon such causes and that emphasizes the imperative necessity of teaching sex hygiene to the adolescent. But serious as are its results, it is both preventable and curable if the right thing be done at the right time in the right way.

The first preventive measure is broader knowledge concerning the infection, its origin, its method of propagation, its dangers. Young men, if they but knew, even if their hearts be not inclined to keep this moral law, would still be deterred from inflicting upon their wives that which causes death and which makes their offspring blind. But the germs may be destroyed, and the eyes preserved, even though they have become infected. Two cents' worth of the simple and harmless germicide that some of the states are now providing and distributing to all physicians and midwives free, and two minutes of time are sufficient to save seventy years of dependence and of suffering, and yet with this knowledge spread broadcast, one-quarter of all the children in the schools for the blind have had their eyes needlessly sacrificed because of the ignorance, the negligence, or the indifference of those who presided at their birth.

Shall we again count the cost of this criminal neglect? Thirty-seven of the one hundred and thirty-nine children in the New York State School must grope their way through life because someone criminally neglected to give them right and adequate care during the few minutes following their entrance into the world. Because of this neglect we, the other citizens of the state, who have become accessories through our not having used proper and reasonable measures to prevent the commission of this crime, have been very properly required to pay a fine in the form of an additional tax for the education and maintenance of this injured group, amounting to $17,500 per annum.

In the State School for the Blind at Columbus, Ohio, was probably gathered the largest number of needlessly blind children ever brought together. Fifty-seven of the seventy-five victims of ophthalmia neonatorum, or birth infection, were brought together in one room in order that they might be photographed, and that by means of this photograph more effectively might be shown and more graphically might be demonstrated the necessity of the prevention of this condition. A child who is blind as the result of an ophthalmia neonatorum is not a beautiful sight. The eyes are bulging and staring, and there is a pathos attached to that form of blindness which is indescribable. When instead of one, fifty-seven pathetic little faces look up to one, and at the end, when they are dismissed, fifty-seven little figures in broad daylight go groping their way out toward the door, it makes one feel that if there were but one such child that could be saved by the measures which the state should take to prevent blindness, the cost would under no circumstance be excessive.

Indiana seems to have solved this problem by a master stroke of genius, which at once secures complete registration and some protection by placing upon the birth certificate the question: "Were precautions taken against ophthalmia neonatorum?" and making "all bills or charges for professional services rendered at a birth unlawful if report is not made as commanded." Would it not be good business if each one of the states were to say through its official representatives: "The time has come when this needless blinding of babies must stop, and we will spend ten—twenty—thirty—fifty or a hundred thousand dollars, if need be, but we will protect them from such a calamity—and incidentally save ourselves from the tremendous burden of taking care of them later."

It is inspiring and hopeful to know that the propaganda which has been so actively conducted for the control of ophthalmia neonatorum is already bearing fruit. The following extract is taken from the last report of the official inspector of the New York State Board of Charities: "There has been a noticeable falling off of the numbers of ophthalmia neonatorum cases, and this fact has been reflected in other reports from other sources. It is but reasonable to suppose that the time is arriving when some noticeable return shall be recorded of the labors of the past few years to combat this highly destructive and yet easily prevented cause, and I take it that the figures examined and referred to in a measure do reflect the situation as a whole."

The superintendent of the Perkins Institute, the New England center for the education of the blind, tells me that his plans for the splendid new structure about to be erected are smaller than they would otherwise have been because of his feeling of certainty that the efforts now being made will, within the next few years, materially reduce the proportion of new accessions to the ranks of the blind.

The propaganda for the control of ophthalmia neonatorum which is being conducted in Ohio seems to me to be so effective and so graphic that I want to stop for just a moment to call your attention to it. The state of Ohio has a Commission for the Blind, and, to sum up, about $3,500 is appropriated annually for the work of this commission. Recently the most active work of the commission has been propaganda for the prevention of blindness. Last year the commission decided that the entire sum of this $3,500—less than the amount, by the way, which would be necessary for the maintenance of one blind child through his school life—should be used in the state of Ohio for an educational propaganda. The commission therefore secured the services of Mr. Charles F. F. Campbell, formerly of Cambridge, Mass., and more recently of Pittsburgh. Mr. Campbell is a man who is thoroughly acquainted with the conditions, and a most effective speaker, a man who presents most effectively facts such as those to which I am referring, and he visited during a rapid campaign of three weeks twenty-seven Ohio cities, including Cincinnati, Cleveland, Springfield, Dayton, and all of the larger as well as very many of the smaller Ohio cities. At the same time the commission used prepared stereotyped plates in the descriptive matter of ophthalmia neonatorum and other forms of blindness, such as have been displayed in the exhibit in the Coliseum, such as Fourth of July accidents and injuries, traumatisms, blindness from industrial accidents which might have been prevented, and all that sort of thing, and these stereotyped plates were sent to newspapers in every county in the state of Ohio. There is not one single county in Ohio which failed to receive this published matter, and in some of them two or three and even more of the newspapers published many columns. When this was accumulated, as it was by the clipping bureau, it was found that hundreds and hundreds of columns of descriptive matter had been used throughout the entire state of Ohio. So there is not probably in the civilized world a place where the popular understanding of the causes of blindness is so well understood as it is throughout the state of Ohio today. The idea of the campaign which was conducted is based upon the thought that before any legal measures can be effectively taken, it first becomes necessary that there must be a public understanding and a development of public sympathy in regard to such a movement. For many years laws have been enacted, and in at least sixteen of the states these laws have been on the statute books for twenty years and more, making certain provisions in regard to birth infections, but they have received no recognition whatever, being in most states an absolutely dead letter. These laws require the reporting of cases of birth infections promptly, in order that they may receive the immediate treatment which is necessary in order to save the eye.

In Boston the Commission for the Blind has secured the services—in this instance paid for by the Russell Sage Foundation—of an exceedingly effective man, who, when cases of this kind of blindness of children appear in the dispensaries, has the cases followed up to the homes, and finds and determines under what conditions these cases have arisen, and why a condition so thoroughly amenable to treatment should have occurred. In several of these cases it was found that the mother had been cared for by a midwife who, contrary to the law, had failed to report to the Board of Health the existence of the infected eyes. In September a prosecution was obtained in one of these cases. In October there was an immediate doubling of the cases ordinarily reported, which was about ten a month. In November the prosecution was forgotten, and the number dropped again so that only ten were reported, but in November three cases of blindness appeared in the Infirmary and three prosecutions followed, which were given the most widespread publicity. The newspapers everywhere were asked to make public the fact that these prosecutions had been obtained and that these women had been convicted for failing to give these children the opportunity to have their eyes saved. Immediately a number of cases began to pour in. In December there were again twenty; in January there were thirty, an increase of ten; and then there was a sudden rise, so that by February there were ninety, and by March of the present year there were one hundred and twenty cases, making it perfectly conclusive that the only thing needed to bring these children who would otherwise have lost their sight under the care necessary was that they be followed up, and that prosecutions, where prosecutions should be obtained, be obtained. It makes perfectly conclusive that in every community in which this blindness has been occurring it is only necessary that there shall be an organized effort on the part of that community in order that innumerable cases may be saved.

In Cleveland last March a very similar process was carried out. The Commission for the Prevention of Blindness, a local commission of Cleveland, had a similar experience. A blind child was brought to one of the dispensaries. It was found again that the fact of the infection of the child had not been reported, although a law had previously been obtained requiring that such cases be reported under penalty of a fine. Prosecution was obtained, and a number of interests were co-ordinated in order that reports might be followed up. Two or three other cases were found and prosecuted, and immediately large numbers of reports came in from all sides, and the report of the commission is that at least twenty-three children in Cleveland were saved from blindness last year by this effective work on the part of that small community. I mention this as an evidence of the extreme practicability of the measures which we are endeavoring to secure throughout the United States for the prevention of this form of blindness.

Another and an equally large group of babies are born blind. It is a firmly established belief with many that these ills which are congenital are also inevitable, and we try to bear them with patience and fortitude—especially if they occur in the families of our friends—but it has been known "since

Jacob grazed his Uncle Laban's sheep'' that in all animals desirable or undesirable traits may be perpetuated in their offspring under the action of certain known laws. The degenerate changes in the eyes that cause blindness or semiblindness are almost invariably the evidences of like defects or of disease in the immediate or remote ancestors. Many of these take the form of cataract, which unfortunately is usually not operatable. Of course, it will not be necessary for me to say to those familiar with the laws of heredity that acquired characteristics are not transmitted. One who is physically normal except for the fact that he has accidentally lost his sight, as from an explosion, may have children with perfectly good eyes. In the case of a person born blind, however, or imperfect sighted, the same defect will or is likely to recur in the children of the immediate or subsequent generations.

Some forty years ago, before the sexes were as carefully segregated as at present, in the New York State School for the Blind, two young people married, both of whom were congenitally blind. Some years afterward their sightless progeny began coming to the school, and then the third generation, and now a little girl representing the fourth generation has recently been entered in the kindergarten. In this family alone, seventeen members have been educated and cared for as state charges, and other members of this same family will come to the school every few years, and they will continue to come world without end unless measures should be taken to stop the development of a defective breed. Each member of the family becomes a factor of a new line, multiplying in arithmetical progression as long as it is permitted to continue to do so. It is well within the bounds of probability to say that that one marriage has already cost the state of New

York at least fifty thousand dollars. All of this might have been prevented by moral suasion if the state had made provision for the separate maintenance of the original pair. But the woeful pity of it is not in the waste of money, but in the waste of lives.

Who knows but Maeterlinck is right, and that the souls of unborn babies are waiting for fit tenements to be prepared for them? Should we not insist on as clean and decent bodies for their souls as we do homes for their bodies? Or shall we invite these innocents, as in that other great class of born-blind babies, into habitations wrecked before they come into the world by one of the most noxious and fatal poisons of the diseases of sex?

It is not only the babes who suffer. The foundation of many conditions ultimately resulting in serious defects of vision and predisposing to blindness is laid during the years of school life while the tissues are plastic and are easily affected by insanitary surroundings. Improper and insufficient lighting of schoolrooms, badly printed schoolbooks, and, more than all, too long and too persistent demands upon the adolescent eye for near work are the conditions that make for defective eyes and lay the foundations of conditions that may ultimately lead to partial or complete blindness.

The necessity of better conditions in many of the schools has for a long time been evident to those who recognize the importance of protecting the eyes of the developing child if it is hoped to preserve them in their normal form for the later work of life. But the appointment of a special committee by the National Educational Association last year gives reason now to hope that this subject will be studied from many sides. This committee consists of an illuminating engineer, an experienced school man, a book publisher, a psychologist and an ophthalmologist. A like committee has been appointed by the American Medical Association, and under the direction of these bodies careful investigations will be made of existing conditions, and from the data secured undoubtedly valuable conclusions will be drawn and recommendations made.

In this connection, the importance of social service will, of course, be evident. The surgeon at the out-patient service of any eye hospital is constantly impressed with his own impotence from a lack of general knowledge of the home conditions. Impaired nutrition affects the structures of the eyes as it does every other tissue in the body, and it manifests itself in ulcers which leave blinding scars. It is futile to give medicine when the hungry child needs milk, or to prescribe drops when he needs bread. Conditions requiring immediate surgery are neglected because someone has not the time to impress quietly and patiently upon the timid and ignorant family, often foreign to our customs and language, the urgency of such a procedure. And here it is that the specially trained and tactful social worker may be most helpful in saving eyes that otherwise would be lost. But the medical profession itself has by no means wholly reached the highest degree of efficiency. Not that the surgeons are not adequately trained, but that the methods of record-taking are so defective as to make exact determinations almost impossible, and it is only by statistics that meet the three requirements of completeness, correctness and immediateness, that it is possible for the value of the efficiency of the work of our hospitals to be determined with the same degree of precision as that employed in our modern business houses. Were such records uniform in all of the hospitals of the country, it would be possible for us to get facts from them which would so impress the public with the necessity of co-operation in the development of preventive measures that the expense of the maintenance of hospitals, which has become a large tax upon the public purse, would be greatly lessened. There is much waste of time that has a money value in having large crowds of patients hastily and inadequately treated when smaller numbers and more complete and thorough examinations would so limit the number of their visits as to leave more time for the correct treatment of those who remain.

The constant interrelation between the various activities of life again is exemplified in blindness resulting from industrial accidents. It is a common misapprehension that every accident is an act of God and that it must necessarily be accepted without complaint or criticism. Exceedingly interesting and valuable in this connection is it to know that the prevention of accidents has so largely occupied the attention of the great casualty insurance companies that one of them has issued a book for general distribution, showing the most common causes for accidents and how they might most effectually be avoided. The writers, Mr. Frank E. Law, M. E., and Mr. William Newell, A. B., M. E., of the staff of the Fidelity and Casualty Company of New York, have consulted the vast number of records of the company with which they have been connected and have visited a large number of factories and other places. In the preface of their book they say: "The desirability of preventing accidents no one will question. Aside from the humanitarian aspect of the matter, which must appeal to every lover of his kind, the financial loss alone due to accidents is so great as to warrant the most complete precautions for their prevention. In the year 1908 the large sum of $22,392,072 was paid in premiums to insurance companies for liability insurance. The prevention of accidents absolutely is, of course, impossible, but much more can be done to prevent them than at first sight appears. It is to Germany that we must turn for exact information regarding the causes of accidents. From statistics collected there in connection with workmen's compensation insurance, it appears that the greater number of accidents, 58 per cent are due to the negligence of employers or employees, and the smaller number, 42 per cent to the inevitable risks of employment." It will be seen therefore that more than half of these accidents are not only not inevitable, but are absolutely preventable and are due to the want of skill and to carelessness, want of guards, deficient factory arrangements, acting against rules and other evidences of neglect which might and should be avoided. In this connection it must be borne in mind that the precautions for preventing industrial accidents are far and away more complete in Germany than in the United States.

American statistics are very incomplete, but it would seem that about 15 per cent of the injuries are those affecting the eyes. The age at which these accidents occur is usually between twenty and forty years, the most productive period in a workingman's life. To show how complete was the loss to the man and how small the compensation, it is reported by Miss Crystal Eastman from her Pittsburgh survey that for the loss of an eye the compensation in eleven cases was as follows: One man received $200; two received $150; one received $100; one, $75; two received $50; one, $48; and three received nothing.*

*Eastman, Work-Accidents and the Law, p. 126.

The United States Steel Corporation has so seriously taken up the study for the protection of men in its employ that a very compact organization has been developed for this purpose. Mr. David S. Beyer, chief safety inspector of the American Steel and Wire Company, writes: "In some of the companies which were brought together in 1901 to form the United States Steel Corporation, organized safety departments have existed for the last fifteen years. In all of them more and more attention has been given to safeguarding employees, until at present each of the main constituent companies has a corps of trained specialists who devote their time to studying the causes of accidents and to devising means to prevent them." New impetus was given to this work by the interest manifested in it and the policy adopted toward it by the officials of the Steel Corporation. Every year, beginning with May, 1906, all of the men in charge of these matters for the several subsidiary companies have been called together at the general offices in New York for discussion of the problems connected with their work. At these meetings the officers of the corporation have given assurance of support to the subsidiary companies in every practical undertaking for the prevention of accidents. This resulted in the formation in April, 1908, of a central committee of safety.

Some idea of the breadth of the field before the new committee may be gained from the fact that it includes 143 manufacturing plants, in addition to mining and transportation properties, employing in all approximately 200,000 men. Meetings of the committee are held about once a month, when arrangements for inspection are made and reports considered. Drawings, photographs, rules, specifications, etc., are submitted for consideration, and such as seem desirable are sent out to all the companies.

During the two years since the institution of this central committee of safety, its inspectors have reported to it in round numbers six thousand recommendations for increasing the safety of employees in the plants, mills, mines, and on the railroads and steamship lines of the organization. Of these recommendations, 93 per cent have been adopted by the committee and carried out by the subsidiary companies.

One of the most common sources of accidents to the eyes is caused by flying bits from emery wheels. A device has been adopted that makes it possible to cover a large portion of the wheel, leaving enough of it for use by the man, and other devices have been adopted by which the men's eyes are shielded from flying bits of the wheels. Many of the companies supply these protecting devices to those to whom they sell wheels, and allow them gratuitously the use of these protecting devices as long as their wheels are used, so that in many cases there really is no excuse for a very large number of these accidents, many of which are exceedingly serious.

Instructions should be given to the workmen, and in every shop some such advice as the following should be posted where it is easily seen: "Never run a wheel above its indicated speed"; "A workman at an emery wheel should keep his eyes and body out of the plane of rotation of the wheel; chips from the wheel will be less likely to strike him if this suggestion is heeded." The grinder will find that large glasses made of plain glass, or indeed his own spectacles should he wear them, will afford great protection from flying particles. Or he may use other protectors made with glass in front and gauze surrounding the glass.

It must be said many of the workmen object to the use of these protective devices, not realizing the dangers to which they are subjected, and it has always been a source of difficulty with employers to secure from the workmen the co-operation necessary in this mode of protection; here again we come back to the same point at which we started—the necessity of intelligent educational work. If the men can be made to understand what an injury would mean and that they are in constant danger, there will be little difficulty, if proper devices are given to them, to make them use them. The reason that many of the men do not use the devices is that improper devices have been given to them, for instance, isinglass spectacles, through which they cannot see clearly.

Another very common cause of injury is from what is called a mushrooming hammer, whose hammering surface is driven beyond the outer edge so that the bits are easily broken off and fly into the eye. Hammers are sometimes, too, made of cheap material, badly surfaced, so that not only the outer edge but the entire surface of the hammer breaks like egg-shells, and bits are carried into the eyes, making it a dangerous instrument in the hands of a man who has to use it daily. The saving of a dollar or so in the purchase of a cheap hammer is often a very costly experiment. This subject is very adequately dealt with by Dr. S. C. Ayres, who submitted such a hammer for expert examination, and the result of that examination was exceedingly interesting, because it demonstrated the fact that this hammer was being sold very commonly and that good hammers can be easily obtained. It was demonstrated that if the hammer was made of good material and properly annealed, such accidents would practically never occur. Of course this applies equally to other tools. The cost of a new hammer is a dollar and a quarter. The cost of the loss of an eye, as determined by the courts of Texas, was $6,500. Would it not be profitable to require that the tools of working-men be made of such material as to reduce the possibility of such an accident to the ultimate minimum?

The use of insufficient or poor lighting in workshops is not only a source of frequent accidents but of defective work. In some of the factories where fine fabrics are woven and great care must be exercised, the loss of a single thread in the woof is sufficient to make what is termed seconds. It has been found that in those factories in which imperfect light is used the proportion of seconds is increased thereby. It may be interesting to consider for a moment how simply adequate lighting might be secured.

On the authority of Mr. E. Leavenworth Elliott, editor of the Illuminating Engineer and a practical physicist, it is stated that the loss of three minutes' time on the part of a workman because of imperfect lighting in a factory would be sufficient to pay for adequate lighting for that man the entire working day, while an uncertain light not only produces lowered efficiency, injures the eyes of the man, but may result in an accident the cost of which would be many thousands of dollars. Good illumination is a paying investment for every employer of labor.

It will be seen, therefore, that there are a multitude of practical and practicable ways in which eyes might be saved at the expense of comparatively little effort. The one thing needed is organized co-operation. It will be seen, too, that the conditions which result in blindness are many, and in a large number of instances they are controllable. In 1906 the American Medical Association, which is the largest organized body of physicians in the world, undertook, by means of this co-ordinated effort, to wipe out infantile ophthalmia as a cause of blindness, and committees for this purpose, working under one general central committee, were appointed in every state in the Union. Propaganda has been made, laws have been enacted, in six states a simple prophylactic is distributed gratuitously, and great progress has been made toward the ultimate accomplishment of what seemed to be impossible, the purging of our country of this blot on its sanitary efficiency by thoughtlessness in humanity.

Last year the work of this committee was broadened to include all forms of preventable blindness, and the committee has been correspondingly enlarged by the appointment of a number of associate committees, each having for its scope the control of some special condition. Eight of these committees are now actively at work under the leadership of men who have given special attention to the subject assigned to them. These committees are investigating trachoma, which has become such a menace to the nation that our ports of entry are closed to those infected by it, under Dr. John Green, Jr., of St. Louis; blindness from toxic amblyopias, such as alcohol and tobacco, under Dr. George E. De Schweinitz of Philadelphia; blindness from wood alcohol, which is far more common than we realize, under Dr. Casey Wood of Chicago; congenital blindness, under Dr. Clarence Loeb of St. Louis; industrial accidents, under Dr. Mark D. Stevenson of Akron, Ohio, and general sanitation and hygiene of the eyes, under the chairmanship of Dr. William Campbell Posey of Philadelphia, while the committee on ophthalmia neonatorum continues under its former chairman, with Dr. J. Clifton Edgar of New York and Dr. F. F. Westbrook of Minneapolis, Minn., as the other members.

Commissions for the prevention of blindness and the care of the blind have been established in a number of states, notably in Massachusetts and Ohio. Under the direction of the Russell Sage Foundation, a committee on ophthalmia neonatorum is a branch of the New York Association for the Blind, with Miss C. C. Van Blarcom as executive secretary, and one on prevention of blindness under the direct authority of the Russell Sage Foundation with Miss Louise Lee Schuyler as chairman is in executive charge of Mr. Samuel Ely Eliot. These have both actively taken up the propaganda for this work. By the former six publications have been issued, and by the latter, two.

These various activities have led the now large number of people interested in this subject to believe that an association devoted to the prevention of blindness which would co-ordinate with the various individual efforts would be of great practical value. Such an association was organized at a conference held in the United Charities building on the seventeenth of December last. The meeting was called by the chairman of the Committee on Prevention of Blindness of the American Medical Association, who, with Mr. Edward M. Van Cleve, president of the Ohio Commission for the Blind, and Mr. James P. Munroe, president of the Massachusetts Commission for the Blind, constituted a committee appointed for this purpose at a conference held in February, 1910. The object of the organization is to unify the campaign which has been carried on by separate organizations in various states and localities. The Committee on Organization, Drs. Munroe, Van Cleve and Woods, recommended that the society include all persons and bodies desiring to co-operate in "prevention of infantile blindness, prevention of blindness from industrial and other accidents, and from disease, and in the conservation of vision through improved hygiene of the eyes during school life and in industrial occupations,'' and that it invite the co-operation of prevention societies now in existence, of state and national medical societies, educational bodies, labor organizations, commercial bodies, women's clubs, and the like. An organizing board of directors was also recommended and is now in the process of formation.

Immediately upon the publication of the fact that such an organization had been planned, communications were received from all classes of interested societies, one from a typographical union in Ohio, asking for literature; another from the New York branch of the Association of Collegiate Alumnae; one from the secretary of the Committee of One Hundred, and one from the American Breeders' Association, Eugenics Section, in which it was stated that that association had already begun to obtain facts on congenital blindness from the various schools for the blind and deaf.

It would seem that the time has fully arrived when the co-ordinated efforts of those interested would be effective in the development of a work of great importance and of national extent. It is believed that the careful study which would thereby be given to preventive measures in factories and workshops would so increase the efficiency of labor as to make employers anxious to co-operate with students of these conditions, not alone because of the awakened business conscience—evidences of which are everywhere present—but because as a business proposition it would pay. When we learn that it is cheaper to save eyes than to destroy them, when humanity and science join forces with capital and labor to produce increased economic efficiency, with added advantages to each, the benefit to all will be beyond our powers to estimate.

THE NUTRITION OF CHILDREN UNDER SEVEN YEARS OF AGE

WINFIELD S. HALL, Ph.D., M. D.

Professor of Physiology, Northwestern University Medical School

Human life, as you probably very well know, is divided into infancy, childhood, adolescence, adult life and old age. Childhood is the second of the five periods and comprises about a decade, perhaps a little more, beginning with about the third year. Childhood is a period of unorganized play; and that makes a difference in the feeding of the child.

I shall confine my discussion to the feeding of children in the period before their school days; that is, before the seventh year. Of course during the sixth year they may be in kindergarten; but a very small proportion of all children go to kindergarten. It is a period, then, during which the child is devoting several hours a day to active play, preferably under the eye of mother or nurse; in the ideal case, under the eye of the mother. I refer to the activities of the child at this age as unorganized play. This has a significance, because the child engaged in unorganized play shifts his attention and his activities every few minutes. He plays at one thing, as "hide and seek" for a few minutes, and "tag" for a few minutes; one game and then another passing in a kaleidoscopic succession during the day. The child fixes his attention upon any one activity for a few minutes only. This, therefore, is thc period of unorganized play.

There is a moderate amount of physical growth during this period. If we consider the amount of weight and of height and growth measurement,

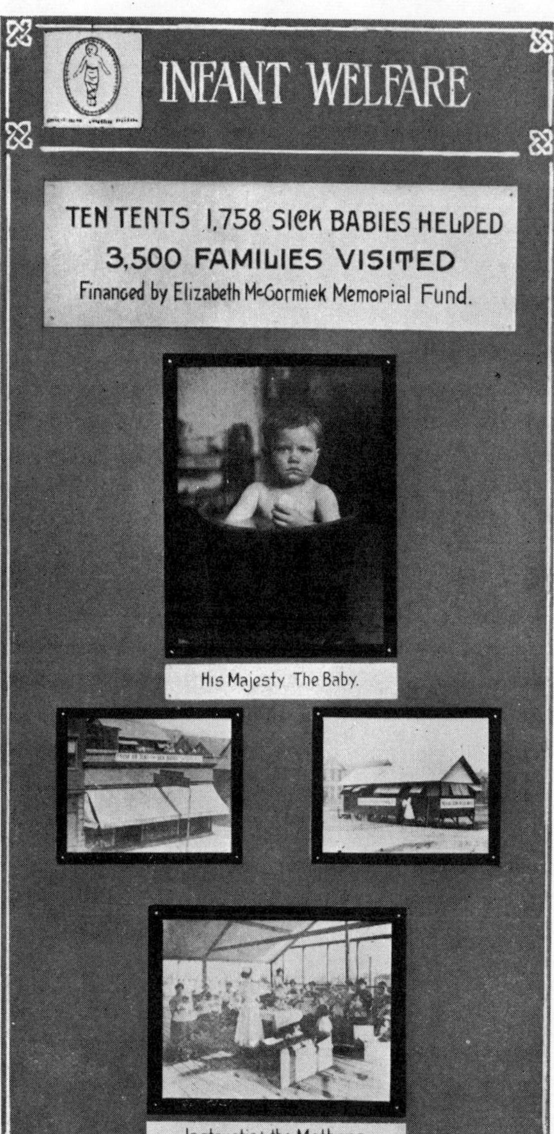
INFANT WELFARE
TEN TENTS 1,758 SICK BABIES HELPED
3,500 FAMILIES VISITED
Financed by Elizabeth McCormick Memorial Fund.
His Majesty The Baby.
Instructing the Mothers.

added to the child's bulk during any unit of time, as a year, for example, we find the percentage rate of growth during this period considerably less than during the period of infancy. The percentage growth at infancy is greater than that at any other time during life. However, the percentage growth is very great during the early years of adolescence. At the age of puberty, from the thirteenth to the fifteenth year in girls, from the fifteenth to the seventeenth year in boys, the rate of growth is very rapid. But the rate in early childhood is somewhat less than at puberty, and considerably less than in infancy. This matter of the growth of the child is a very important one when we consider what the child should eat; and the importance of it will be emphasized presently.

I would emphasize another feature of child growth, namely, the incessant activity. A common expression for parents to use in referring to a child, particularly to a boy, is: "He is a perpetual motion machine"—which means that from five or six in the morning until a similar hour at night, or even later, the child is continuously moving. Even when he is supposed to be sitting still, he is wriggling about. It is actual pain to a child of that age to sit really still for such an interminable period as five minutes. The meal-time period at table is one during which the child is wriggling and twisting around; and in some families the child gets down off his chair, takes a turn around the room, and then comes back to finish the meal with the rest of the family. That was not considered good discipline in my childhood, but is accepted now, I believe.

Habits

Let us now consider the relation of habit to the physical and psychical well-being, including its relation to the nutrition of the child. This period of early childhood is the period during which the child is acquiring habits which may last him through life. No parent can do justice to his child if he ignores the fact that, during early childhood, life-habits are being formed. Some of us, I am sure, would emphasize the importance of considering seriously the influence of habit before childhood, i. e., in infancy; and many a mother will begin almost with the first day of the life of her infant to guard its habits and to introduce the element of regularity into its life. If the mother has given no attention to habit-forming during the first three years of the child's life, surely she cannot longer put it off, and must begin very carefully to guard the eating habits as well as all other habits. During this period the character of the eating will be established—whether the child gobbles his food or whether he eats in an orderly way, and whether he eats regularly or irregularly.

First, consider the habit of regularity. Regularity should be introduced in all the life habits of the child, particularly in eating, sleeping, and care of the bowels. As to eating, any of you who have had an opportunity to study child life can call up many instances where the nutrition of a child has been completely upset or disturbed very seriously, requiring months to get it straightened out again, by irregularity of meals, eating whenever there is an inclination. I have seen mothers with little infants in their arms, offering the little child something to eat whenever he cries, assuming that the child is hungry because he cries. Of course the mother who is so unwise as to do that is the mother who belongs to the dark ages of the nineteenth century! Twentieth century mothers have learned that they must introduce regularity into the eating habits of their infants.

The child comes home from school "starved to death." Are you going to give him a lunch? Yes. If he is hungry enough to gnaw at a dry crust, give him a lunch. If he is not hungry enough to gnaw at a dry crust, but just hungry enough to eat some bread and butter and jam or some cake, then he is not so very hungry; he is not starving; you need not worry about him. If he is hungry enough to eat a dry crust of bread, he will because of the hardness and dryness of the bread be forced to chew it fine, thoroughly mixing it with saliva. This bread will digest very rapidly; and within an hour and a half's time, the regular time for the next meal, the child will be ready for it. But let the child eat a lunch of bread, butter and jam or of cake, and when the regular meal time comes he is not ready for good, wholesome meat and potatoes or bread and milk or cereals. He may be ready, however, to eat cake or pie, which will, of course, further disturb his digestion. I have seen many a child have his digestion disturbed, his general nutrition disturbed, and his general health disturbed, by this irregularity of eating. I would emphasize, then, with all the force the English language will put at my command, the importance of regularity in the eating habits of children.

As to the sleeping habits: they must be regular, too; because if they are not, that irregularity will interfere, at one end of the day or the other, with the eating habits. A child of three, four, five or six may get up and have breakfast with the family if he has gone to bed early enough the night before. That means introducing regularity into the sleeping habits of the child. A younger child, younger than six or seven, ought to have a nap in the afternoon; then he can rise with the rest of the family and go regularly to the table in the morning with them.

As to regularity in bowel movement, we learn as we study the nutrition of children that it is a matter of the greatest importance that they have a passage of the bowels regularly every morning at least, preferably twice in the day. A mother or nurse has not done her fundamental duty by the child if she has not looked carefully after this matter. It is a matter of considerable importance—perhaps hardly understood until we study the psychological influence of habit over the physical body—to go to "stool" at a regular hour, and wait for the inclination. Every child in this period of its habit-gaining existence should be taught that habit. It can be introduced into the regular régime of the child's life.

The next habit is that of simplicity. We are living in a complex age. There is a tendency for all of our living to be made progressively more and more complex. Our eating habits become complex along with the rest; also our drinking habits—we are not satisfied with plain "Adam's ale." There is nothing better to drink in all the world for man and beast, even for the plants of the field, than water, just plain water, water that is so abundant on every hand. Of course, we who live in crowded cities must give no small amount of attention to the purity of the water, to guard it from contamination; but it is possible for us to get ample quantities of pure water, and there is nothing better to drink, and yet there is a tendency to put tea and coffee and fruit juices into water to make something "better than water." It tickles the taste. Let me tell you something; this tickling of the taste of the child with spiced foods, rich complex foods and flavored drinks is for several reasons a most unfortunate tendency. In the first place, it establishes in the child an unnatural taste for foods and drinks that are not simple and wholesome. Furthermore, there is another side to this question that I wish to emphasize in passing, though it has nothing to do with the nutrition. This giving of highly-spiced complex foods and highly-flavored drinks to little children is a catering to sense gratification. Eating a thing because it tastes good, or drinking a thing because it tastes good, is doing a thing that gratifies the sensual! Mothers, if you begin that way with the child on these simple senses of taste and smell, and the flavor of food and drink, what are you going to do fifteen years later when the primordial urge gets into that young person's blood and he looks out upon the world and turns to the right and to the left for other forms of sense gratification?

I do not want to do more than suggest the possible final result of giving free rein to sense gratification. Teach the children of three and four to be satisfied with simple things. Do not cater to sense gratification; that is a most unfortunate thing to do. Those of you who have studied pedagogy, those mothers who have seen their children growing up into adolescence, will vouch for the truth of the matter. So much is to be said for simplicity in eating and drinking.

There is another habit that is of the greatest importance for the mother to establish in her child. It is the habit of a thorough mastication of food. We have had the importance of that brought to our attention especially during the last few years by our friend, Horace Fletcher. He has caught the public eye. And one might think that we physicians had never discovered the hygienic importance of mastication; but in a quiet way we have been preaching it to our patients for decades. The great importance of a thorough mastication of the food has been well recognized by the medical profession for ages long. To emphasize very briefly the reasons for the need of mastication: (1) If the food is thoroughly masticated, thoroughly chewed and mixed with the saliva, it will be very much more rapidly and easily digested. (2) The food can be very thoroughly masticated only by consuming more time than would be taken if the food were simply bolted, or washed down with water. During the time that one is thoroughly masticating food, the food taken in the early part of the meal is being rapidly digested and absorbed. It has satiated the hunger; and the person satisfies his appetite, within twenty or twenty-five minutes of chewing, even though in that time he has chewed only a very moderate amount of food. If he bolts his food as rapidly as he can wash it down with water, he will have gorged himself in fifteen minutes and still be hungry and go away from the table hungry, ready to eat more if he could hold it. Do you see what that means? It means that he is going to over-eat, and he is going to learn the habit of over-eating in childhood. When he gets to be about thirty years old he is going to begin to lay on flesh, and this process will progress until by the time he is fifty he has distorted his proportions out of the human type altogether. So it is a matter of the greatest importance in the nutrition of people in general to get the habit of thorough mastication of the food early in childhood. You cannot teach an old person to chew his food thoroughly and properly; that must be taught in childhood.

The Physical Needs of Early Childhood

The physical needs of early childhood may be subdivided into two general groups: First, the need of constructive material; second, the need of fuel material. The body may be likened to an engine. When an engine is built certain constructive materials are used, iron and brass and babbitt and so forth. After it is constructed, fuel is needed to make it go. The total amount of fuel that an engine will consume during its life-period of perhaps a decade is many hundred times the weight of the engine. In a similar way the amount of fuel material that we in our life activities consume and use as fuel is many hundred times as great in the aggregate as the amount of constructive material that is actually built up into body tissue.

What are the materials that the body must have for construction? They are nitrogenous material and certain mineral salts. The latter are very common, every-day materials that are found on every hand; they are soil constituents that are built up into the structure of plants and pass from plants into the bodies of herbivorous animals and make a part of their construction, so that whether we eat vegetables, fruits, cereals, milk, eggs, or animal flesh, in any case we get these salts incidentally in sufficient quantities. Therefore, as a rule, we need pay little special attention to the salts, with, perhaps, the one exception of iron, which I shall refer to a little later.

To emphasize now the great importance of the nitrogenous foods as constructive material—what are the nitrogenous foods? They are the foods that contain the half dozen most important constituents: carbon, hydrogen, sulphur, phosphate, nitrogen, and oxygen. The constructive foods are lean meat, eggs, milk, and the nitrogenous portion of cereals. Cereals are rich in these nitrogenous constituents. They are so sufficiently rich that the herbivorous animal readily builds up his body from the nitrogenous material that he finds in plants. Man also could build up his body with equal ease from the nitrogenous material that we find in cereals. However, man seems to be rather omnivorous so that human nutrition is best maintained when we have a mixed diet—mixing with our cereals, vegetables and fruit, such foods as eggs, milk and perhaps lean meat. The people in the far northern latitudes, where they have almost no vegetation, are confined very largely to a meat diet; while the people of the torrid zone, because of the abundance of fruit that actually falls into their open hands, are habitually fruit and nut eaters; and people of the temperate zone who have to hustle for either fruit, vegetables or lean meat have the mixed diet.

We find, then, that the constructive foods needed by the child are furnished by the most natural things, the things that are easy to obtain, milk, eggs, cereals, and such legumes as beans and peas, all of which furnish abundant proteins or nitrogenous food. I should like to take this occasion to emphasize especially the importance for little children of three of these and to minimize the importance of the fourth one. The three are cereals, milk and eggs. The fourth, the importance of which I should minimize, is lean meat. Children of the age under consideration would be very much better off if they ate a very small amount, if any, of lean meat. Cereals, milk and eggs all contain not only the constructive material, salts as well as the nitrogenous material, but also some fuel material—milk and cereals being particularly rich in fuel material.

As to the fuel foods: I have called your attention to the fact that we find some fuel foods mixed in with the constructive foods. But there are foods that are fuel foods par excellence and are not in any sense constructive foods. They are the carbonaceous foods; these are the starches, sugars and fats. Where do we find them? We find them especially abundant in vegetables, fruits and cereals. I have already discussed cereals with milk and eggs. In vegetables and fruits we find practically no nitrogenous material of any importance; but they furnish much of our starches and sugars.

Nuts are very wholesome foods, but they should not be used late in the evening, as postprandial desserts. They should be made a definite part of the meal and should be chewed to a creamy consistency. When they are thus made a definite, organic part of the meal, a regular course—a nut course—and are thoroughly masticated, they are not indigestible. Nuts are just as digestible as anything else if they are properly chewed and taken in proper relation to the rest of the diet; and they are exceedingly nourishing. You cannot get so much nourishment for the same amount of money in any other way as in nuts.

Let us emphasize the importance of abundant fuel material. I called attention to the fact that children of this age are perpetual motion machines. They are continually on the move from six in the morning until six or seven at night. That continual activity is a manifestation of motor energy and demands fuel food. The body has the wonderful power of transforming fuel energy into motion; you have to feed your locomotive, or it cannot pull your train; you have to feed your engine, or it cannot drive the wheels of commerce; you have to feed your child, or he will not be active. So let him have sugar; let him have starch in abundance, plenty of potatoes. Let him pile sugar on the cereal if he wants to. Of course, this thing must always be considered: that some children may have an idiosyncracy in regard to sugar. In the stomach of an occasional individual sugar shows a tendency to ferment; and nutrition is seriously disturbed.

However, this idiosyncracy is early discovered by the mother and the physician. Such an individual must go through life eating sparingly of sugar, perhaps occasionally tasting it; and if it always produces the same results, he must practically leave it out of his dietary. Such an experience, however, must be taken as a personal peculiarity, an idiosyncracy. The average individual can use starch and sugar; and they make wholesome fuels, though they do not build up muscle. If eaten in excess, of course, they do tend to increase the adipose tissue; but if the child observes the rule of very complete mastication of food, excessive eating will be obviated; and the child will not show a tendency to lay on fat.

In closing, I wish to discuss briefly two things: iron and fasting. I mentioned iron as the one inorganic or mineral constituent to which the mother may well give some little attention. It seems to be the mineral constituent that is the most difficult to assimilate, the most difficult to hold in the body. In certain disturbances of nutrition, the body seems to lose iron through excretion and seems to fail continuously to get the proper amount of iron out of food, though the proper amount may be present. The result is that the child gets paler and paler as the months go by. Every mother ought to know what that pallor indicates and she ought to see to it that the child has an abundance of easily digestible, nourishing foods, a good proportion of which should be rich in iron; for if the amount of iron in the food is increased, the tendency will be for the disturbance of nutrition gradually to be corrected. Eggs, particularly the yolks, are rich in iron. Green-colored plants are very rich in iron—especially spinach, chard, dandelion greens, and so forth. Lean meat is also very rich in iron—

especially red meat. Let me emphasize the importance of egg yolk. Let the child have egg lemonade when he comes from school. I do not know of any child who does not like egg lemonade if it is rightly made. Let him have eggs in all kinds of ways, but especially the yolk; and instead of the yolk and white of one egg, preferably the yolks of two eggs. As to the relative importance of these iron foods, eggs come first; greens, second, and lean meats, last. All of these perhaps, but especially the first two, should be used very freely in the diet of the anaemic child.

And finally a word about fasting. Many mothers seem to feel that, if the child does not eat three meals a day, something very serious will happen because of the failure to fill the stomach. Here is a fundamental rule for child and for adult also: Never eat unless you are hungry. Never force food down yourself or your child. If you are not hungry, do not eat; nature is whispering to you to fast. And if you have not an appetite for your dinner when you get home tonight, do not eat, but trust nature to give you an appetite for breakfast. If your child comes in from play or comes home from school or gets up in the morning with no appetite, do not urge him and almost force him to eat something; that is the height of unwisdom. Nature is working out the best good for the child and is protecting him from overloading his system and so has removed his appetite. Let the child fast. Nature will remedy that as the child gets over his temporary indisposition.

THE CLOTHING OF CHILDREN

NELLIE CROOKS
Milwaukee—Downer College

There is nothing more vital to the life of the child than clothing, for this is necessary as a protection both against heat and against cold. Changing styles affect us all, but unfortunately most of all they affect the child. Not many years ago all infants and children were dressed in low-neck and short-sleeve dresses in spite of cold houses. With the introduction of furnaces and steam heat into our houses, however, we changed the dress of children and put them in heavy flannels. Why these two things went together no one knows; but for many years it was the custom to use the heaviest kind of all-wool flannels. Now, I think, we have come to a more rational state of mind and realize that there is a connection between the temperature at which we keep our rooms and the clothing of our children.

The essentials in all clothing for children are warmth, lightness, looseness, and cleanliness. Many people think that weight and warmth are synonymous, but that is far from being the case. Warmth is due to material, texture, the number of layers, and color. Wool is our warmest material and is the only fibre that has on its surface little serrations, or saw-like edges. These tiny serrations, which cover each fibre of wool, produce warmth by friction.

The question of the use of wool is very important. For many years we thought, as I have said, that only pure wool should be used. Now we are going to the other extreme and use material largely of cotton but with little wool. Year by year raw wool is higher in price; this is due to a great many causes, but the result to the consumer is the same. These prices, if they are maintained as they have been, mean that for the same amount of money a very much poorer material is given. In some little children's shirts that I analyzed to see if they contained the amount of wool as represented—they were sold as all wool at eighty-six cents—I found the amount of wool to be only 57 per cent. While a certain amount of cotton in wool keeps it from shrinking, still we do not wish to pay for wool when we are getting something that is adulterated with cotton. The United States Government provides that the shirts worn by the soldiers shall contain 30 per cent of cotton; so you may take 30 per cent as a very fair allowance of cotton. In the case of children, however, where the garment has to be washed so often, it is essential that underclothing should be of materials that will not shrink too much; we can assume, therefore, that 50 to 75 per cent of wool is as great an amount as is desirable in underclothing for children.

The question is, how shall we know whether or not we are getting the proper per cent of wool in the materials we buy. I have tested some materials that were sold as all wool and I have found that they had only 11 per cent of wool. The best and simplest test is to make a 5-per-cent solution of caustic potash. Take a piece of caustic potash four inches long, which you can buy for a few cents at any chemist's, and put it in a large tin cup of hot water; place it on the stove and let it come to a boil. Put your material in this caustic potash and leave it for a minute or so. The wool will become a jelly-like mass, but the cotton will remain. Take out what is left and wash it; and this gummy substance, which was once wool, will wash out and leave the cotton.

And in that way you can have an idea, though it may be only a rough estimate, of what is in the material.

While this is a very satisfactory way to test the materials that are sold by the yard, how can we judge of materials that are already woven into garments? Underclothing for children is generally bought in the finished garment. The best way to judge when one is buying woolen garments is by feeling the wool. There is a certain feeling that one gets in the fingers by passing one's hands over good wool. In buying it is well to remember that there are many little children's shirts sold as all wool that have only about 20 per cent of wool, which would give, of course, a very small amount of warmth for a great deal of weight. And as I have said before, weight is not at all synonymous with warmth. Therefore, if it is impossible to get good wool, if it is too expensive to obtain, it is far warmer to have two layers of a thin material than it is to have one layer of a very thick material that is not woolen.

The question of children's stockings is a very important one, as children's feet and legs are exposed to the weather. We have the idea now that the short socks are not good for children three, four, and five years old and that wool should be worn by little children except in very warm weather. Here are some stockings that I bought at a store in a poor district. They cost forty-eight cents a pair, and they are the most miserable things I ever imagined. They are made of short bits of wool, from tailor's clippings and the refuse that comes from old materials, composed of cotton and wool. These are exposed to the fumes of sulphuric acid, the cotton is burned out and the wool is left; and these little short ends are rewoven again. These stockings are just as hard as boards; I should pity the poor child whose feet would have to walk in them; and yet they were forty-eight cents a pair. A little good wool would be better than shoddy, which not only is poor, but will begin after a few washings to rub off and will keep rubbing off, the stockings getting poorer and poorer with every washing.

When children are older than four or five, it is thought by many that cotton stockings are as good for them as wool. It is impossible to test stockings because each pair is a separate article. Even when you buy stockings that bear a label you know, you are not always sure that they come from the same place, because the practice in many of the big stores is to import stockings and label them in their own stores. One of the characteristics of a good stocking is elasticity. Whether a stocking is of cotton or of wool, it should be elastic. The pair of which I spoke has no elasticity at all. It is also better to have the stocking ribbed; this gives more elasticity. The shape of the stocking is also very important, as the shape makes a great difference in the wearing quality. If children are active, the least that they can get on with is six or eight pairs of stockings a year.

As to the question of night clothing; for the poorer people who cannot afford thin wool, there is a substitute in cotton called flannelette. Flannelette is cotton that has been combed up, that is, its soft outside fluff or surface, the nap, is caused by a machine. There is one great objection to flannelette, and that is its inflammability; it is as inflammable as cotton batting. The advantages of flannelette are that it is soft and warm. The thinner wool material is also warm, but it is not so much used, the mothers preferring this flannelette, which can be bought for ten to twelve cents a yard.

For the petticoats that little boys and girls wear,

thin flannel and flannelette are very good materials. And for their little bloomers there is a kind of flannelette that has a plain surface on the outside and the fluffiness on the inside, which is very warm and does not catch dirt. Very often, of course, the bloomers are made of a wash material like the dress; but for warmth the flannelette is a much better material.

The rompers that children wear are a blessing and are very inexpensive. When bought they are only twenty-five to fifty cents, and when made are, of course, less expensive.

When it comes to the question of dresses for children, there are several materials that may be used, calicoes, ginghams and percales. The thing that I should like especially to emphasize is the great difference in wearing quality as an advance of two cents in price is made. For instance, the wearing quality of a cotton that is ten cents a yard is certainly nearly half as much again as that of one which is eight cents a yard; and twelve-cent cotton has almost double the value of ten-cent cotton. The material that has been found of greatest value in an orphan asylum in which I am very much interested, where the children are very well cared for, is nurse's gingham, which stands washing and is very serviceable material. At retail it is twelve cents a yard, and at wholesale it is much less.

It is possible, as illustrated in the exhibit, to weave cotton very loosely; it can be woven almost like a fine mosquito netting; the threads can be starched, then the finished web can be starched also, and the material, when it is ready to be sold after being pressed and given a gloss, has the outward appearance of a good material. When it is washed, however, all this dressing comes out, and the resulting article is a very poor, flimsy stuff, which when used for children's clothing will tear, and which wears very badly. This cheaper cotton shrinks a great deal.

For the little boys who are wearing blouses a heavy cotton material like duck is very warm and not at all expensive. When the little boys outgrow the cotton suits and go into woolen suits, it has been found very much more economical to buy with each coat two pairs of trousers. This enables a boy to wear a good pair for school and have the other pair for other occasions, and the two pair do not more than outlast the one coat. The proportion of wool in these suits is from a half to three-quarters per cent. This amount of cotton enables the trousers to be washed without shrinking. The question of the washing and shrinking is of course a great item in both wool and cotton materials. The question of shrinkage means that with a growing child, even if the garment is large at the beginning, it will not be large enough in a short time.

While the adulteration of wool makes a difference in the underclothing and dresses of the child, it makes more difference in the outside clothing. A coat or overcoat that a girl or boy wears must be warm; that is very essential in our cold winters. The price of the overcoat or the coat is a serious item, but if it is possible in any way to get it, the better coat will outlast by two to one the coat of the poorer material. And there is another thing, if there are several children, it can be handed down to the next younger.

The question of the home-made and the factory-made outfits for children is so fully dealt with in the exhibition that I did not take it up. The difference in cost is several dollars per year, and I think for the cheaper garments it may be said a hand-made one will outlast a factory-made one of the poorer quality twice the length of time.

It has occurred to me that in connection with the work that is being done for children, if there could be some way by which the poor could get materials at cost it would be a good thing; if it were possible for them to get, for instance, good twelve-cent gingham for eight cents; if some of the institutions that get a large amount of materials could sell the materials at cost to the people who want them for children's clothes, it would certainly make a great difference a year in saving. The very poor mother who has to buy the things ready made is of course the prey of the cheaper shopkeepers who are very conscienceless.

A year or so ago there was an investigation of the cost of living among the wives of switchmen in Chicago. They gave their testimony as to the rise in the cost of living in all the different branches of their housekeeping, and they said one of the things which made it so much more expensive to provide for their families was that the clothing did not last, as it had formerly done, to pass from one child to the next; it simply fell to pieces after a short time and was of no use.

I think, then, we may conclude that anything that we can do to help the people in selecting better clothing will be a great saving of income. If we can show by tests or by experiments or by any practical way that a few cents a yard or a few cents a dress or a few cents on underclothing, or even fifty cents or a dollar in a coat, will make a wearing difference of a year, and the difference of its being passed down to another child, I think we shall have done a great deal. I wish that there were some way in which those of you who are working in settlements, working in large institutions, could pass on the knowledge that you have gained by experience to those people who have no chance to learn, who have no chance to have the experience which will teach them, because they get their clothing in such small quantity. The only thing by which they learn is their experience, which is often very disastrous.

And as to the question, what are we to do when we are trying to get all wool and pay for it and get cotton, the only thing that we can do is to agitate as much as we can and help the Murdock Bill, that goods shall be labeled for what they are. There is no law in this country that prevents anyone from selling anything that is not as represented. We should have a law like the Pure Food Law. There was a decision this winter in New York that was the first decision ever given in this country, of a wholesale merchant who received a lot of material to be made into men's clothing, and who found that while it was labeled "all wool," it was largely of cotton. He sued the manufacturer, and for the first time the defense was made that it was a common usage and therefore it was proper to misrepresent goods in labeling. That defense was not accepted, and the suit went against the manufacturer. If we had a law, there might be occasionally times when the large dealers would sue the manufacturers who sold goods that were not as represented. The individual, I think, has very little chance, but in union there is strength.

UNSETTLED PROBLEMS IN REGARD TO THE PHYSICAL CARE OF CHILDREN

J. M. DODSON, M. D.

Professorial Lecturer on Medicine, The University of Chicago

Notwithstanding the gratifying advance during the last century in our knowledge of childhood and infancy and all that pertains thereto, the one thing that impresses one most is the immensity of the field, the multitude of things that are yet to be learned about it. What we do not know about children would fill a great many volumes. Realizing that, the next question is how are we to lessen this field of ignorance with regard to childhood.

I should say in the first place that the most essential thing in the study of all these problems or of any other, is the method of scientific exactitude. We have wasted in former years an enormous amount of time in guess work, in speculation, and in theories about these things. What we have needed is exact scientific information. The methods of science must be applied to these things if we expect to arrive at definite conclusions.

Particularly is this true in connection with the problem of childhood, and this scientific spirit must be combined with a human attitude and the kindest sympathy for the child in all his relations. That adult who has forgotten all about his childhood, who has forgotten, for example, the spirit of play, is not likely to make very satisfactory headway with the study of the infant or child mind or of his needs.

The student of these problems must have access to materials, and we must recognize the fact that it is the function of institutions of all sorts that have to do with the care of children as, for example, the cure of sick children, to afford a place for the study of these problems of childhood and for the dissemination of information in regard to them. In other words, research and instruction must go hand in hand with the effort to care for and cure these sick children. What is more, these three things cannot be dissociated; no one of the three can be carried on successfully without the presence of the other.

And finally the various agencies concerned in the care of children, the school, the home, the hospital, the dispensary, the juvenile court—all of these agencies must co-operate with each other. With all of these organizations here in Chicago, I am more impressed from year to year with the fact that we are wasting an enormous amount of energy, and of well-meant effort, for lack of co-ordination and of co-operation of the proper sort.

In approaching these problems of what we do not know about infancy and childhood, the most fundamental thing of all is undoubtedly nutrition. As physicians we must recognize the intimate relation of mind and body; we must remember that happiness, health, and effectiveness are absolutely dependent upon a healthy body and that in this building up of the body the problem of nutrition is fundamental. Nutrition and growth go naturally together to form the very fundamental problem in the whole matter of childhood. Notwithstanding the immense amount of study that has been devoted to nutrition, particularly of infancy, in the last ten or twenty years, it still remains a field about which the universal feeling is that we have yet very much to learn; and the reason of this is that when we approach the study of nutrition, we enter one of the most difficult fields of science, organic and biological chemistry. One must know and understand the chemical changes that go on in the body, before he can know much about nutrition.

Closely associated with the problem of nutrition is the problem of growth. The adult who is healthy in body, stature and size has only, in the matter of nutrition, to supply that amount of fuel or food which is necessary to maintain the heat of the body and to do the work which it is called upon to do. With the infant child, however, nutritional processes must be such as not only to take care of the body from day to day and to keep it normal and able to perform the various processes, but it must be of such a sort as to build up tissue by intricate processes, which we do not as yet well understand. We can study, however, the processes of growth in the child, and the more exact and scientific the method, the better and more exact will be the knowledge that is derived from such observation.

This is a field that was almost wholly neglected until recently. It was about fifteen years ago, I think, that the late Dr. Christopher, sometime member of the Board of Education in Chicago, introduced into the city schools the Department of Child Study, whose function it is to make an accurate and exact study of the child by scientific methods, to keep track of the weight, the stature, the development of the various parts on the physical side, and to examine carefully into the condition of the several senses, the sight, hearing and the like. This department has given the Chicago schools a foremost place among the school systems of the United States.

We shall not attempt to touch upon the education of the normal child because that is an enormous field in itself and is well covered by the other discussions held in connection with this Exhibit. The study of the subnormal child, however, is very intimately associated with the study of the normal. The line between normal and subnormal is by no means a sharp line, rather it is a very indistinct line. There is indeed a very gradual series of steps from the completely normal child down through the various gradations, the lesser degrees of acuteness, to the completely subnormal child or idiot. And the methods which are adapted to the study of the subnormal have a direct bearing upon the pedagogic methods that are to be used successfully with the normal. Some of you may have read in a recent issue of McClure's Magazine (May, 1911) a most interesting article describing the methods of Maria Montessori, an Italian teacher, in dealing with the subnormal and normal child. She found that certain methods which she had adopted in connection with the training of the subnormal were remarkably effective in training the normal child and that observation has led to the adoption in several schools in Rome, Milan and elsewhere of these methods of the subnormal as applied to the normal. It has produced some remarkable results, and is of much interest as showing the relationship between the two.

While the proper nutrition and growth of the child are essential to his development, the subsequent maintenance of health is equally essential. There has been a remarkable and very gratifying advancement in our knowledge of disease in the last forty or fifty years, and it is rather interesting to note that most of this progress has been along the line of those diseases which are incident to early life. This great development of exact knowledge was born of the demonstration by Pasteur that certain diseases are due to micro-organisms. These so-called infectious diseases are for the most part diseases of early life.

The fruits of this great discovery have already begun to show in our mortality records. About eight years have been added to the average duration of human life, but this increase in longevity pertains almost wholly to the ages under forty. In other words those of us who are under forty may expect to live considerably longer than we would have lived half a century ago; those who are past forty can expect to live no longer than our forefathers at corresponding ages. There has been but little impression made upon the diseases of metabolism that obtain in later life. If we are to increase our knowledge of this group of diseases, if we are to lessen this enormous field of the unknown, we must have, in the first place, opportunities for study; and, secondly, we must make use of the knowledge that we have by the dissemination of that knowledge among the public, and by the securing of those regulations, statutory and otherwise, which are necessary to make such knowledge effective.

May I say a further word at this point with reference to the infectious diseases? We know a great deal more today than we did twenty-five years ago about diphtheria, scarlet fever, smallpox, and the other infectious diseases. So complete and accurate is our knowledge of these infections, that I think it is actually safe to say that if we could put into operation those procedures which every medical man knows to be effective, such as the prompt and complete isolation of every case of scarlet fever, of diphtheria, or of measles, and universal vaccination against smallpox, these infections could be permanently abolished. Notwithstanding these facts, here in Chicago we have about as many cases in proportion to the population as were observed fifty years ago. Every autumn when the schools open these diseases appear and spread with absolute regularity. Why? Simply because children still in the infectious stage are allowed to go back into school.

Concerning possible additions to our knowledge of disease there is another essential about which the general public is not fully informed and in which the attitude of the public mind is neither wise nor helpful. If we are to extend our knowledge of disease by accurate observation, then the places where sick children are cared for, and especially hospitals and dispensaries, must be just as much places for the investigation or the obtaining of new knowledge and for the instruction of the coming generation of physicians who are to deal with disease, as they are places for the curing of the sick. Grant that the primary function of the hospital is today, as it always has been and always must be, the care and the cure of the individual who goes there, another indispensable and co-ordinate function of the hospital is the scientific investigation of disease and the instruction of students. Show me the hospital where no work of that sort is done, where no scientific investigation is pursued, where no students are instructed, and I will show you a hospital where I would not take a patient if I could help it—a hospital in which every patient receives less care and effective attention than he ought to have. The attitude of most of our hospitals and hospital authorities is wholly foreign to this idea, antagonistic to the very notion of investigation and instruction.

Possibly this has been in some measure the fault of the medical staff, who have seemed to forget that the prime function of the hospital is the care and cure of the sick. Possibly medical men have sometimes been a bit thoughtless and a bit neglectful of a humane and sympathetic attitude toward the patients, but that is certainly the exception. The physicians, especially those connected with the charitable institutions who have given so freely of their service, have as a rule, a keenly sympathetic and humane attitude towards the individual patients. These physicians have not received and are not receiving in our public institutions, nor in most cases in the private charitable institutions, that assistance and that encouragement to scientific investigation and to the instruction of the coming generation that are so essential to the future welfare of the community.

Pardon me for speaking at such length at this point, but it seems to me one of the most important things that can be developed in connection with this discussion. We have in Chicago some hospitals that have manipulated this intelligent and helpful spirit, and one in particular, which has recently been making some magnificent strides forward, should be a lesson to other hospitals everywhere. In this hospital not only is the investigation of disease of the highest type encouraged, but provision has been made for it by the establishment of a thoroughly equipped pathological department in charge of trained pathological workers who are doing splendid work along these lines. I refer to the Morris Institute which has recently been established in connection with the Michael Reese Hospital. There will be made in this institute, I am sure, in the near future, discoveries of great moment.

UNSETTLED PROBLEMS IN REGARD TO THE NUTRITION OF CHILDREN

CLIFFORD G. GRULEE, M. D.

Professor of Pediatrics, Rush Medical College

The subject of nutrition of children is that about which least is known of any of the subjects of medicine. Perhaps there is no one branch of medicine about which so little is known as the nutrition of the infant and the child. Much is known of nutrition in the adult, but the nutrition of the infant and the child presents problems that are peculiar to themselves. In the first place the infant organism is a growing organism; therefore the nutrition of the child must be of such a nature as not only to supply waste as in the adult, but also to supply material for the growing body.

In the second place this nutrition must be afforded to an undeveloped gastro-intestinal tract and an internal metabolism, which is in the process of growth. This organism, which is providing the material for growth, must do more work than is required of the perfected organism of the adult.

With these two things in mind, you will see the difficult problem that we have when we approach the problem of nutrition of the infant or the child. The problem is more difficult the younger the individual. One of the few things, or rather one of the many things, that is attracting the attention of those interested in children's diseases today and will in the future attract more attention, is the nutrition of the new-born infant. It is a problem that has not been solved nor has any approach to its solution been brought about.

It is a practical impossibility to be sure that you can artificially feed a new-born infant from birth on and have him remain normal. Everyone should know that even a few weeks of nourishment at the mother's breast means much to an infant.

Another problem, a problem that is as yet not at all solved, is the nutrition of the normal infant after the first two weeks of life. Although, compared to nutrition of the infant in the first two weeks of life, nutrition after that period is very easy, still we cannot say in a given case whether the child will be a normal child or not; nor can we give any formula that we can be sure will fit a majority of these infants and that will not lead eventually to gastro-intestinal troubles.

The next question that presents itself in point of time is the problem as to what we shall feed these children after they pass the infancy period, or rather when they have come to the period when they demand something other than milk and starch and sugar mixtures. When are they ready to start with solid food? What shall that solid food be? We know a great many things that we cannot give them but we do not know in a given case, we cannot set down any general rule in a given case, as to how soon we should give the child solid food. These are all problems that perhaps many of us thought were definitely solved. They are not. These are all problems that will have to be worked out in the future. Our ideas in respect to the food of even older children have changed materially of recent years; whereas formerly it was thought that eggs were especially good for young infants, now eggs are not given nearly so often nor nearly so early in life. On the other hand vegetables are given much earlier. This is only one of the points in respect to infant feeding.

A vaster field than the normal child is the child with nutritional disorders. If we do not know how to keep a child normal under all circumstances, how can we tell how we shall cure a child who is sick? Peculiar as it may seem, the problem of curing certain nutritional disturbances is a much easier one than the problem of keeping children well, because in this field a great deal of work has been done and definite clinical symptoms have been shown of certain disorders; therefore, when these disorders appear, their presence is indicated by these symptoms, and we can have the materials at hand to overcome these disorders. In a normal child we have nothing to go by.

We do not know the nature of the disturbance in such a common thing as summer diarrhoea. It was formerly thought that summer diarrhoea was purely and simply an infectious disturbance, that it could be overcome by pasteurization of milk and by giving clean milk to the baby. It is unnecessary to show you how that idea has to a large extent been exploded. There may be some cases of summer diarrhoea that are due to infections, but it is certainly true that if the child is not given proper food the child is led on to summer diarrhoea, no matter whether the infectious organisms are there or not; and it has been proven conclusively within the last few years that a large percentage of summer diarrhoea are due to overfeeding of sugar, that is milk sugar or cane sugar, which have been regarded heretofore as almost harmless. This field is a comparatively large one and the most important of all.

We see poor, puny children, the victims of malnutrition, who will go sometimes for months without gaining an ounce and who still seem to take care of the food without any gastro-intestinal disturbance, for the internal organism is so constituted that it cannot make use of the food that the child takes. This is probably the most difficult of all problems that confronts us with respect to the infant's food. These children, if you give them a certain amount of food, not only will cease to gain but will lose weight; if you do not give them a certain amount of food, there is starvation and it requires nice judgment to tell how much or what kind of food the child should have.

But aside from these disturbances of nutrition, there are other disturbances that are intimately connected with nutrition, and of these probably that best known to the lay mind is convulsions. Now how definite the connection between convulsions and nutritional disturbances is, we do not know. We do know that very frequently with sudden gastro-intestinal attacks these children do have convulsions, but what the definite connection is, has not as yet been determined. We do not know whether the convulsions themselves are purely and simply the result of nutritive disorders or whether the nutritive disorder is simply the causal factor or medium that brings on the convulsion.

Another disease that is not commonly connected with nutrition but that probably is very intimately connected with it, is eczema. Eczema in the child very frequently can be relieved by changing the food—not always but very frequently. This gives us the idea that there is some distinct connection between eczema and a nutritional defect of some sort or another. What we do not know as to the nature of the defect is another problem to be solved.

But these are not all; if you do not feed the child proper food, you lower the child's resistance not only to nutritional disturbances but also to disturbances such as diphtheria, sore throat, colds, pneumonia and other diseases. These disturbances are all more or less dependent upon the nutrition of the child. Not that every such case is due to poor nutrition, but poor nutrition not only predisposes to these diseases but accounts for the lowered resistance.

What is America doing to combat or find out about the nutritional disturbances? So nearly nothing that I am almost ashamed to tell you what little is being done in this country. There has in some way grown up the idea that the scientific spirit could never be humanitarian, and this idea holds in the work of pediatrics (children's diseases) and nutrition, more than it does in any other. As a result we have not the laboratories; the medical profession has not the facilities for finding out the conditions that underlie these problems. In Berlin there has recently been established a hospital, known as the Kaiserin Augusta Victoria, which is devoted entirely to the study of infant mortality and the ways of reducing infant mortality. This was established some two years ago, and since that time practically all the work which has come from that institution has been on the question of nutrition. We have nothing in this country to equal that. There is one thing that must be done: our efforts must be devoted to realizing such an institution. No matter how much your charitable organizations may do, no matter how much good the nurse may do in the homes in teaching the mothers cleanliness, no matter how much may be done in furnishing these mothers with proper materials to work with, all these must go for nothing if you do not enlighten the medical profession and keep it working. That enlightenment of the medical profession can only come in one way, and that is by affording the men who do this work sufficient chance for investigation so that their interest will be aroused—not only their interest but the interest of the coming generations. America must start now where Germany was perhaps twenty or twenty-five years ago to build up a pediatric profession in this country; we have to start now and build up a scientific knowledge of children's diseases. As far back as America is at this date, she is so largely because of a sentiment that prevents progress—the idea that scientific investigation is not compatible with humanitarian instincts. I do not know of any class of men that devotes more time either to the individual or to the community than the scientist, and none gets paid less for its trouble. Whatever the physician does, he must do purely and simply from his own humanitarian instincts. These are the things that the people must do ultimately if we are to reduce the ravages that gastro-intestinal disorders are making among the infants in this country.

QUESTIONS TO BE ANSWERED IN REGARD TO THE THINKING OF CHILDREN

JAMES R. ANGELL

Professor of Psychology, The University of Chicago

There are so many things which we do not know about the thinking of the children that one might say we know almost nothing about it. There is one thing, however, which we do know and that is that children think very concretely and very specifically and in terms of great force; but beyond that we know little.

As a matter of fact, children do not think in the sense of reasoning, any more than adults think, unless they are obliged to. Many people spend the major part of their lives without ever having indulged, in any definite way, in the luxury of real thinking. Like adults, children think only about the problems that actually confront them. They think only when some obstacle is presented to them and they are obliged to solve a difficulty. Thinking is a device which has been used for ages in overcoming obstacles that present themselves to us, perplexities of one kind and another.

By what method then shall we lead the child in his thinking? It is really a question of dealing with the thought processes of the child in such ways as have been outlined to us here today—seeing that those things which come to the child, those difficulties with which he is confronted and which actually stimulate his thinking are on the whole of an intelligent and wholesome character. Evidently that brings us back to the social and moral problems of the home, to the general conditions of the neighborhood, the general opportunities for exercise and play, to the thousand and one things which present themselves to the child as problems. Our primary obligation is to provide surroundings such that the child's mind shall not be soiled through the material given it to work upon, shall not be rendered diseased or morbid. The thinking will largely take care of itself if these conditions are properly safeguarded.

Our schools face not only the problem of supplying material for thinking but also the necessity of furnishing a motive. Formerly, this motive was largely found in the fear of punishment. Of late, a persistent effort has been made so to arrange the work of the school that it may appeal to the fundamental native interests of the children and so elicit a more vital reaction. In many directions this movement has met with great success and, despite its mistakes, it merits encouragement and sympathy.

Possibly of more importance than thinking, in the sense in which we have been using the term, is imagination. Particularly is this true of little children. Imagination, like reasoning, feeds upon the food supplied it; and in even greater measure, because of its greater spontaneity, is it essential that it should find pure and wholesome experiences to work upon.

From every point of view then, we may feel assured that, when we aim first at a solution of the social problems of childhood, we are beginning at the right point, and that the best and strongest forms of mental development will follow largely of themselves upon a successful solution of these difficulties.

UNSETTLED PROBLEMS IN REGARD TO THE HEALTH OF CHILDREN

ISAAC A. ABT, M. D.

Professor of Pediatrics, Northwestern University Medical School

A great improvement has occurred in the reduction of the infant sickness and death-rate in the past few years. The diseases of infancy and childhood were about the last of the diseases to be studied and to receive attention. Other branches of medicine that related to the cure and treatment of the adult were much earlier the subjects of inquiry and were more quickly developed. There was a time when the pathology and the exact knowledge concerning the diseases of infants and children consisted largely in such empirical thought as referred to teething, and disease and symptoms supposed to be produced by worms. Nearly all the practitioners throughout this western country during the first half of the nineteenth century were of the opinion that the infant could not be successfully treated medically; that if he did not make a spontaneous recovery, he could not be helped by medical treatment. In other words, because of the limitation of medical knowledge which was so great, physicians expressed the thought that they could not help the infants. While knowledge concerning infantile diseases has been slow in developing, nevertheless we may say, to the credit of the medical profession and in the interest of infantile and child life, that mortality has steadily diminished through the efforts of physicians.

Another point that we note is that the highest death-rate in all large cities occurs in the poorer districts. A great many of those individuals who have poor homes and who live under poor sanitary and hygienic conditions contribute the largest number to the mortality. The fewest deaths occur in the better districts, where intelligence and sanitary conditions prevail and where disease not only is prevented but, if it does occur, is more efficiently and more intelligently nursed and treated.

Now, there are reasons why the death-rate is so large in the poorer district of the city. The traditions of taking care of infants and young children are very, very bad; we must break down these old traditions if we would do anything toward diminishing morbidity and mortality. Many people have been taught to believe that when an infant is sick, he is merely teething; and a week or ten days or two weeks may elapse before the doctor is called. By this time, the infant is beyond rescue. Who that has worked in the hot beds of infantile disease has not learned the traditions or the prejudices against bathing and against everything that means cleanliness? The lack of knowledge concerning food and all that tends toward baby's comfort and health is appalling. The difficulty is to teach the people the simplest rules of sanitation and hygiene. The problem is not altogether a medical one. If it were a medical problem, it would be easier to deal with. It is equally a sociological problem. The eventual solution of the underlying difficulties is not by the individual, but by the municipality or the state, or by the legislative body that has to do with the health and the comfort and the happiness of the people. So the protection of infant and child life requires the activity of all agencies that have interest or knowledge to contribute to this subject. We must not throw the entire responsibility on the doctor and say that he does not know how, or that his profession is behind the times, or that medicine is not keeping pace with the march of progress. There is a philanthropic and sociological side and there is a medical side. We must do our duty medically, but the philanthropists must do theirs, too. The physicians must tell them the best they know concerning the care of children, but the philanthropists must do their part in providing ways and means.

Child welfare, as I understand it, refers to the prevention of disease and the protection of child life. This movement had largely its inception through the efforts of Professor Budin. It was he who held that if the infant could not come to the clinic, the clinic should go to the infant. The infant should be supplied with proper food and sanitary care, and in this way receive the necessaries that he stood in the greatest need of. Professor Budin's method was to send from the laboratory each day a bottle of milk for the children, thus bringing them under his control. It seemed to be the most important thing that children should be under intelligent care. In Austria, this infant-welfare work has been extremely interesting. The work has been largely experimental; methods were tried and abandoned. They found that what they thought was progress was not progress at all; experience showed that some plans were impracticable and impossible. They found that distributing bottles already prepared and mixed for infant feeding was not a perfectly satisfactory measure. It was found better to teach mothers how to prepare milk at home.

One of the greatest developments of this welfare endeavor is the propaganda concerning breast milk. It has been demonstrated that there is only one specific natural food for the baby, and that is mother's milk. This knowledge has been taught and disseminated to mothers throughout all the land. There has sometimes been a feeling among mothers that the baby did not need the breast milk, that he was equally well nourished with artificial food; but this idea has been dispelled by the dissemination of knowledge concerning the value of breast milk.

The interest in the propaganda for the protection of child life is a worthy theme. But we must not make mistakes. We must not disseminate views in a dogmatic way unless they are susceptible of proof; they must be sound and useful. In other words, we should not today tell mothers to give the baby a milk diet according to one man's method, and then tomorrow say that it was all wrong. This is confusing, to say the least. We should not tell the public to let the baby sleep on a cake of ice in the summer time and then put him in the incubator in the winter time. In other words, we need to be definite and accurate; our instructions should be well founded and consistent. It seems to me that there should be uniform instructions, based on sound experience and exact truth, for the purpose of educating the masses. If possible, we should not be compelled to jump forward, and then retrace our steps backward all the time. We must make sure that we are traveling in the right direction, that what we are teaching is correct. Should we spend time and money and brains and every possible form of energy without getting tangible results? We must not deprive the infant-welfare movement of all the good we can do for it by disseminating unfounded or half-baked precepts. In order to save child life and to make homes and all people happier and better we should determine the knowledge that is most efficient to help them and proceed to disseminate it.

Now, that leads me to say this: that there are definite problems confronting us. For instance, a man of great genius, ten years ago, sat down by the bedside of a child and told us what we never knew before concerning tuberculosis in infancy. He told it in such a way that it reflected not only knowledge on the disease of childhood but the knowledge on tuberculosis of all ages and all stages. So that there is work to be done by sitting down at the bedside of the little patient, to watch and study and interpret his symptoms.

A man not long ago sat down by the bedside of scarlet-fever patients and told us facts and conditions that we had not previously known about scarlet fever. He wrote a clinical history that hitherto was unknown to us. The story of scarlet fever must soon be rewritten; the chapter must be retold. We must soon rewrite the chapter on measles. Possibly measles as it occurs here in Chicago differs from measles in London or Berlin; soon we must rewrite the chapter as it occurs here in Chicago. During the last month or six weeks, we have had an epidemic of measles. One physician meets another and he comments on the fact that this disease is running atypically this year. Consequently, there is work to be done at the bedside or in the clinic for a better understanding of this ancient disease.

There is work to be done along the food and clothing line. There is also work to be done along other lines. For instance, it is not always the feeding of the baby that makes him sick; it is not always because he is not receiving sufficient food; it is not always because the food is not adapted to the baby; it is sometimes the baby himself—his constitution is wrong. Perhaps the baby comes from nervous parents; he is a neuropathic individual. We must care for his nervous system and must not at once condemn the food. Many a baby has gone for weeks and months without gaining weight and the fault has not been the food; it has been a constitutional defect in the infant.

Then there are other problems that must be studied with regard to breast milk. One set of doctors will tell the mother: "Do not eat this and do not eat that and do not eat the other thing, because it is bad for your milk." And another very intelligent class of physicians will advise the mother, "Eat anything; it produces no effect on the milk." Another class of men will say, "Be careful about the baby's nervous system; be sure that he gets sufficient rest." Now, these are matters that should be settled, and must be settled. These are definite laboratory and clinical problems. So there is work to be done in the clinic, in the hospital, at the bedside, and in the laboratory, in order that more knowledge may be obtained and a more perfect agreement arrived at, so that our propaganda may proceed along the right lines and in the proper direction.

There are not always opportunities at hand for doing this research work. We have not the facilities in Chicago at our hospitals for doing clinical work in the proper way. In the matter of caring for contagious diseases, for example, we lack hospital facilities. In the Isolation Hospital, there is not room enough for the patients. Some of them are compelled to wait before being admitted. Those who are in the hospital are obliged to lie three or four in a bed. That is absolutely true. And why? Because the citizens of Chicago are not sufficiently interested to demand that suitable hospitals be provided. By private bequest money has been at hand, and the offer has been made to build the hospital, but the Common Council of the city of Chicago would not allow it to be built and consequently no provision for this private munificence has been made.

There are other reasons why we cannot forge ahead in the building of laboratories, because we are meeting opposition. We are meeting opposition from different "isms" and "pathies" and anti-vivisectionists. This is the class of people who are opposing every progress, every step that is leading us ahead to a point where we may acquire knowledge and render service. They are opposing progress and opposing it sometimes in a very material way.

It is a fact, perhaps not widely known, that in the state of Illinois it is a penitentiary offense to perform an autopsy on a human being unless consent has been obtained. A great many times, it is absolutely necessary that an autopsy should be done in order to study the disease, to study it from the inside of the body. It is necessary to study disease in the most detailed way, in order that we should understand the complex processes of the human body. But we are being opposed by the very laws of this state. So it is not always easy to make progress along the lines of scientific or clinical work. First, we have not adequate hospitals; second, we have not opportunity for work in research laboratories, or perhaps the men are not equipped, or not willing to do the work. But there is one institution which has been established in Chicago for a long time, the McCormick Institute, and there is the more recently established Morris Research Laboratory, both of which have great promise for future work.

Then there are one or two other points that I have not touched. I have not referred to those who know it all, who go back to the old traditions, the wiseacres, the grandmothers, the neighborhood sages, the nurses who think they have drunk deeply from the spring, who go about disseminating knowledge as though they really knew it, but who need first of all to replenish their knowledge, to keep abreast of the advance. We should look after the young men who are starting out to be doctors; we should insist that they must know something definitely about the diseases of infancy and childhood, as very many do not. We must say to our medical schools that they must provide adequate knowledge; they must provide adequate facilities for the education of young physicians in infantile diseases. We must say to the young physicians that they must know at least something instead of nothing about the cases that they will have to treat.

PART THREE

THE SCHOOL AND THE CHILD

"Enforcing soberly the self-control that makes and keeps a people free."

THE HOME AND THE SCHOOL

FRANCIS G. BLAIR

State Superintendent of Public Instruction of Illinois

(An Uncorrected Stenographic Report)

A literary critic has said of Shakespeare that he was more the product of the time in which he was born than he was the creature of his natural parents. What that critic meant, I suppose, was that Shakespeare with his fine nervous system, with his fine physical make-up was more the creature of that literary atmosphere into which he was born than he was the creature of his physical parents.

Whether that is true or not, it leads me to this statement, which is very old fashioned, that every child born into the world is a creature of two different forces; one set of forces is, of course, heredity and the other set of forces, those things that happen to him after he comes into the world. Oliver Wendell Holmes said that a child's education should begin two hundred years before he is born. He wanted to emphasize the tremendous influence exercised by heredity in determining the career of any child. And when Ralph Waldo Emerson on a certain great occasion pointed to a certain man and said "that fellow has been to school for a thousand years," he meant that every child born into the world is in a true sense "the heir of all the ages, standing in the foremost files of time," that the influence of one's ancestors has a large influence on the life of one's children.

I can remember in our country debating society how I used to maintain that a child was an absolute fatalism, determined to be what his ancestors had been, or less, that he was really the product of circumstances that had brought him into the world.

And after I had taken one side in a debate and convinced myself that it was all heredity, and had taken the other side and convinced myself that it was all environment, it came to me somewhat as a subtle surprise to conceive the idea that what the child comes to be is a composite thing, that he is partly what his ancestors through their lives, through their thought, through their endeavors, have determined that he should be, and that he is largely what he is determined to be by what has happened to him after coming into the world. If we as teachers believe that what a child is to be has been absolutely determined by what his ancestors have been, then the influence of the teacher would become nil; then the influence of priest, parent, preacher or social reformer would become as nothing. If I am to have influence, if I am to be a teacher, a formative worker in the world, I must believe that a large part of what the child is to be, is determined after he comes into the world.

If you want to see the relationship that heredity and education bear to each other, go down to the lower forms of animal life. You will see there those lower forms hatched or born into the world precisely like their ancestors with no power to be altered by constructive influences. If on a June evening the windows are opened and the June beetle is allowed to fly in, he immediately flies to the lights just as his ancestors have done through æons. One may say, "Have a care, Mr. Beetle, pause and consider, everyone of your ancestors throughout the ages have flown into the flame with disaster." One might try innumerable educative devices, but no education that can be given him will change an iota of his action, for he is absolutely predetermined by ancestral forces to fly into the flames.

If one would go a step higher, Baskett tells in his interesting little book on birds that there is in Australia a bird of the very lowest type of animal intelligence known as the brush turkey. It lays its eggs in the brush and goes away and leaves them to be hatched out by the heat of the sun and of decaying vegetation, and as soon as the young brush turkey is hatched, he is able to go about, to feed and care for himself, and the services of the parent bird are unnecessary. The writer says that every attempt to domesticate the brush turkey of Australia has failed; surround him with new conditions and he is unable to adjust himself to those conditions.

As we go higher, into the higher order of animal intelligence, we notice that as the animal becomes more and more intelligent the young is born into the world in a more and more helpless condition; and another thing, as the young is born into the world in a more and more helpless condition the period of postnatal infancy stretches out longer and longer as compared with the period of prenatal infancy.

John Fiske tells us in his great essay on the meaning of infancy about the excursion of evolution. He said first of all that the child in the course and economy of creation is born into the world helpless, that he would perish unless ministered unto by his parents, and the first great result of the helpless child being born into the world is the influence of that helpless child upon the mother and the father. I wish to bring it home to you how we need the influence that comes with this helpless little fellow into the home, into the community, and into civilization. We come together, we parents, and speak in rather large terms of what we should do for the boys and the girls; we rarely ask ourselves, what have our sons and daughters done for us; what has come with these helpless little children into our homes, bringing with them tenderness, sweetness, gentleness, and a centralized force that will hold together the home in all circumstancs. Christianity always turns to the picture of the mother and the little child and keeps his presence everlastingly before us, with the softening, transforming, civilizing influence of the helpless and dependent infant.

I am reminded of the story about Mr. Huxley, when his child Leonard died. Mr. and Mrs. Huxley had several children; but this particular child, who was frail physically, was the joy of their hearts. When he was three and a half years of age, on a Thursday afternoon he was taken with scarlet fever and on Saturday afternoon the little fellow died. Mr. Huxley was standing by the bedside, and a friend standing by him, who was anxious to say something comforting, said: "It is too bad that when you and Mrs. Huxley have cared for the little fellow during the time that he was so dependent, just as he reaches the stage where he could care for himself he should be taken away from you." The story runs that Mr. Huxley thought for just a moment and then said: "You do not understand it at all. This little fellow came into our house helpless and dependent; he meant much to us in the development of sweetness and gentleness that we never should have been able to touch." The parents preferred to remember the little fellow for what he brought with him in his coming rather than what he took with him in his going.

In a little cross-roads station in Illinois as I was sitting on a long bench, I discovered sitting by my side a blind man. After awhile he addressed me, saying: "Sir, may I ask you if you will help me on the train when it comes?" "Certainly," I said.

After a moment he remarked, "My people do not like to have me going about selling shoe strings and little novelties and bothering people by asking them to help me on the trains and to help me across the road"; and with a sweet smile lighting up his face, he said, "I say to my people that every time a man helps me on a train, he gets just as much out of it as I do; every time a man leads me across the road, he gets just as much out of it as I do." Then I thought I knew for the first time what St. Paul meant when he said, "I am a debtor to the Greek and the barbarian."

And so when we stand in the presence of a little child, as he is born into the world, a little pulsating mass of flesh and cartilaginous tissue, we think of the influences that are to come, of the opportunities there are before this little mass of flesh and cartilaginous tissue, out of which is to come a man, strong and virile, able to stand erect, to do without complaint the work set before him, to be one of the great forces working in the world, to become, as it were, the foundation of the world. While a great part of his inheritance will come into his nervous system from his ancestors, the greater part will come from his environment and his training. This is not a gospel of doubt; it is as I see it a gospel of hope. When the child comes into the world, he has already a great deal of good wrapped up in his nervous system, and we may see infinite possibilities in him.

As the child goes along, there come occasional outbreakings, and we cannot tell where in the world he got his disposition. These breakings out happen with children who come from the very best homes, where the father and mother have cared in the best way for their children. It used to alarm and surprise me beyond measure that a boy or a girl coming from such homes should do those things. I am, however, no longer alarmed by such occurrences. A little fellow comes to the school and tells a lie; and a young schoolmaster places him in the category of liars; or he steals some little thing and is called a thief. I believe such classification is erroneous and harmful. You cannot be friends with individuals if you are going to classify them in such terms. The old proverb says that no chain is stronger than its weakest link. That may be true of chains, but it is not true of human character, which must be recognized and classified in terms of its best virtue rather than in terms of its worst fault.

It is said that when Constantine was converted to Christianity, he was besought by some zealous people to issue an edict that every heathen temple in Rome should be destroyed. His reply was that instead he would issue an edict that across the road from every heathen temple should be erected a Christian temple. So it is with every teacher who comes into the school, and so it is with the mothers. They should discover the source of evil and root it out. Too much attention has been paid to the evil itself; but, if we take it at its very beginning and root it out, the results will disappear; the good is there and if given a chance, it will come forth and express itself.

In these modern days there is a tendency to blame the schools for the shortcomings and failures of the parents. The school is not, however, a formative institution; the home is the formative institution and there this formative work must be done. It can never be done in the public schools. In regard to discipline, in answer to the charge that the boys and girls were growing up without any respect for authority, an educator once called attention to the fact that although the school might have deteriorated, the home had deteriorated even more. Illustrations would not be difficult to find.

SCHOOL WELFARE

Parents' Clubs have secured Reading, Rest and Lunch Rooms. Branch Libraries, Pictures, Pianos, Manual and Domestic Equipment. Bubbling Cups. 1st Aid Cabinets. Other Health Agencies.

Reading Room
Parker Practice School

Co-operation
Parent-Teacher Club
The School
Englewood Woman's Club

Parent-Teacher Association, Parker Public Schools, spent $300.00 for pictures

Pianos secured by
Lewis Champlain Club

Domestic Science
(Pontiac School Club)

Lunch Room
(Englewood Parents Club)

Summer Class
(Perkins Bass Club)

Secured by
"Beidler Club"

Secured by
"West End Mothers' Club"

The efforts of the Mothers' Congress

to secure a Parent-Teacher organization or Mothers' Circle in connection with every school is worthy of commendation, and should receive the hearty co-operation of every teacher.

Ella Flagg Young,
Supt. of Schools

F.G. Blair,
State Supt. Public Instructor
and pres of State Normal Schools

Parents Clubs
are formed to consider

Relation of home and school.
School and home hygiene.
Physical culture.
Personal hygiene.
Adolescence habit.
Play grounds. Pure food.
Environment. Recreation.
Childrens' books. Stories.
Moral Training.
Industrial education

Prevent the first offence by co-operation

And yet, the formative influence of the home must be made a part of the public-school system; it must be reckoned with. Ten thousand fathers and mothers of Illinois should be interested in their public schools, so that they would assist in teaching the children this fundamental law of obedience, and put into the child's character that which is useful.

Imagine a situation in which a sovereign power should issue an edict to close the school houses in this country. Can you think of a more terrible calamity, more terrible consequences than that the sixteen million boys and girls now cared for by the schools and not otherwise provided for, should roam the streets without care and without instruction?

I have witnessed in our public-school system many objectionable things that have fairly made me tremble. But out of it all comes a great ability, and the association of these boys and girls together makes our American children into our American citizens as they mingle together in this great school system.

In an Illinois town, the mayor on the occasion of a great school convention, presented the welcome of the town to the teachers, saying: "We heartily welcome you teachers to our city and to our homes." A teacher in reply, said: "You have welcomed us into your city and into your homes. We come into your homes whether we are welcomed or not; when you send your little boys and girls to school, the school comes into your home. If you watch, you will see in your child the public school; the influence of the teacher will be found at your table." I am glad to say that I think that our teachers are worthy of the place, that the teachers found in our public schools are unusually fitted for the honor. Of course, there are some who have not been so successful as others; but on the whole they are worthy.

One of the greatest things that our public-school system has undertaken for the children is to care for the physical side of their natures. We must have more light, more ventilation, less congestion. There is nothing more important than the physical training of our school children. Every worker in our school today is pleased to see the robust youth, the bodily health, the physical activities of the children. I do not know of anything more noble than strength in body and strength in mind. Our schools must be provided with better light, better ventilation and they must make it possible for the boys and girls to preserve their health, their physical activities, and their physical powers. We must work for great power, greater effectiveness in our public-school system, and that can never be accomplished without the hearty co-operation of the parents and of the home. We are coming to appreciate that more and more as one of the things most essential. It seems to me most essential of all that we should have the co-operation of the home, of the fathers and the mothers, of the preachers and the teachers in the community, so that our schools may have adequate revenues, so that we may pay our teachers adequate salaries, so that we may accomplish the greatest good for the boys and the girls, the greatest good for the city, for the state, and for the nation, and secure the greatest number of boys and girls healthy in their mental makeup, in their physical makeup, and in their social quality and worth to the nation.

THE PROBLEMS OF SEX HYGIENE

FRANK R. LILLIE

Professor of Embryology, The University of Chicago

The conspiracy of silence that has existed so long on the subject of social or sex hygiene is breaking down, and the prejudice that has so long prevented any serious discussion of sex problems is rapidly disappearing. The central problem, of course, of much of our modern literature is the sex problem, and whether or not as generally presented it is very helpful from the standpoint of instruction in social hygiene, the fact indicates at least a very keen interest. The ostrich plan of burrowing with the head in the sand with reference to these problems is giving way to an attitude of study and examination. Many are convinced that much of immorality and unhappiness has had its root in ignorance, and propose that, so far as may be, that particular reproach shall be removed.

To the biologist, the problem of sex and of reproduction is about half of his subject matter. We divide the functions of animals into those that make for self-maintenance, and those that make for race maintenance, and to these there correspond the instincts of self-preservation and of reproduction; and in the higher animals, reproduction is invariably sexual. Sex occupies an equally prominent place in human biology. Whenever we look beyond individual needs, whenever our outlook becomes in the least social, we come immediately in contact with the problems of sex and reproduction; yet our system of education hardly recognizes the problem. We teach all the arts of self-maintenance, and none of those of race maintenance; or, if we touch on social problems at all, we avoid so far as possible the basic fact of sex, the very foundation of society. One may even read the school textbooks on physiology without suspecting that man is an animal that propagates his own kind. In our dealings with children, owing, perhaps, to our own self-consciousness or to the crude fear of awakening that which is the most vivid spot in the consciousness of young people, the really fundamental knowledge is avoided, or consciously concealed. We retain some of the old foolish fear that knowledge of the truth will remove some of the bloom of youth, by loss of mystery. But those who love mysteries may be reassured. We shall not destroy mystery with a little knowledge; the knowledge should only render it reverent.

The recent report of the Chicago Vice Commission has brought home to the community certain very dreadful aspects of social pathology and done a good deal to arouse public sentiment in favor of instruction in social hygiene. The full problem of social hygiene, however, cannot be grasped unless it is realized that the revelations of the Vice Commission show but the waves breaking in on the shore out of a whole ocean of ignorance and ill-regulated living. Conceivably the whole public business exposed in this report might be eliminated, and yet the problems of sex hygiene, of social hygiene, if by it is understood the best possible regulation of sex life, would be touched only on its borders.

The problem is no less than this: to help to produce conditions under which the sex life may be lived in the best way, both for the individual and for the community. The latter is, of course, more properly the immediate problem of eugenics, but at the same time no sharply dividing line can be drawn between the problems of eugenics and those of social hygiene.

Very little is known about sex development from its psychological aspect, although the studies of Havelock Ellis in England have contributed very materially to this important subject. However, knowledge is very far in advance of its application in education, and there is no need at all of waiting for more knowledge before proceeding with education. Knowledge which is now common should be available for grade boys and girls, so that they will be prepared for the bewildering sensations of awakening sexual life. These children should be impressed with the responsibility resting upon them as the fathers and mothers of future generations, with sincere and intelligent respect for their pro-creative functions, and also with the serious consequences of the abuse of these functions. These things involve the education and the co-operation of the present generation of parents. The great problem that remains to be worked out is the way in which the knowledge of social hygiene shall be presented.

At the same time the fact should be emphasized that there is a real need of more exact knowledge with reference to many parts of our subject and therefore a need of further investigation. Certainly no error will be made if avoiding all traces of sentimentality, instruction is placed as firmly and as broadly as possible on the scientific basis.

SEVERAL ASPECTS OF THE TEACHING OF SEX PHYSIOLOGY AND HYGIENE

R. E. BLOUNT

Waller High School, Chicago

I shall not make any attempt whatever to discuss the needs of sex instruction; for I think that most progressive people have come to realize that our method of treating sex matters needs to be changed. The miserable failure of our policy of silence on the subject is very apparent. And it seems to me that whatever we do, we cannot do any worse than has been done. So I propose that we go ahead and do something, and do it boldly.

I want first to speak of the proper time for presenting instruction in the matter of sex physiology and hygiene; second, to ask what instruction should be given; and third, to inquire how and by whom the instruction should be given.

It is the art of teaching to give instruction when the children demand it. As our schools are now organized, we must often cram information down the throats or into the minds of children, knowing perfectly well that that is a perfectly miserable way to do. The ideal way is, of course, first to arouse the interest of the children so that they will begin to ask questions and demand instruction; for as soon as children want to know, their wants can be supplied very satisfactorily. Usually one will find children, three or four or five years old, beginning to ask questions about the origin of little brother or little sister. Then, of course, is the time to begin instruction. Nobody can deny that, and all sensible people nowadays are giving what instruction they can. Children differ very much as to their power of asking questions, as to their inquisitiveness; some children will ask very few questions and be satisfied with very little; other children will, after one question, ask another and another, and so their inquiry will lead them on until they have called for the main principles of the whole subject.

I know one little boy who at the age of five or six got the main principles of the whole subject of reproduction; not because it was urged upon him, but because he kept demanding and insisting until he got it all, because he found a ready response from the persons of whom he inquired. So I say that the ideal way is to take up with the child year after year, as his horizon broadens, the new questions that come to his mind and answer them just as fully as he is able to understand.

There are certain children who never will ask questions very freely; they are naturally retiring. Upon such children sometimes influences must be brought to bear to arouse their interest, some information must be volunteered as it is needed; for, at certain ages, certain information is needed by the child, and he suffers severely if this information is withheld. And so we cannot rest wholly upon the best scheme of answering questions when they are asked, but we must sometimes stimulate the child to ask questions, to want to know, or we must volunteer information as it is needed.

Just when information is needed, one cannot say. At the age of puberty certain matters must be taught the child if he is to live the best sort of life. Comparatively few things need to be forced upon the child's mind, need to be volunteered and given to the child without inquiry, but a few things he must be taught.

So much for the time at which to give the information. Now, what information to give. And my first point has brought out the answer to the second one: give such information as will fully satisfy the child's mind, fully satisfy it. I would not hold back one single scientific fact. Give him all the facts so far as he is able to understand, so far as he wants to know, and needs to know—and his needs will be largely though not usually perfectly equivalent to his demands. I do not know of a single scientific fact that will harm the child. There are many sentiments, many ways of looking at the facts that the child would better never have. The prude's way of looking at matters of sex, the child ought never to receive, and that is what we have been giving him all these years. The scientific way of looking at sex cannot possibly harm a child, and it is for that reason I say give him fully all the information he is able to understand, and just as fast as he calls for it. There will be certain things of course that the child will never ask about, certain questions will never come to his mind unless put there by evil-minded people; for questions about immorality do not naturally spring up in the child's mind very early; he learns them from other people. I should a great deal rather tell the child myself about the immoral sexual practices than to have him pick them up from some person who suggests them with a wink and a leer. It will harm the child much less to have the teacher or parent tell him, than to have some lewd person bring them to his mind. And so if any knowledge at all is to come to the child's mind about immoral practices—and it is sure to come sooner or later—it is better for the parent or teacher to put that information into the child's mind than to let him pick it up from the alleys and street corners.

There is another matter, too, that would scarcely come to the child's mind: sexual passion is altogether outside of his life. When the child is young, he will not ask any questions about it—nobody need fear that. Before the child becomes old enough to experience sexual passion, he will have heard about it, he will have picked it up in literature here and there; and it would be a great deal better if this were to come from the lips of the parent of the child than from some disreputable source. One need not fear but that, if the question of sexual passion should come into the child's mind, it is all right to make a clean, frank statement of it.

Who shall teach the child, the teacher or the parent? That question has been raised again and again. At first I was quite inclined to sympathize with the people who said it is no part of the teacher's business; that it is too sacred a subject for the teacher, and must be handled by the parents. But the more I have thought it over, the more I have thought this a mistaken attitude. It involves the fundamental question: what is the function of the school? In all time, every new thing that has been proposed has been opposed by reactionaries on the ground that it is not the function of the school at all; that the province of the home is being invaded; that something is being taken away from the parent that he should provide for. It was just so with manual training, with cooking; people said, "Our girls must learn cooking in the kitchen; it is preposterous to teach it in the schools." And so it was with this matter; people said at first: "Oh, that is the parents' duty; it is a sacred thing and must not be assumed by the teacher."

The function of the school, it seems to me, could be put in a very broad way; and, when so understood, the school must supply for the child everything he needs that is not supplied by the home or some other agency. Of course, it is desirous that the parents shall clothe the child and feed the child, but if he comes to school without a breakfast, the school would better feed him before it tries to teach him. If the child comes to the school without adequate instruction in matters of sex hygiene, it is the duty of the school to give him that instruction. One can not get around that conclusion. Moreover, in many cases the school can give this instruction better than the parents can give it, so the school ought to assume that duty and carry it out.

I have talked with mothers and fathers on this subject, and at first they were inclined to say: "No, you are encroaching on our province." I have asked them, "Well, what do you teach your child, your boy or girl, about sex matters?" They say: "I have never taught him anything about such matters." I say: "Why don't you do it?" Their reply is: "I cannot do it; I haven't the heart to do it; I haven't the scientific information to do it. You teachers must do it." They have come to that conclusion, those I have talked to, rather reluctantly most of them, but just as soon as they are pinned down to conditions, they see that they cannot give the instruction, that it must be done by the teachers. I heard a professor at the University say not long ago that he didn't care so much for the instruction his child was getting at school in reading and writing and arithmetic; he could teach those things, but the thing he could not teach the child was the social life, the relations with his fellows. That is a tremendously difficult problem. So the school should be allowed to go ahead with the subject of teaching sex hygiene. The teachers are more capable of doing it, and ninety-nine out of one hundred parents will not do it. And how shall they do it? All through the course; it must begin with the little child and go on up through the grades, changing, however, constantly from grade to grade. To turn to certain of the details: When teaching nature studies, teachers should show the children that a large part of their structure is devoted to maintaining their own lives, but a part of their structure is devoted to perpetuating the species. The children will take it simply and innocently as it is given to them; so the foundation is laid, the main principles, of the whole subject. The conjugation of two cells for sexual reproduction can be given to the child in a way that will absorb his interest, and be perfectly clean and wholesome. It can be discussed in mixed classes without the least embarrassment, and it prepares the way for the more difficult instruction that comes in the later years, instruction that really is embarrassing to a good many boys and girls, and sometimes to the teachers. With the lower plants and animals it is comparatively a simple matter. Of course, most of the teachers have not prepared themselves to teach that subject. It will be years before it can be done well, but the plan suggested here is an ideal scheme to which we should approach as nearly as we can. In connection with the question of human reproduction, which ought to come somewhere in the seventh, eighth, or ninth grade, the children ought to be given a good many details of the anatomy and physiology of the reproductive organs, and of course above all the hygiene. It needs to come along about the age of puberty; a little before the age of puberty is better than afterwards, for better a year too soon than a single hour too late.

We have had some experience in the ninth grade in one of the schools in Chicago in giving such lessons. We have taught seven hundred boys and girls in connection with the regular physiology lessons, three or four or five lessons in sex physiology and hygiene, beginning with the main principles illustrated in the lower animals and the plants and coming on up in the last lesson to the human reproduction, the anatomy of the reproductive organs, the physiology, and finally a good, strong discussion of hygiene.

We began by sending notices in sealed letters to the parents, stating our purpose and giving a little discussion of the needs of such instruction. From the parents of about seven hundred children, we had only seven or eight requests that we should excuse their children from these lessons. In addition, in our letter of announcement to the parents, we invited them to make objection, if they had any to make. One father objected to having his boy study these lessons, because they were a shameful thing. Two mothers said that they had given their daughters instructions; so it was quite unnecessary. One mother was a believer in Christian Science; she did not want her daughter to study any physiology at all. The half dozen others did not give any reason. All the others (seven hundred) consented and we got letters from two or three dozen of them commending the work and congratulating us for the stand we had taken.

Then the children themselves appreciated the lessons. I was surprised to see how they appreciated them, and in what a frank and clean spirit they received the instructions. The boys and girls were divided into separate classes. I gave the instruction to the boys, and a woman physician who had had a good deal if experience in teaching gave the lessons to the girls. After the lessons were over, in order to make my questions less personal, I said to quite a number here and there, "This is a new thing; shall we give the lessons to the class next year? I want you to help me decide this matter." They did not feel that I was asking about the effect on themselves, but the effect on the next year's classes. I got the answer: "Surely, give the lessons next year; they are valuable." Then again to another class I said: "Write on a slip of paper two columns; in one of the columns write a list of the topics of instruction you have had this term in physiology that have been very beneficial to you, and in another column a list of the topics that have been less valuable, so that another year we shall be sure to give the topics you approve of, and shall, perhaps, omit some of the topics you do not approve of." I did not suggest their speaking of the matter of sex hygiene at all, but I told them not to sign their names because I wanted them to be perfectly frank. A good many of those boys and girls said that among the most helpful lessons were the lessons on sex physiology and hygiene. We entered upon this instruction with fear and trepidation, prepared to endure obloquy, no end of censure, and we received only one letter of condemnation and numerous letters of congratulation. And so we feel we have a reason for planning to go ahead and repeat these lessons just as often as we have a class in physiology.

One thing, though, I think ought to be made very important in this discussion: We must be scientific and avoid sentimentality. We should go to the bottom of the scientific explanation, perfectly frank and perfectly clean in every detail, not holding back a single thing scientifically demonstrated. But one may be misled by the statement that we should avoid sentimentality, and conclude that we should never appeal to sentiment. A large part of our instruction must be not the physical anatomy, not the bare physiology, not simply how to keep the body in good health; it must be a discussion of the ethical relation of this whole sex matter. It must be a discussion, with the older child largely, and to some extent with the younger child—it can be taken up in some form at all ages—it must be a discussion of the social aspects of the whole subject; not simply in avoiding disease, but how sex matters can contribute to a high spiritual life. We have been so accustomed to excuse sex, to say, "Well, people may have sex relations, people may marry; it is permissible." Some religions have taken that sort of an attitude; but we are getting beyond that now. Occasionally a bold man or a brave woman, who sees the larger life clearly, sees that sex contributes to spiritual life, and does not detract from it, when sex is properly managed. And we ought to make it one of the main points of our whole discussion of the sex matter to show how sex contributes to the better life; not to excuse sex relations at all, not to justify them, but take them as simple facts in the world and see how we can bend them to the best life we know.

Just a suggestion as to what to do with older people and the older youth—those in the last year or two of the high school, and people after they get out of high school. Their needs are quite different from those at the age of puberty and below that age. Young men and women are particularly susceptible to the influence of ideals. Boys and girls in grammar school, even in the high school, respond very quickly to the suggestion of an ideal. So in our teaching of physiology in the ninth grade, we have always tried to put before the boys and girls a high ideal of sex matters and they have responded to it quickly. They have taken it as their ideal when they might have taken—if we had been quiet—as ideals the things they hear on the street; the things that degrade their character.

As to young men and women in the upper year of high school, and those who have been graduated a year or two, some means must be taken to give them instruction in sex matters. With them must be discussed in great detail the relation of the sexes, the economic relation, the proper spirit of entering into marriage; the conduct during courtship. Much disaster comes from improper methods during courtship. The continental method is to have some adult person by as a spy, to see that no impropriety is committed. We have flown to the other extreme in this country. We have seen that proper courtship requires the young people to be by themselves, but we have omitted the essential thing, and that is the proper instruction as to their conduct when together. We must give them, not such negative instruction as we commonly hear given them; we must teach them the meaning of all their relations with each other, so that they shall see what their relations should be when they are together; to the end that their relations may lead up to the best sort, the highest sort of spiritual life. And they will be able to control themselves intelligently, voluntarily; and not remain within bounds because there is a spy watching them. They can never develop the proper relation, the proper thought about marriage, if they do not have a chance to work it out by experience, by discussion, by frank communication of ideas between themselves.

Just a résumé of what I have tried to say: that the instruction should begin as soon as the child is asking about the matters of sex life in any of its phases, social phases, physical phases, whatever it may be. And the teaching should be full and frank just so far as the child is able to understand it. He will get no harm from a clean lesson. All the harm comes to children from the immoral way, the prudish, and the slighting, leering way, in which most of the information comes to them. So give them frank instruction all through their infancy up to adult life. Give it to them just as rapidly as they are able to receive it, as rapidly as they demand. Make the ideal sex relation, spiritual as well as physical, the most prominent thing, and whatever the instruction may be, do not omit the ideal.

THE WORK OF THE CHICAGO WOMAN'S CLUB IN SPREADING KNOWLEDGE OF THE SOCIAL PROBLEM

ELLEN M. HENROTIN

About three years ago, the chairman of the Reform and Philanthropic divisions of the Chicago Woman's Club felt that there was an urgent need for teachers in the schools who had had some instruction in sex hygiene. To carry out that plan committees of women physicians and of other members of the club were formed, and courses on sex hygiene were offered. The meetings were at first not so largely attended, but as time went on they grew, until now two or three hundred teachers attend each course. The first year we gave a few isolated lectures, but this year we have given two courses for the teachers, which have been largely attended.

This year I have been working as a member of the Vice Commission, and I am convinced that there is nothing so needed for young girls, say from fourteen years on to young womanhood, as instruction in sex hygiene. So many mistakes, so many sad things happen through utter ignorance, because the child goes out into the world, which presents so many temptations to her, so utterly unprepared for what she is to meet. And the parents seem unable to perform this task. And when we think of the economic conditions under which women and young girls work today, it becomes a sacred duty to arm them at all points. And how can that be done, unless they are given some definite instruction?

Of course not only knowledge should be given but also appeal should be made to the sentiment, and to the ethics of the whole subject. Do not say to the girl, "You must be modest"; but tell her how to be modest. It is like saying to a little child, "You must tell the truth"; but few people ever tell the child or explain to him what truth is. It is necessary to be very practical in one's instruction to young girls. It is a crying sin in this generation that parents are so careless with their young daughters—not only in one class, but in all classes; and therefore it becomes doubly important that girls should be given some sound knowledge of the temptations which they are to meet and be armed at all points with knowledge and righteousness, in order to resist those temptations.

The Chicago Woman's Club has tried to present programs suggesting to teachers what road they should follow in the teaching of sex hygiene to these children. Many aspects of the subject must be suggested so that where a phase will not be acceptable to one teacher, another may take it and formulate her instruction along that line.

The programs that have been presented will give a more definite idea of the work. They include such topics as Anatomy and Physiology of Sex; Sociology of Sex; Interpretation of Life Through Art; Development of the Ovum; Critical Periods; Sex in Plants; Venereal Diseases; Heredity; Motherhood; The Child; The Dangers of Venereal Diseases to Mother and Child; Ethics in Sex Relation; Readings from Spring's Awakening.

THE HIGH-SCHOOL TEACHER ON INSTRUCTION IN SOCIAL HYGIENE

MARY BLOUNT
The University of Chicago High School

The problems connected with the teaching of social hygiene are among the oldest of educational problems; and at the same time they are the newest, for the science of biology is young, and embryology the most modern phase of biology.

There has been a great deal of discussion from time to time as to whether the subject of reproduction, especially the subject of mammalian reproduction, should be taught in secondary schools. There was a time when it could not be taught because the subject was not well enough understood. But since the science is now well enough in hand, I take the position that the subject of mammalian reproduction should be taught in secondary schools. There may be some prejudice against it among certain classes of people. But in my own experience I have not had to overcome prejudice; I have dealt with the pupils themselves, and with the children there is no prejudice. One can do anything in science with children, for scientific truth appeals to them.

Unfortunately in the University High School there is no course in human physiology. However in the department of physical training, a course of five lectures on hygiene is given; Dr. Monilaw gives the lectures to the boys and Dr. Norris to the girls. In these lectures there is time for one lecture on pelvic hygiene. Both Dr. Monilaw and Dr. Norris feel that they have very little opportunity in so short a course.

My work is zoölogy. The course in zoölogy in the University High School is elective for sophomores, juniors, and seniors—boys and girls both. It is given wholly in the laboratory. I shall briefly outline it. First there is a little work on protoplasm and the cell. Then we pass immediately to the study of the mammal. For convenience we use the white rat for dissection. The ease with which these animals can be kept in the laboratory and their size make them convenient for handling. There is a very short study of the skeleton and the muscular system and then a study of the various systems of organs that perform life processes: the digestive system, the excretory, the reproductive, the circulatory, the respiratory, and the nervous system. Each pupil has a white rat for dissection. For the reproductive system, each pupil dissects both sexes. We always have in the laboratory some non-pregnant rats and others containing embryos. The rats are raised in the laboratory and are mated at such times as are needed.

Just a brief outline of the study of the reproductive system; I shall discuss only that, but it must not be thought that we give any more emphasis to that than to the other systems I have named. From the white rat we see the size and position of the ovaries. We see the corpora lutea and understand their meaning. Unfortunately, the Fallopian tube is very small in the white rat, but it can be demonstrated. The microscopic size of the egg is demonstrated from the sections of the ovary. The egg passes through the Fallopian tube, and if fertilized it attaehes to the side of the uterus and develops.

There is the greatest interest in the freshly killed specimens. For much of the work we must use the alcoholic or formalin material. But a freshly killed rat, in which the organs have their natural color, in which the blood vessels show up plainly in the mesentaries, and in which the increased blood supply to the pregnant can be seen in contrast to the non-functioning uterus, appeals to the student very much. We always have the freshly killed material for at least two or three demonstrations, though we have to use the preserved material for more detailed study from day to day.

We notice the relation of the embryo to the mother, the amniotic sac, the umbilical cord, and the placenta. We have some young male rats for demonstration, and from them see the position of the testes in the abdominal cavity, and contrast them with the mature rat in which the testes have descended into the scrotal sac. The inguinal canal is very large in the rat and gives a good demonstration of the fact that the cavity of the scrotal sac is continuous with the abdominal cavity. So we compare both the young and the adult of the male rat so far as its anatomy is concerned.

Besides the microscopic study of the sections of the ovary, we also have microscopic study of the spermatozoa of several vertebrates. For the early development of the ovum, we use the amphibian egg, in which the cleavage shows so beautifully. The cells in the early stages are large enough to be seen without the hand lense. We trace the development from the two-celled stage to the four-celled, eight-celled, and so on; and from this the pupils generalize and learn that all development takes place by multiplication and differentiation of cells.

This work is given in the year. We begin our study in zoölogy with the mammal, rather different from the plan that is used in many schools where the first form studied is the frog or toad or the insects. We begin with the mammal, and having worked out the system of organs that perform the life processes in this very complex animal, we turn to the study of smaller animals, beginning with the simplest, the amoeba, and go on as complexity increases. All through the year we are interested to see how reproduction takes place in the various groups of animals. And over and over again, with every new type of animal, the questions come spontaneously from the pupils: "How does this animal reproduce? Where are its eggs laid? Where are they carried? What becomes of them? How does the process of reproduction go on?"

SCHOOL ATTENDANCE

W. L. BODINE

Superintendent, Compulsory Education Department, Chicago

School attendance is one of the great constructive factors for the conservation of childhood. It is gratifying to note that Chicago has as good school attendance as any American metropolis. The Coliseum has been the scene of many events, political and athletic—expositions of all kinds; even a President of the United States has been nominated there. But this week and next week we find it the capital of childhood, to which all roads lead, the children's city, with its columns of white and screens of gray, and any man, woman, or child who walks through those broad aisles and looks at the facts and the figures in that exposition can lift his head above any prejudice he may have and come to the conclusion that Chicago is a child-saving city—in its great Juvenile Court, its schools, its school attendance, its playgrounds, its work of prevention, and the character of its children. Moreover, in the conferences that have gathered, many people actively engaged in juvenile welfare work in the city are coming together. Truant officers and principals, probation officers, nurses, medical inspectors, Humane Society agents, policemen, Parental School people, the Juvenile Protective League agents, factory inspectors, representatives of every possible phase of the work are gathered in these meetings. The great standing that Chicago has won and will maintain as a child-saving center has been brought about largely by such persons. They are the people who do the work, who visit the homes, who help straighten out these tangled lives of children. The truant officers last year took care of 3,614 truants, and it was necessary to send only 511 of them to the Parental School. Thus the truant officers practically saved 3,103 truants, and saved that cost to the taxpayers. They are a great force for prevention. They made over 20,000 calls at the schools. Here is one reason why Chicago has a great school attendance. The result is that out of the total enrollment in this city of 204,000 pupils in not only the public but the private schools, the number of truants is less than 1 per cent, and the number of absences, including repetition due to truancy, is 1.21 per cent.

Another great agency of prevention is the staff of probation officers. Between the truant officers and the probation officers over 5,800 children are being held in line in Chicago today. The Juvenile Protective Association officers have to combat the destructive agencies that are ever in the path of childhood. They are doing a great work of prevention. Prevention, that is the word! We know these facts, we face this problem of truancy and delinquency. We know the conditions of these homes, of these children; the environment that creates the truant, the delinquent, and the unfortunate child. But the great public, a great portion of the public, does not know these conditions. The great value of the Child Welfare Exhibit is the open door for the public, for every man, every woman, every child of every nationality and every creed to come and to see. And when this great public visits this mirror of truth and sees therein the picture of fact, the living picture of fact, more pathetic than any of the wildest dreams of fiction, I am satisfied that it means in the future a greater interest of the public in the work in which the agencies gathered here are interested. Possibly it portends in the future a revolution in method by which the number of institutionalized children shall be reduced to a minimum and by which dependent children shall be cared for in a home instead of an institution. There are in this city 642,776 children under sixteen years of age. Of that number 251,556 are of compulsory-school-attendance age, 80,466 between fourteen and sixteen, 11,665 of whom are regularly employed. The question of the fourteen to sixteen period is a serious one in school attendance, the question of the boy who will neither go to school nor to work.

There are two laws to be noticed: First, the Compulsory Education Law, which imposes a responsibility upon parents or guardians to see that the children attend school the entire time—for violations of that law parents are taken into the court of domestic relations or municipal courts and fined for not keeping a child in school; second, the Parental School Law, which provides for habitual truants and classroom incorrigibles between the ages of seven and fourteen.

THE CHICAGO PARENTAL SCHOOL

PETER A. MORTENSON

Superintendent of the Chicago Parental School

In administering a large system of education, we find certain abnormal types that cannot be made to conform to the conditions maintained for the average normal child. Manifestly, these must be treated as special problems.

It has been found advantageous to segregate the blind, the deaf, and the subnormal children. The truant or the incorrigible child is abnormal in so far as his moral development has been arrested, or through the exercise of positively bad habits he is detrimental to other pupils.

When it is possible to correct these tendencies through the efforts of parents, teachers and truant officers, the course is obvious; when all such efforts fail, the case is a proper one for the Parental School.

Waste in Truancy and Incorrigibility

The average retardation due to truancy is a little less than three years, in the case of boys committed during the last year. The retardation of boys committed for incorrigible conduct is not quite so great. The waste, however, can not be measured solely in terms of the retardation of the individual.

Doubtless any good teacher can manage an unruly boy—it is simply a question of how much time and attention one pupil should demand at the expense of the other members of the class. If computed in terms of the waste of time for the members of the class who have a right to the teacher's time, the waste is more apparent.

The average school is organized to teach the great majority of normal children. Its methods of instruction and means of discipline and control are, of necessity, adapted to those who wish to learn rather than to the occasional trouble-maker. The Parental School, on the other hand, is organized to care for just these types. It is doubtful if it would be wise to organize all schools for the benefit of this small minority, even were the question of economy not considered.

History

The Parental School Law was passed by the legislature in response to an urgent demand on the part of the public-spirited men and women, who realized that the Compulsory Education Law had failed largely because nothing could be done with a chronic truant or habitually incorrigible child whose parents could not be held responsible. This law authorizes the Board of Education of Chicago to equip and maintain a school of detention for boys and girls of compulsory school age who cannot be made to attend school regularly by ordinary means or who while in school will not submit to authority. While the law authorizes commitment of girls for truancy or incorrigibility, no provision has ever been made for their care. The proportion of girls who are truant or incorrigible, however, is very small. Boys charged with delinquency or boys who have been in penal institutions cannot be admitted to the Parental School. It is the province of this school to assist in solving a distinctively school problem.

Method of Commitment

When the efforts of principal, teacher and parents, aided by a truant officer, have not succeeded in securing the regular attendance of a boy at school, or if the boy continues to violate the rules of school to the detriment of regular classroom work, the principal may file a petition with the superintendent of compulsory education, recommending the boy to the Juvenile Court for commitment to the Parental School. The parents are summoned to appear with the boy before the judge of the Juvenile Court, where an opportunity is given them to state their side of the case. The judge may commit the boy or release him on probation to a truant officer, at his discretion. Boys who are committed to the school are conducted to this institution by the sheriff, and receipted for by the superintendent of the Parental School.

Time of Detention

No definite term is assigned by the Juvenile Court. It is understood that each boy earns his own release under established rules, as follows: The school is divided into three divisions, corresponding to good, fair and poor. A new boy is entered in second division, or fair. If his work in school and deportment is satisfactory for the first month, the boy is placed in first division. If he maintains this position for a period of three months, he is recommended to the Board of Education for parole. Should a boy's record be very bad he may relapse to the third division or he may remain another month in second division. It is difficult for parents and friends to realize that this arrangement is for the boy's good. Frequently it is thought that political influence or other pressure is necessary, or will assist in the release of boys. The attitude of school officials and others connected with the Board of Education in this respect has been commendable. Every effort is made to encourage the release of a boy as soon as there is evidence of his willingness to comply with the conditions of parole. The fact that the capacity of the school is limited and that there is a desire to accommodate as many boys as possible during the year has tended to shorten the period of detention. The first boys at the school were kept fifteen months. The average time now is between six and seven months.

Causes of Commitment

As a general rule, the causes that lead to commitment either for truancy or for incorrigibility do not lie within the school. Boys come from all types of schools, depending somewhat on the disposition of the principal and truant officer in the matter. The manual training in special centers has had no perceptible influence.

Parental weakness and indifference; poor physical or mental inheritance; bad environment and street influences; intemperance and incompatability of parents; and improper nourishment and hours are noted most often as contributory causes. Many parents who mean well by their children, are so engrossed in making a living that the training of their children is left to chance till it is too late.

As long as inefficient parenthood exists, the best schools will probably fail to reach all abnormal children. The Parental School, with all its advantages, fails in many cases, particularly when boys are badly endowed by birth.

Schools Represented

Because of economic and other conditions, the larger proportion of boys come from congested and industrial districts. On the last day of the year three private schools had four boys, three private schools had three boys, five private schools had two boys, twenty-four private schools had one boy, one public school had nine boys, one public school had seven boys, five public schools had five boys, four public schools had four boys, eleven public schools had three boys, twenty-five public schools had two boys, and one hundred and fifteen public schools had one boy each in the Parental School. At that time 197 schools were represented by one or more boys as the membership was then constituted.

The Parole List

The Parental School Law provides that paroled boys shall remain in the legal custody of the Parental School for one year before being eligible for discharge. On the last day of the year, 406 paroled boys were attending 234 schools throughout the city, subject to return at any time for violation of parole. Reports are sent to the school once a month by the principals of the various schools, and an accurate record of these reports is kept.

Nearly all boys have good reports at first. A majority continue to have good reports, while others fail to keep their record after parole. The Parental School endeavors to co-operate with teachers and principals by looking up boys or writing to them or their parents when the lapse begins. As many of these boys are leaders of gangs at home, they are returned promptly as soon as their failure is established.

Organization

As an institution the Parental School is organized on the cottage plan; that is, the boys are divided into eight groups of about forty each. Each group of forty boys is placed in charge of a family instructor and his wife, who is known as assistant family instructor. This group is made to conform as nearly as possible to family life under the direction of these instructors. The boys live, sleep, and eat their meals in their own cottages. In the cottage they are trained in manners and morals, and every effort is made to lay the foundation of good character. The family instructors are men and women of high ideals.

They are not merely guards, but leaders. They avoid nagging, scolding and threatening, and strive to gain the confidence and respect of each individual boy.

The family instructor trusts his boys, but is always alert. He sets the example of industry in working with the boys. He seeks to develop a sense of pride in the good name of the cottage and school, and strives to instil habits of personal cleanliness and to inspire politeness, courtesy and respect for true manhood and womanhood.

Were it possible from a financial standpoint, it would be very desirable to have smaller groups or families. It is better, however, to have a family large and in charge of efficient instructors, than to decrease the size of the families and to place them in charge of inferior instructors.

An effort has been made at the Parental School to do away with the old-fashioned idea of bolts and bars and walls, and the boys are trusted a great deal. They are not trusted, perhaps, so much as they think they are, but they are never walled in, there is nothing at any time to keep a boy from leaving, or "sneaking away," as the boys call it, if they so desire. They are, however, promptly returned if they succeed in doing so; there are very few escapes. During last year there were forty-six boys who escaped or attempted to escape from the Parental School during the twelve months. The year before there were fifty-one such escapes and attempts at escapes. All of these were brought back without accident or delay.

Growth

The school was opened in January, 1902, with thirteen boys. All were housed in one unfinished building. The project was largely an experiment, as very few similar schools had at that time been organized. The expense of maintenance proved to be greater than some of the promoters had anticipated, but the Board of Education has shown a disposition to support the school in a loyal manner. From time to time improvements have been made and buildings erected, until today this school is probably as well equipped as any institution of its kind in the country. In March a new cottage was completed and an additional classroom occupied. Twenty acres of land were made available for farm and garden use. During the year a dairy was added, which has supplied the school with all the milk needed—approximately 250 quarts per day. Better drainage and fertilization have improved the condition of the soil, thereby making the farm and garden a source of considerable revenue.

The School

This is not a penal institution although in effect it is intended to deter those inclined to truancy and incorrigibility. On the other hand, it is a good school in which an effort is made to form the school-going habit and to interest boys in their school studies. Boys are built up physically through exercise, regular habits and nourishing food. The temptation to use cigarettes is removed and real work is demanded.

To form a good habit it is necessary to focalize the attention upon the matter in hand and to repeat this process in an attentive manner and to permit no exception or deviation until the habit is formed. In the last point lies, largely, the strength of the Parental School. Any good school can fulfil the first two conditions, but, if children are away from school nineteen hours of the day, it is impossible to prevent deviations and exceptions natural to abnormal children.

Manual training is a prominent feature of the school work. One hour a day is set aside for wood work and other forms of construction. The manual-training room is well equipped with benches and lathes. When the weather permits, one hour daily is given each boy on the farm and in the garden. Each boy has the sole care of a plot of ground under the direction of his teacher, and on this plot he plants, cares for, and harvests a crop of vegetables. Throughout the year occasional assignments are made for one day only to the kitchen, laundry and farm. This work is greatly enjoyed by the boys and stimulates their interest in school work.

Military System

Military formation and tactics are used in the moving of classes in companies, so far as it can be made of service. About one hour a day outside of school time is devoted to training in military tactics and battalion. These exercises provide good physical training in which all take part and they have been of value in correcting faults in attitude and attention, which are common among our boys. On the other hand this is not a military school, but conforms as nearly as possible to the routine of the public schools.

Examination of Boys

On entering the school all boys are examined by Dr. F. G. Bruner, of the Child Study Department, who reports on each case.

We have now come to recognize that boys are very bad often, not because they are perverts or moral degenerates, but simply on account of some defect in bodily structure which has made it impossible for them to do normal mental work even of a purely mechanical kind. Of course, there are other important factors which contribute to bad conduct, as for example an inefficient home atmosphere, positively bad street environment, and vicious companionship. Wherever an irregularity in the workings of the sense organs, the muscular mechanism, the vital organs, or the nervous tissue obtains, corrective work proceeds under a handicap, and indeed it will fall short of permanent results unless the physical stress is removed and the corrective work is founded upon a healthy, well functioning organism. By no means the least important feature of the work of a parental school consequently lies in the line of correcting the physical deficiencies from which many of the boys suffer on entrance. Efficient work in such an institution must include looking after such things as defective vision, ear troubles, nervous disturbances, poor bodily postures, and undesirable motor habits, as well as a bracing up of weak wills, the dampening of spontaneous and thoughtless responses, the development of normal, healthy interests along the lines of children's innate capacities and natural inclinations, and the cultivation of wholesome attitudes toward social institutions and moral problems in connection with the home and community life to which they will ultimately be returned.

Means of Correction

Boys improve under regular feeding; they develop good habits through military training; they become alert through manual work; occasionally they improve through the removal of physical defects; the farm and country life have their influence; restraint and the suppression of bad habits under the direction of men and women of character make an impression. Let it not be inferred that the abnormal types can be corrected through feeding, by surgical operations or even manual training.

With all of these, the formation of good and wholesome habits is a slow process and often fails to last. The greatest factor is earnest, personal effort directed with sympathy and the least possible interruption.

Corporal punishment is not permitted at the Parental School, but other means are used to impress prompt obedience. No punishments are severe, but they are sure to come if merited. Extra duty and the deprivation of privileges are the most effective.

The Parental School seeks to form good habits of study and conduct, in the hope that these habits will persist after boys are paroled. Each boy is required to practice these good habits for a definite period before being paroled. Every effort is made to return boys to the home school at the earliest possible time, to avoid institutionalizing and to make room for other boys.

The Problem

In theory, if all schools were good schools, and all homes were good homes, schools of detention would be unnecessary; all children might be cared for if not in regular rooms, in special classes. As a matter of fact, bad boys do come from good schools and, apparently, from good homes—perhaps the traditional black sheep. They come also from mediocre schools and from bad homes. As long as inefficient parenthood, inebriety, indifference and poverty exist, complicated by the gang in the alley and the cigarette lure, as long as individual differences and retarded development are recognized, there will probably be truancy and incorrigibility.

Irregular attendance, with consequent repetition, is a recognized form of waste in school systems, and great waste may be traced to the efforts of the teacher to control the individual boy who will not conform, except at the expense of the entire class.

The average citizen is likely to think of truancy as merely an incident. But in the crowded city, every call to the truant is toward deliquency, and especially when school is in session and the truant finds companions among older boys who loaf about the streets, these older boys will encourage him to do what they themselves do not dare.

The point is made that a detention school removes a boy from his surroundings and from temptation and places him in an artificial world, and that the life becomes attractive to him—that he becomes institutionalized. The facts do not seem to indicate this. Statistics may be misleading, but reports seem to indicate that Chicago's method of dealing with young offenders is improving. Without claiming too much for the Parental School, attention may be called to the fact that the John Worthy School has less than half the number of inmates registered in former years before its establishment; the same is true of the reformatory at Pontiac, whose inmates are recruited largely from Chicago.

SCHOOL ATTENDANCE FROM A BUSINESS MAN'S VIEWPOINT

MODIE J. SPIEGEL

Chairman, Finance Committee of the Board of Education, Chicago

I find myself in a somewhat awkward position; for, as a business man and from a business man's viewpoints, I strongly advocate prevention as the keynote in the treatment of cause of truancy as that for which the Compulsory Education Department of the Board of Education of the city of Chicago stands; and as chairman of the Finance Committee I must provide the funds necessary for that preventive work. As this method of treatment is costly, the undertaking is difficult and my position is embarrassing.

When I first became a member of the board, I found on investigation that the average attendance in the schoolrooms of the city of Chicago was in the neighborhood of sixty pupils to one teacher. I was not an educator, just a plain business man; but it was apparent to a layman that no teacher could do justice to sixty pupils and that this crowded condition might have a tendency to create truancy and deliquency. We have been working on that theory from year to year, trying to provide the moneys necessary for more teachers in the schoolrooms and for the erection of more school buildings. Between $11,000,000 and $14,000,000 a year of the public money have been appropriated for the purpose of educating the children and preventing truancy. It has been necessary for me to find more moneys whereby more schools could be erected and more teachers employed; and the result has been that the average has been brought down, so that today it is in the neighborhood of forty-five children to a teacher.

If that attendance were further reduced to the neighborhood of thirty-eight or preferably thirty-five, the teacher could observe the children even more closely. I believe that Chicago's showing in the Compulsory Education Department in the last four years is largely due to the fact of the reduction of the number of children in each room, and that if the teacher were in a position to have classes of thirty-five or thirty-six and to give more personal attention to the children, to study their home life, to see what little things appeal to them, to be more of a theoretical mother to the child who seemed backward, the number of truant children would decrease.

The Board of Education welcomes suggestions from social workers. The Finance Committee asks their support and their advice. Under the leadership of the Superintendent of Schools, who understands the situation thoroughly, we will lend every assistance possible to prevent truancy.

THE HOME AND TRUANCY

JOHN D. SHOOP

Assistant Superintendent of Schools, Chicago

I have been interested in seeing the interest that is awakening in some of our eastern cities along the line of the discovery of the causes which lie behind truancy. It is my particular interest to tell of schemes that are being launched in Chicago as well as elsewhere in the effort to take care of truancy as far as possible from the standpoint of the school itself. All who have given any consideration to the natural tendencies of children know that they are not all built on the same plan or after the same kind of architecture. More and more it is being acknowledged that cognizance of the individual tendencies of children must be taken. The psychology and the pedagogy of today is centering itself more and more upon the distinct personality of the child and yielding to him in the argument all of the advantages and conditions possible, and catering, in so far as the educational scheme will permit, to the diversity of characteristics found in the children.

Brief reference should be made to one feature of the Parental School Law. It is being realized that every possible effort must be put forth in order to avoid the brand of disgrace, as it were, that comes in the life record of the child by having his name recorded in the court proceedings. I wish that Chicago might have the law so changed as to conform with that which is now found in the state of New York. In New York, when a boy refuses to go to school, the superintendent of schools may assign him to the Parental School without going through with the processes and routine of court proceedings. That is, the Parental School is an organic part of the general school system, and, when the superintendent decides that in the education of that boy it is necessary to turn him over to the full charge of the management of the Parental School, the boy goes there without any reference to the juvenile court, except in cases where there is an appeal on the part of the parents.

I believe that we are looking toward better things in the way of child welfare when we are considering it from the standpoint of legislation. The less punitive we make our institutions, the less we institutionalize the children, the better is it going to be for the children. It has been stated that the home is the unit of our civilization, and that the boy ought to be under the home environment and under the home influences, where the loving touch of the mother may come in contact with the cheek of the boy, and where all of those conditions which teach the boy to know that there is someone in the world who cares for him may weave themselves into the warp and woof of his own life experience. So long as we can keep him in the home, let us make every effort to see that the boy does not lack that training.

But homes are not all alike. And I do not wonder at the fact that some of the children want to go back to the Parental School. I remember the case of one boy who said to me when he got back from the Parental School: "There is one thing that I like there; I had a little white bed all to myself." If in our child welfare discussions we can look to the creation of a better home environment; if we can turn our energies as we are doing, largely through visitation agencies of the organizations that are working co-operatively along this line, to build up the standard of the Chicago home, we are doing that much as a preventive measure against the truancy of the child. We have not realized in the past how much encouragement the homes in Chicago need. It is not to be wondered at that one of the greatest and most widespread organizations that we have in our city today is the Mothers' Club. Why? Because when the father goes off to his business at seven, eight or nine o'clock in the morning, comes back late in the evening, and scarcely gets acquainted with his children at home, the great burden of responsibility that used to be shared equally between father and mother falls upon the shoulders of the poor, burdened mother. They do right to meet from time to time to discuss the policies and the best means for the management of the boy. It is a part of our civilization; we stand committed to this task as teachers and as members of the organizations that are governing the educational forces of this country to give the best of our lives and the best of our efforts to the building up and fortifying of the American home. Someone has said that when the home is right, the city is right; and when the cities and the homes are right, the state is right; and when the state is right, the nation is right; and when the nations are right, the world is right.

WHY WE HAVE TRUANTS AND DELINQUENTS

D. P. MacMILLAN

Director, Child Study Department, Board of Education, Chicago

For the investigator of social relations, information is divided into two parts, that which one has in his possession and that which one has not, and the latter is by far the greater portion. Concerning any custom our information must have two aspects: the first relates to matters of fact; the second concerns the history or setting of that fact. We must know the custom and in addition the environment in which that custom lives. I think that there is no more lamentable fact extant at this the beginning of the twentieth century, with all its boasted informations and achievements, than ignorance—and the most pernicious kind of ignorance is that which concerns childhood. And further be it added, the most baffling and the most vital feature of that atmosphere of ignorance is summed up in the fact that we know very little indeed about the best motives to be ingrained to effect human improvement.

It is a truism to assert that to know the means and measures of improvement of humanity we must know the children; and with reference to truancy we must know more about it than the mere fact of its existence.

If I were to attempt to discuss first causes of truancy and delinquency or attempt to attribute truancy and social mal-adjustment to any one predominating cause, I think that I should have to do so with some apologies. But I will make no reservation in discussing the characteristics and traits of the truant and the delinquent. My observations are made and my judgment founded not alone upon truants who have been committed to the Parental School, but also upon truants chronic and temporary who have not been so disposed of, as well as upon the delinquents of one kind and another who have come to the attention of the department during the course of its history.

The most important features that one ought to bring out center about three things—strictly there are only two, namely, that the truant and the delinquent are born in an inferior environment out of which they must make a fresh start for themselves; they receive an inferior education to that of their fellows, and are handicapped by physical and mental inferiority. I may qualify these statements as I go along, but cannot withdraw them; and such qualifications as I shall insert, will be made for the purpose of preventing wild and worthless generalizations. Judged by every form of physical test that can be given, the truant and the delinquent are inferior. If one takes the body as a whole—I refer to the external features of the body—and examines it with reference to increase in size and weight, increase in diameter at different levels of the body, as well as with regard to changes in proportion and symmetry of the whole and its parts, one readily discovers on the one hand what we may call defects of structure and organization; on the other hand, one finds defects of function, which center about nutrition, circulation and respiration. Then one must consider defects of strength evidenced in the diminished force of muscular contraction as well as in the diminished resistance against fatigue.

But apart from the body at rest, it is in the expressions of the body, such as movements and attitudes, that one finds defects most apparent and most significant. These features may be discovered in terms of excess discharge in motility and in irritability; but I think that I can make the whole subject-matter plainer to you in terms of the captions "growth" and "motor control," if under the former are included all the marks resulting from past functioning of the body, and under the latter such excesses or defects in action as actual observation reveals to us. It is apparent that structural deficiencies, such as defects of structure of the head, of the trunk, of parts of the trunk, of the extremities, and so forth, are by no means uncommon, some of which are vital or real indices of disturbances, and some of which are not. Moreover, the motor defects, which mean the exaggerations of movement when the attempt is made to keep still and the excess discharges when there is an attempted co-ordination in serial acts, are nearly all indications of abnormal functioning, whatever be the special features of behavior that one considers in detail. In these two features we have the most significant ways of measuring physical defects, and if the growth defects are combined, one will find that among truants and delinquents as compared with the average group of children, there will be seven growth defects to five found among so-called normals, and with regard to motor defects it will be ascertained that for every three deficiencies of motion in the average group, six will be found in these wayward pupils. This means to us simply that the body has not been trained, that in the widest sense of the words the mental content of physical acts does not have the proper setting before that act is begun, while it is being carried on and after completion.

But you will inquire: Are there any grave defects of the so-called internal parts of the body that are significant, such as, enlarged tonsils, adenoids, and swollen cervical glands, and all that sort of thing, and will not the pupil be normalized by curing and correcting these abnormalities? Certainly they must be considered defects, but one cannot pick out a particular child with a defect, be it ever so marked, and say that because of that defect, he will go wrong or that he will not attend school. Again with regard to sensory defects, that is maladjustments of the organs of sense, particularly eyes and ears, it is found that about the same number of children are afflicted, irrespective of whether they willingly go to school or just as willingly flee from it. It seems to be evident, however, that we do find graver defects among truants, incorrigibles, and delinquents; and the farther they depart from normal children in action, the more serious are the defects found to be. But, again, it must be remembered, that, although bad vision, for example, is an important thing, it is not a bad eye in itself that makes significant the child's actions in not attending school or in becoming a delinquent; and so, even when all defects are corrected and the physical status is normalized, there remains the problem of training.

I am not going to review the means taken to measure defects of one kind and another, but will simply revert to the fact that our experience is gathered from the individual records of certain pupils and cases that have been examined in the offices of the Board of Education, from a careful study of their school progress while in the regular grades, as well as from an extended survey of the characteristics of pupils in the John Worthy reform school. Furthermore, the teachers' study of the truant and incorrigible, with special reference to their attitude toward work and people, reveals many important things, although again these estimates must be interpreted. The teachers of the Parental

School may feel that a great majority of the pupils make rapid advances in their studies during their stay with them, and improve in demeanor, yet it should not be overlooked that they are the pupils who were previously regarded as so markedly inferior by the regular teachers in the day schools. Every child must, of course, be judged in terms of the place in which he is found and the group to which he belongs, and so estimates of relative standing and comparative progress in school work must be carefully evaluated in and of themselves. Nevertheless, school standing and amenability to the kind of training that schools give, have some significance. From this point of view it is found that a review of the school standing of pupils committed to the Parental School shows that, for example, more than half the thirteen-year-old boys have a standing in scholarship that is usually attained by the nine-year-old pupils coming from average American homes, and all of these children of all ages not recommended for commitment are below their fellows of equal school opportunity. Moreover, judged in the same way by like standards, delinquents are found four years below where they ought to be for their age, and the worst types of moral transgressors examined in the laboratory are below for their age in every particular. All this is indicative, but when it is remembered that these pupils come from an environment that is even farther below the average than the pupils are below their more favored fellows, our attention is directed, not to the boy or girl in and by themselves, but in relation to the medium where they live and attempt to work. Even those homes from which the best of the groups that we are discussing come—those sending pupils to the Parental School—are very far from desirable places for children. The history of the cases seems to show this, for taking the average of the ratings of homes of the four years' attendance after the year 1902, it is found that between 75 and 80 per cent come from poor homes and unfavorable environments.

But beyond school tests and standards, the best evidences of the comparative ability of truants, incorrigibles and delinquents is shown by a series of mental tests that appeal to inherent ability or native power. Whenever any test is made that appeals to native power, it will be found that these children do not differ very much from the ordinary pupils, that in that which appeals to their understanding they are rated very high, whereas, in that which draws upon their power to execute or to perform, they show at once the same qualities that we have observed in structural and functional defects, that is, their acts are uncertain and indefinite.

In reviewing the most general characteristics of all, summed up from all these methods of testing, it is seen that the truant and the delinquent are pupils whose minds are not trained to perform specific things regularly in definite ways with and for persons. I repeat, the general trend of their growth and education is this: They have not acquired the training to do specific things regularly in specific ways for persons and with persons, and this general characteristic shows itself not only in the body externally, and not only in the acts which the body performs, but likewise in the mental tasks that are put before them. To be sure these characteristics go much deeper than first observation indicates, and it is more than probable that a social investigator, studying the home-life in detail, would find that the child's food was irregularly taken, that it was poor in quality, that his rest was irregularly taken and that it was disturbed, that his work was fitful and undisciplining, and that his play was not carried on in the real social spirit. These are the formative factors governing his life-habits of which school-life constitutes only a meager portion.

I have said that the mental attitude of the child is the significant thing. Therefore the question arises: What are the first steps that ought to be taken in the line of ameliorative and corrective measures? Taking our departure from the pivotal point, it may safely be said, that changing the physical status will, in the great majority of cases, favorably affect the mental, and that changing the environment, the surroundings, will likewise modify the physical. We must, then, get all the information possible with reference to the child, with regard to the medium in which he lives and further with respect to the best means of bringing these two together, and all this ultimately means more knowledge of persons and personal relations.

I will conclude by repeating that the delinquent and the truant come from a social medium which is inferior and out of which they must make a fresh start for themselves, they receive an education inferior to that of their fellows, and are handicapped physically and mentally. Our obvious duty is to develop the physical, awaken the mental, and give a start in the right direction, and that means the necessity of securing more information concerning the three aspects of the problem of which the central point is the child.

ESSENTIALS IN EDUCATION

MARY S. SNOW

Supervisor, Household Arts and Science, Board of Education, Chicago

To formulate a plan for discussing essentials in education, it is necessary first to decide what is the purpose of education, in order to assemble the methods that shall accomplish this aim.

What may fairly be expected from a boy or girl at the end of elementary school, of high school or of college? Indeed the question may be profitably narrowed to what may be expected from the boy or girl at the end of elementary training, since of the next hundred children to be met on the highway ninety of them will never reach high school. The ratio of one in ten may well provoke the old question of "Where are the nine?"

Most of the vast machinery of the public schools is kept in motion for the ten. We treat all alike as if they all had the long stretch of years up to eighteen for the more or less pleasant task of absorption. No mention of what life is like in its practical phrases, no allusion to labor—unless it be accounts or teaching—no pretense at dignifying the hands as the skillful servants of the brain, must be made for fear of subtracting somewhat from a presumable accumulation of culture that will be recognized by the final diploma.

When the remnant of the vast army who entered first grade is graduated from elementary school, those people who expect to see them move in unbroken ranks into high school have their first shock of disappointment. If these spectators have been exceptionally keen after knowledge of what happens to the children, they have seen them dropping out all the way in pathetically large numbers as fast as the gate was opened by the fourteenth birthday. The pathos of their eagerness is the sharpest rebuke that the characteristic course of study can possibly receive. The Industrial Commission of Massachusetts revealed 25,000 children between fourteen and sixteen years of age out of school. Recent investigation brought out the fact that practically the same number of children are to be found in the city of Chicago. Further inquiry shows that this vast number are out, not so much for economic reasons as for the reason that to neither parents nor children did the work which the children were doing in school seem to be "worth while." Whether it is or not, is a matter for educators to thresh out, but the fact that neither parents nor children can realize its value or have sufficient conviction of its effectiveness to keep the children in school when the law permits them to leave, is a matter of grave and tremendous moment. The fate of these children is the fate of the unskilled worker, with the increased pathos that they are unskilled children. They drop into the various occupations which are mechanical, deadening, and empty of growth to future efficiency. They weary of the soul-breaking monotony of their tasks and shift intermittently to others. They suffer from the enforced idleness of the "seasonal" occupations and many of them find the only excitement about work to be "hunting" it; and so their time is spent in a sort of industrial vagabondage. To such as cling to their tedious and paralyzing tasks comes inability to move on to anything that requires thought or responsibility. They have ceased to be able to do the one or bear the other, and the disintegration of soul and body becomes at last a question that knocks at the door of church and state and is finally turned back to the school. And since at the end of eight years of training this seems to be what happened to the children whom the schools had let slip and whom the trades would not take, the question is pertinent—What have we left undone?

What, then, must we do? It is a question which was asked one John the Baptist and he gave a very short and practical reply; and if we have aught of wealth, of wisdom, or even of faith, it should be placed at the disposal of these children whom we assume to educate. By "educating" we mean to say we are to place the experience of the race at the disposal of the child that he may meet his needs with intelligence and effectiveness.

Certainly some essential is missing. Children are not dull about significant truths. They wish to know how to read and to write and to manipulate number processes. They have wholesome and often keen interest in the movements and experiences of peoples and the great figures in history; they work hard and cheerfully to know somewhat of the countries of the earth. Musical expression satisfies and delights them. Art entices them up to the point when they find that it misses practical application, and then interest dies and with it power in expression. Then they begin to reach after further reality with passionate earnestness. They long to express themselves in tangible ways. They have a right consciously to experience the sensations of knowing that they know and knowing that they can do. If opportunity for "doing" has been opened to them, they will have gained in strength of character through their authoritative wills commanding their powers, and the purposive and coördinate work of the motor phases of education will have furnished a kind of test of progress, a mental verification of accomplishment that can never come through any academic work. They have many measuring rods in the evaluation of the finished task—the eye, the muscular tension, judgment, comparison, trial. There is necessary integrity since no amount of vanity will make the tangible result reveal anything but truth. William James, with ever brilliant insight, said that manual training did more for the moral strength of youth than any other subject in the curriculum.

The artificial prejudice in the country against labor with the hands is the almost insurmountable obstacle to the sufficient introduction of manual training for boys and girls into the public schools. The economic question is perplexing, but, if labor with the hands had the sympathy and admiration of all classes, the matter of expense would seem trivial. The outward march of the 25,000 children would be halted by its own will, and the recognition that thinking was about to culminate in action and that it would be well to stay on a bit in the midst of reality, would be assured. The chief interest of children, as with all of us, is to live—and what promises to prepare them for life will make irresistible appeal.

The average industrial life of a girl is less than seven years. She marries, undertakes the administration of a home, and if she is without training or experience, the experiment is expensive and full of tragic failures. She is self-conscious, supersensitive under criticism or raillery, and finally drops all and goes back to the shop or office, preferring to earn the money to pay the bills. The significance of the home is weakened, children must not come, little good-will having gone into the home-making effort none comes out, and at last comes the inevitable crash. It is almost a "haec fabula docet" to sketch the picture of the other girl who, in school when interest in stimulating the activities of grown-up people ran high, performed all household processes, cooking, cleaning, serving, laundry-work, sewing, millinery, marketing, care of the baby and cooking for the sick. All these activities followed one another; anticipation of the coming and keenest interest in the present occupation carried her forward with singular and unexpected power of comprehension and perfection of technique.

Having met all her needs in school in simple effectiveness and with joy in the doing, she faces life outside with consciousness of power and dignity, and when she goes into her new home it is with anticipation and confidence. It has no surprises for her as it has no terrors, and her life is the confident life of one who knows that she knows.

The medium in which a boy works is usually either wood or iron, and he has the experience of always making them obedient to his will. Like the girl he is daily measuring himself in terms of his own results. Both media are unswervingly faithful to truth and they will demand the same from him.

Manual training for boys or girls must not be measured by results in material but by what is left in the pupil, of resourcefulness, of self-reliance, of confidence, of integrity, of respect for and faith in the dignity of labor.

The classicist and the educator, tradition-bound by the hundreds of years of devotion to the themes of monastic education, take alarm at motor training, fearing the crowding out of the so-called culture subjects and the robbery of the child. The contention is that the state's best gift to the child is the placing at his disposal the culture of the race—meaning by that the subjects which are hoary with tradition and crystallized in the practice of education—and the giving him power to think; having been so furnished, he can dash out at the age of fourteen or eighteen and make his way successfully in a world which is going at an innumerable number of vibrations a minute. They further contend that applied art, applied science, applied mathematics and applied humanity have no place in the school life of the child, but are the problems of the after years. The terms applied art, science and humanity, are much like the terms applied truth, health and courage. They exist only for the sake of the application. Would it be too exaggerated a contention to assert that there would be quite as much culture resultant in the practice of the art, science and humanity as in the study of them? May it not be claimed that the application of the study of proportion, form, line, the science and art of textiles, the realization of living conditions and the habit of conscious conquest, if analyzed and scrutinized, are, after all, culture? Benvenuto Cellini thought so when he wrought his miracles in precious metals; Michael Angelo believed thus when he wrought the marvels of his mind in every possible medium; William Morris took his place in the assertion of the dignity and nobility of labor; and springing up on all sides are groups of people who have obliged their hands to execute in a fine way the rarest and best workings of their minds. Doing has preceded art in the history of the world, as musical instruments antedated singing or the art of music, but the conscious stage of the life necessity having been passed, immediately came the grace and idealism of art as a recognition of facility and a reaching out of the soul.

The school tardily recognizes this, letting the ideal set up its throne with no kingdom of the real for which to plan and dream, and since it is indeed life that is the deepest interest of the child, as it is of us all, this most potent factor in training should be in intimate relation with all formal theory and academic knowledge.

Youth needs all the wisdom of adult life for its direction and progress and, though knowledge comes, wisdom does not always result, much less linger. It would be well to keep our practice as well as our hope directed toward the final result which we expect in the child—self-reliance, constructive ability, courage, industrial integrity and sympathy, power of judging, and intelligent attitude towards life experiences outside the school.

THE SCHOOL OF TOMORROW

HENRY SUZZALLO

Professor of the Philosophy of Education (Educational Sociology) in Teachers College, Columbia University

The Method of Prophecy

It is quite a task to assume to prophesy what any institution will be in the future. If one had stood at the beginning of the seventeenth century and had tried to prophesy the democracy of the American states and their political institutions, one would have been subject to severe criticism. At the opening of the twentieth century we stand in the position of forecasting an institution that is just in its beginnings. The only safe way by which we can gain a view of the school of tomorrow is to project it from the angle of educational history. Once we realize the changes that have occurred within the three centuries of American history, we must admit the tremendous radicalism that has overthrown previous conservative traditions. In this twentieth century, when affairs move with even greater rapidity than they did in the eighteenth and nineteenth centuries, we are justified in prophesying even more radical reform.

The Contrasts in Our History

Go back with me for a moment to the Colonial period of American educational history, and examine the various elements where social pressure registered itself upon the school. Contrast these points under pressure with the actual situation as we find it today. In the first place the school as an institution was largely under the control of the church; now it is the servant of the state. It was supported by voluntary agencies; now public taxation is the major resource. Once we educated the select few, those among the leisure class who had a gift for formal and abstract thinking; now we educate all—the rich and the poor, the gifted and the defective. Then, the arts and sciences taught were almost exclusively concerned with mathematics and the languages; now the course of study is as broad as human knowledge itself. The schools of that day were concerned primarily with ideas and symbols; today they are busy with impulses, ideals, things and actions. The three R's have made room for play, sociability, fine arts, literature, moral training, nature study, geography, history and self-government. Once the teacher ruled his school with tremendous authority, in terms of divine and civil sanction; today the teacher rules for the most part through a leadership of mind over mind, that is reverent and tolerant of childhood while clearly conscious of social ends. In view of these significant and revolutionary changes which have so greatly modified the school, largely within a single century, we have a right to expect that within the next century the school will be greatly reconstructed so as to be a fit and mighty weapon with which to protect and maintain the democracy of the future.

Basic Influences at Work

Having once put ourselves into that receptive state of mind which our historic perspective suggests, we have only to turn to the basic differences between our century and the last to realize whither our educational reform will lead us. The two basic differences which the school of the future faces are: (1) A school population recruited from wider differences of natural ability, economic and social status; (2) a rapidly changing social organization which is vastly different from that in which the original traditions of the public system were fixed. All of the specific modifications that will mark the reform of the school will find their causes and sanctions in one or the other of these fields of basic change.

Vocational Education

Turning now to a specific statement of what the school of the future will be as compared with the school we now know, we may say, first, that to the traditional function of general or cultural education will be added the new function of special or vocational education.

It is not quite accurate to say that vocational training will be a new function of the school. That higher series of vocations, which have been called the professions, has long had a place in the educational scheme, but the lower and wider series of employments which are associated with manual skill and economic products has been cared for by the institution of apprenticeship rather than by the school. But under modern industrial conditions the system of apprenticeship has become less competent to train men efficiently. The labor union and the capitalist have manipulated the system of apprenticeship for their own special economic ends. The subdivision of labor and the appearance of machine industry have deprived the young apprentice of a chance to learn the business in every aspect—from the ground up. Modern industry, too, has become an increasingly scientific matter, dependent upon the application of laws that the onlooker and the imitator cannot perceive.

Rapid change in the use of machinery, materials and methods, which is characteristic of modern industrial evolution, soon throws the unversatile and inflexible man into the ranks of the unemployed, and present day apprenticeship with its training for a microscopic task does not train adjustable men. The fatigue of labor where the machine dominates the man rather than the man the machine, dehumanizes the operative and suggests the necessity of some antidote. New class problems arise among these men; for the protection of their interests requires class solidarity on many economic issues, and this class consciousness, too frequently narrow and selfish, becomes a menace to the public welfare. For all of these reasons the worker must be trained for his vocation by some other agency than apprenticeship, and the school is the obvious institution at hand to train him for his life's business.

The school of the future must add vocational training. It is inevitable. To perform this task it must double its organization, and widen the spirit of its traditions so as to give roof to the new as well as to the old functions. The school cannot longer be interested exclusively in ideas and ideals; it must show capacity to deal with things of more immediate practicality. It may occur, and probably will, that the present general elementary curriculum may be condensed into six years, and that the seventh, eighth and ninth years of school life, for the ordinary child, will be given over to anticipating and preparing for a vocation. This does not necessarily imply a mere imitation of apprenticeship, but something broader. The fundamental principles and skills underlying a group of vocational activities will be taught in a practical way, the child being allowed to specialize within the group, while a general training for the social problems associated with his vocational life will not be left out.

The program for vocational education will not merely include the old professional training at the top and add the industrial, household, commercial and agricultural training at the bottom. It will provide for many groups in between—for the shop foreman, the factory superintendent and other lesser captains in the army of workmen.

We may have a high school with a six-year curriculum, beginning, for those who do not go into the lower vocational schools, at the seventh school year. This secondary school may be divided into junior and senior high schools, so that technical training may begin, for some with the tenth school year and for others with the thirteenth.

One thing is certain—vocational education will enter the school system. Our competition in the world markets requires it. And when it does come it will distribute a series of special schools along the route of general culture in such a way as to affect the articulation of our present school units—elementary, secondary and collegiate. The wall of school tradition cannot keep out vocational education. Nor will special education enter and crowd the old general, moral and cultural education to the wall. As the two interests are supplementary, each equally necessary in practical life, their interests must be reconciled and a place given to both in school.

A School Supervised Apprenticeship

It must not be implied that the schools will completely do away with the old apprenticeship. The schools may be superior in many respects, but they also have their limitations. When a child has obtained his general cultural equipment and received his vocational knowledge and skill, he will still have to fit himself snugly into the industrial scheme. Within the leisure period of any youth's life, before he is compelled to earn a full living-wage, time must be left for gaining mastery over concrete industrial or business conditions as they are at the particular place where he establishes himself.

For reasons already stated it is unwise to let labor union or employer dominate even this new apprenticeship, and it is probable that the school as an impersonal agent will come to assume a dominant supervision of these last stages of training which the boy or girl receives in his trade. The difficulties of establishing this new principle are obvious. But it is no more difficult than many other reforms that have been established in the past.

Three Stages of School Education

Thus the whole scheme of school education must provide three stages of education: (1) General or cultural training; (2) vocational training; (3) supervision of apprenticeship. In our traditional school, the first function is well established; the second only partially so; and the third not at all.

Three-Fold Function of the School

The second great change in our system of schools will be a broadening of the functions of the common school. The school of the past has stressed one function to the over-subordination of all others. Its sole conscious business was to instruct, though incidentally it protected the child from the dangers of his environment and selected one type of mind to the exclusion or discouragement of others. The school of the future will hereafter consciously pursue three functions: (1) It will protect the powers of children; (2) it will train them broadly; (3) it will distribute its school population to the positions in life best fitted for them. In other words, a school will not be exclusively a collection of classrooms; it will be a substitute environment competing with the city street and it will be an instrument for guiding a child into a vocation. All three of these functions, protective, educative, and selective, have been associated with the school from the beginning, but not consciously.

What do I mean by such a three-fold definition of the school? First, we must ask: What is a school? The school is an institution which came into existence because the instincts of the child were such that, left to themselves, they would not adjust him to a certain knowledge of life. Our scientists tell us that the children of today are born with about the same instincts as the children of our primitive ancestors; the child at birth is about the same as he always was. His instincts were born for efficiency in the hunting and fishing period of human culture, for a period of adventure. Today, under the artificial conditions of civilized life, the gap between the child's instincts and the situation into which he must fit is a tremendous one. It must be bridged by education through special institutions. So it may be said that the school is an intermediary institution that stands between the child and his complicated social life. It holds back the world from the child until he is ready for it; it protects him from over-responsibility. It restrains the pressures of the world that would tie his plastic nervous system into a definite knot and make it impossible for him to remain adjustable. It is a protective institution because it is tolerant when the child makes a mistake, because it is patient and instructive when he does things that are quite at variance with the expectation of grown people. Only as a child becomes strong enough to bear the load, does the school put it upon him.

The School a Protective Institution

The true sanction for the playground movement, for plays and games in the school curriculum, for sociability of every sort, for medical inspection, and for attractive surroundings in the elementary school is found, not so much in the educative power of these things, as in their protective function. These congenial activities conserve the powers of childhood till they are ready for training. They stimulate them in the direction of natural growth, yet leave them free of the vicious prejudice that street and alley environments would give.

The whole careful gradation of school tasks in terms of simplicity and complexity, interest and strain, is a protective device. We know that there are two ways by which we may break a man. In the first place we may give a man tasks that are too heavy for him to bear. Under the discouragement of constant failure he loses his impulse to go on. When a man's labors are too hard for him he breaks down under his load, physically and morally. In the second place, we see innumerable examples of the breaking of men's powers where leisure is too plentiful. We know men who have lost their power to achieve because their instinctive impulses have not been given a sufficient load for normal exercise. Too light a load and too heavy a load—these are the two means of breaking youth before maturity. Therefore the school has a carefully graded system of responsibility quite different from that of the adult world which it has shut out from the child.

In classroom and out, the school will organize its activities so as to make itself a protective institution, one which will conserve childhood. It will make of itself a recreative center, a public playground, a congenial and attractive center of child sociability. To the degree that it can make the school premises a likeable place to children, to that degree the school of the future will meet its important function of being a protective institution.

The School's Selective and Distributive Function

The old school was a selective institution. It had a certain kind of information to give according to certain established methods. If the child had a mind that could fit the school situation, he received an education; if he did not, he was soon discouraged. The school of the past selected a few students, then educated them. The elementary school of the future must take all the students that come and train every one of them. This the compulsory attendance law requires, and we shall not go back upon it.

What has already happened in the elementary school, will occur in less degree in high school and college. These institutions are not now as selective as they were; they will be less so as higher education becomes popular. To keep their own intellectual spirit intact they will have to modify their modes of classroom instruction so as to attract the boys from the athletic field and the fraternity house. Otherwise the student activities will become the dominant interests of college life.

The selective function, already decaying at its old post at the entrance to school, will find new vitality at the exit from school. When the school has done all it can for children, it will try to distribute them into their appropriate places—into the higher schools, aside to the vocational schools, or out to the work of life.

The Basis for Vocational Guidance

The school of the future will interest itself scientifically in the problem of vocational guidance. The school system will have an organized bureau for this purpose, and every teacher will, under competent direction, be active in trying to settle the youth into life. This work will take into account three factors: (1) The capacities of the child in so far as they are revealed negatively or positively; (2) the economic capacity of the family to provide further training; (3) the vocational opportunities open to the boy or girl. The necessary vocational surveys of the community must be undertaken by a special bureau in the department of education and each school must establish the needed co-operation between school and home.

The School's Broadened Educational Function

The school of the future will greatly amend its conception as to what constitutes its educational function. It has progressed far already. The old formal linguistic curriculum is already gone and something richer stands in its place. The present course of study may present a more chaotic situation than the three R's, but it holds more promise of efficiency than any return to the simple formal instruction of the past can ever offer.

Socializing the Teacher

But we shall never arrive at a clear notion of the school's true educative function until the profession of teachers has accepted a conscious social point of view. We are too institutional in deciding what is or is not our business. We look back to the educational past, not out upon the social future in determining our educational work. There are many causes for this biased and narrow vision of teachers, which we need not now enter upon. It suffices to say we need more social and less academic mind in our profession. The problems of social life are growing so urgent that no amount of respectable, conscientious academic blindness to changed conditions will avail us. The school of the future must train men for twentieth century life, not for the dead seventeenth century which revives only in books. The formalism and the narrow intellectualism of the old-time school teacher will pass. No more will grammar be more important than speech. Already the right use of words seems a better test of linguistic power than an accurate definition; and literature begins to be in school what it is in life—a thing of joy!

When our social life was simple, and traditional moral agencies were effective, the school could be a place where children were trained to acquire and use the linguistic tools needed in the personal acquisition of knowledge. But with home, and church and neighborhood life weakening, the school has an additional business upon its back. It becomes one of the chief moral teachers of the nation. So from petty alphabetic business we come into a larger undertaking. There is then the need that the school shall train the total personality of a pupil for the total obligation of social life. How different this educative function is from teaching the alphabet, the spelling of words, and the forms of penmanship!

The school of the future will perform an educational function as broad as human life itself. It will still give the tools of language, but it will teach all the fundamental information the child ought to have about life, cast his emotions into the mould of right social attitude, give him stable habits, train him to think, and give him that expressive outlet for his own powers that will make him co-operative and masterful among things and men.

Broadened Intellectuality

The intellectual work of the school will broaden constantly. The child will know more than forms and facts; he will be an independent and unbiased thinker. Society cannot accept less. The nineteenth century added the content subjects. The

HOME AND SCHOOL GARDENS

Used as Dumping Ground

Sand lot with boys garden

Prize Vegetable Garden So Chicago

Used by School for Study

Oasis in a Desert

Vacant Lots

Plus Garden

Needs A Garden

Back Lot plus Care

Better Gardens - Better People

Successful under Difficulties

child now knows the facts of geography, history and civics. The twentieth century will teach him how to obtain more facts when he needs them, and how to think about those he has. The recent movement for teaching children to study, points in that direction.

Enlarged Emotional Control

The school of tomorrow will not content itself with a superficial manipulation of the conscious mind of childhood when the school authority sets it to a task. It will, because it must, remould the instincts and emotions of children, for here are the sources of conduct, the mainsprings of morality. It will consult the interests of childhood when it teaches, the modern theory being that the whole child is to go to school, not merely that small portion of him that the attendance officer can bring to school, or the teacher compel to attend when he teaches. The school is not going to be a dull place: it will be rich in its stimulation and powerful in its control of the emotional life whether this registers itself in conduct or in art. Play, manners, music, the plastic arts, dramatization—all these are to be more conspicuous in the future.

Increased Opportunity for Expression

The school, too, will be a more active place. The pale imagery and verbal forms will have deeds and expressions as companions. All the knowledge and stimulations of school life will finally emerge in the test of action. As the manual training shop tests one's knowledge of things; the nature study laboratory or garden, one's knowledge of plants and animals; so will the play and sociability of life test one's command of men and morals, for the social life of the school is its human laboratory. Speech, supervised play, students' organizations, self-government, manual training shops, and school gardens will play a more prominent part than now because they provide an outlet in terms of action. It is action that the world cares about. The man of intellect, the man of emotion—these are only important because they determine the man of deeds.

The school of the future will educate boys to be men, by a broad course of study rich enough to attract and hold all types of mind. The methods of teaching used will be as variable as human heredity. The facts taught and the problems solved will be vital rather than traditional, vital to society because of their power to illuminate its life, vital to the child that he may grasp it largely, fully and lastingly.

The School as a Social Center

The school of the future will do far more than care for the children of the community during the school hours. It is inevitably destined by force of surrounding circumstances to become the center of community life, whether the community be urban or rural. In the United States, where education is to be maintained through education, it is absolutely essential that we enlarge our means for educating adults upon the current issues of our social, political and economic life. The school building, which is the one institution near at hand to every citizen, is the one agency, the machinery of which is appropriate to the purposes of disseminating knowledge and encouraging discussion.

The school plant will be used for all clubs, societies and other voluntary gatherings of the community. Its doors should be open night and day for community purposes. Certainly in the large cities the children will find here their after-school playground, recreation centers, and, in the poorer districts, their evening study-rooms. The school of the future will educate the entire community and will be the center of its new sociabilities. It will be open for service, not six or eight hours, but fourteen or sixteen. It will deal with the pleasures as well as the serious responsibilities of the community. It will administer to adult need as well as to the training of children.

We have indicated, in a broad way, all the larger changes, already incipient, which mark out the major structure of the school of tomorrow. The more detailed changes suggested by these gross modifications will become apparent with future analysis and with additional experience. But this much is certain: (1) the school which is coming will provide vocational as well as cultural training; (2) it will be a substitute environment for childhood; it will compete with the city street; (3) it will greatly enlarge its educative functions, so as to touch every type of human being and every aspect of human nature; (4) the school will provide machinery for the vocational guidance of youth; (5) it will become the institutional center of neighborhood life.

[illegible] will [illegible] the entire community and will be the center [illegible] organization. It will be open [illegible] five days a week [illegible] or [illegible] fourteen [illegible]. It will deal with adult [illegible] as well as [illegible] responsibilities [illegible] community. It will minister to adult need as well as to the [illegible] of children.

We have indicated [illegible] all the major changes [illegible] which might [illegible] structure of the school and community. [illegible] changes suggested [illegible] will become apparent with [illegible] and with additional equipment. But as much is certain: (1) the school [illegible] will provide [illegible] (2) it will be a [illegible] for child [illegible] it will compete with the [illegible] (3) it will greatly enlarge [illegible] to reach every type of human being and every aspect of human nature, (4) the school will provide [illegible] the vocational guidance of youth; (5) it will become the [illegible] center of [illegible] life.

PART FOUR

SPECIAL GROUPS OF CHILDREN

"Unto the least of these"

THE DISCOVERY AND TRAINING OF EXCEPTIONALLY BRIGHT CHILDREN

D. P. MacMILLAN
Director, Child Study Department, Board of Education, Chicago

My topic at the present time specifically is exceptional children, with particular reference to the superbly gifted. Although the term "exceptional children" is wholly unscientific in the common acceptation of the words, nevertheless it carries a meaning that has its value in practical affairs. The word "exceptional" immediately recalls to your minds the fact that reference is made to some common rule, principle, or standard; and when it is prefixed to "children," it makes a direct allusion to the norm, the typus, whether indeed this be thought of as the average, medium, or mode, or the most frequently appearing characteristic of a group, or of all species coming under the generic term denominated by children.

There were examined last year in the Child Study Department in the neighborhood of five hundred such children. They came because they presented difficulties—sometimes difficulties of management in the home and in the school, sometimes because of nervous disorders, among them incipient epilepsy. They usually gave evidences of some unusual gift or special aptitude that ought to be attended to. Sometimes they come from perfectly normal homes and are simply precocious. Their precocity is often due to the fact that they come from unusually intelligent homes and receive that stimulus that comes from an enlightened social environment. By social imitation they grow up to be of an inquisitive turn of mind, become interested in things that adults are primarily interested in. Sometimes, indeed, that cultivation means separation; sometimes it means emphasis upon the attractive, and separation of the deterrent qualities that are associated with them. It is very important that attention should be given to the promise that comes, not from the care of the subnormal and the backward, but from the unusually gifted—four probably in ten thousand—who require a special education and will be our glory and our interest.

Two problems arise in considering exceptional children: First, that which is concerned with the discovery of their special traits, with the information which can and which ought to be secured with reference to them; and secondly, that which has reference to their education and their social service. When we speak of "exceptional," of course, there immediately comes to our minds the necessity of knowing what we mean by normal children; and this imposes upon us the desirability of examining a very large number. And if this is not practicable we must have recourse to other measures, keeping in mind three ends: First; we want to know how much of this or that characteristic each child whom we succeed in testing possesses. Then we must know the traits of the majority of the group investigated, and the number that actually stand above and fall below that central mark. After that, we must ascertain how universal that common trait may be, or rather, what is the representativeness of that central characteristic; or in what way and in what degree what we find out in a small group is true about all children. By this means, the degree of departure from the majority indicates to us a new type or an exception; and an exception in this connection may be in all-around ability, or it may be in one or in more special aptitudes.

The problems concerned with all this are so large for our present consideration that we cannot touch upon them in this symposium, but simply indicate in broad outlines the mode of procedure, the plan of operation that must be adopted in the evaluation of the mental and physical characteristics of children, and indeed, some appraisement of what is meant by simple standards. If we have at command norms of physical growth, strength and control, and if we have access to measuring-rods of mental traits of one kind and another, and if we have not only the mental and the physical standards before us but also the codes of right conduct or of right thinking and doing, we can read off the characteristics or the defects from these norms as readily as we can apprehend a physical object or a material process; we read off the characteristics, the excellencies and the defects, and those constitute for us, or exhibit for us, the exceptional child.

It has been said that your attention was to be directed not to the subnormal, those that fall below in one feature or in general characteristics, but to the superbly gifted. These children may be superbly gifted in all-around ability, or superbly endowed in one or in a few particulars. The question at once suggests itself whether indeed those who are superbly gifted can be reached by public organizations, or require intervention by external measures, or private assistance. My impression is that those two agencies must be in operation before the end desired can be achieved.

Another consideration presents itself. How should one proceed after having determined the status of children both as to their physical standing and as to their mental equipment, to effect changes in the mental and physical aspects of their growth? There immediately emerges the question as to what means can be adopted to effect desirable changes in the status of children found classified in those respects. This in turn leads still further. It becomes then desirable to know the causes that have been instrumental in bringing children to the standing in which they are found; to determine the agencies that have been effective in bringing about the relatively static condition of the children, that have made them what they are. The next question to be answered will be what agencies, educational, hygienic, medicinal, would be effective in bringing about desirable changes in the mental processes—changes that will reach a desired end.

Furthermore, there emerges the question of ideals or objects aimed at. What is the end to be attained by the education of exceptionally bright children? An illustration with reference to the physical nature of the child is in point. If one thinks of a person who has to undergo a course of prescribed physical training and who is found by the demonstrator or instructor as deficient in strength in one group of muscles, and probably excessive in others, or in weight, or in some other direction, there arises the question as to what will be necessary in order to make of him a symmetrically developed body—and we are attached to that word, "symmetrical." But when the question of symmetry is raised with reference to the mental, it is very much more complex and very much more difficult. If a child is found who is strong in one particular and weak in another and still only mediocre in a third, the problem arises: Are we going to level up these symmetries and these idiosyncrasies, the peculiarities and the strengths, that appear in one direction, and going to level down in another, so that we have more uniformity among children; or are we inclined to accentuate as early as possible in our education the peculiarities of this or that child so that at the end of the time of preparation we have the child growing not only in the easiest path for him but in the path of his surest success?

The question, then, of the end to be attained in the education of exceptionally bright children is an exceedingly important one, if only because of the confession growing out of lack of careful analysis. We are interested in the examination and in the training of exceptionally dull children from the point of view of philanthropy; we are interested in seeing that each child secures the best education of which his powers are susceptible. We want to bring him up so that he can share in the duties and privileges of citizenship and in the benefits of civilization. We are really concerned with the dull child for the child's own sake. The case of the superbly gifted child is different. Such a child must be educated in accordance with his special gifts, in line with his special requirements, and our interest in his behalf is, from one point of view, really selfish, although it is, on the other, strictly in accordance with the claims of justice. It is necessary to provide the very best possible education for him; and this should be brought about in the most economical and surest way, so that in the minimum time he can attain to the maximum of his strength and bring back to society as a whole some equivalent and some power; or, in other words, promote the group to which we belong. Finally, such a point of view is more social than the other; we are interested in the individual who is weak for the sake of the individual; we are interested in the superbly gifted for the sake of what he shall bring to humanity.

I am interested in public-school education, and I am assured you will agree with me that we cannot for an instant minimize the importance of class or group instruction. I do not believe that there ever will be a general return to the days of individual instruction. But as you know perfectly well, it is largely an economic question, and means for the present and for some time to come, large classes for teachers. Of course, the result is that the children tend to become relatively uniform in type; they pass through the same régime, receive a minimum of individual attention, and are turned out of the schools on the principle that equal opportunity for each means equal accomplishments for all. That we get a maximum gross result which is beneficial, nobody can question. Nevertheless, there is at the present time growing up a feeling that we are in the lock-step system; that children are promoted only at the end of a definite time and at the end of the accomplishment of a certain definite task or work. Accordingly there are about a dozen schemes in this country now in the experimental stage, attempting to break away from this lock-step system of promotion at the end of each year.

In Chicago, and in other cities, we have the double promotion system, which means that, in the middle of the year, when the children are ready, they pass on to the next grade. In addition to this double advancement, we find in certain cities the double course of study, one course of study for the bright and the mediocre, and the other for the lower grade of mediocres and the dull. In certain other cities, the group system, or multiple promotions, is being tried. There are thirty-two of these groupings in the school system of St. Louis, and in Elizabeth, New Jersey, I am told that there are from thirty to sixty grades from the sixth year up to the fourteenth. Then again, recourse is had to repetition of studies —that is, at the end of the ninth or tenth year, the child goes rapidly over the course, and then the next class coming in by double promotion enables him to go over the course more in detail with them, so that, all in all, from the end of the ninth year on, each child who has been over the course once schematically now goes over it in detail, with the idea of getting a surer foundation.

Then again, there is found in certain smaller schools what may be called the "review system," in which, instead of a general and then a detailed study as obtains in the schemes last referred to, they have a regular study plan and then a period of review of the material gone over; and in the nature of a further duplication of the review scheme, what is termed a "three-ring system" is found to obtain, in which the children are made to repeat twice or go over the particular subject-matter of the course of study three times in all.

Moreover, we find prevailing in other portions of the United States and in parts of Europe another great plan of operation, which may be termed the "laboratory method." It is purely or largely individual instruction, with the idea in view of picking out the bright pupils so that they may be guarded and carefully selected and educated. The laboratory method, or individual system, is susceptible of application in certain small towns where the grade of intelligence is above the average, and wherein the race, family, and stock is relatively uniform. A further modification is found in what may be called the "double teacher system." By this is meant that there is an alternation between the individual method and the group methods. That is, the children work in class or in groups for a certain period of time, and then they work individually for the rest of the time. Still further mention may be made of the "minimum-work system," promotions made, not according to time spent, but according to the work done. And finally, we have the multiple promotion and the multiple course of study—four or five courses running parallel, thus enabling the teachers early in the school life of the children to pick out the bright ones, and put them in a selected group, the next brightest in a particular group, and so on, placing them in accordance with their requirements and their powers. This scheme is no more and no less than the attempt to pick out the bright children as well as the dull, so that the individual capacities of the children may be appealed to, and that each may have training according to his needs and his powers.

It has been said that some features of these schemes are applicable to public official organization, and some are only susceptible of organization under private endowment. The time will surely come very soon, when in addition to some such scheme in our public organizations for picking out the bright and training the leaders as early as possible in the several lines in which they may be proficient, there will be a scheme by which the élite, the selected group, may as early as possible be brought to be contributing agents in appropriate environment. This will necessitate not only public organization, but a philanthropic interest as well. It might take the name of "educational aid society." Such a society or organization will assist by this early discovery of the bright, in the prevention of the growth of prigs and precocities whose history shows that they appear bright all the forenoon of life and are really dullards all the afternoon. It will probably be found necessary in some instances to protect the child from the parents; and therefore among other things there will emerge the problem of the conservation of funds for poor children. The bright child of the rich or of the well-to-do will be taken care of by private means, provided their financial ability and civic desire are supplemented by the assistance that this educational society will render them in discovering the really capable and the superbly gifted.

In addition to that work of selecting the bright, specialists will have to be engaged who will determine not only the natural gifts that ought to be cultivated but as well the most adaptable methods and devices for assisting in the natural maturation of these powers. In this way, therefore, the poor child who is really gifted—and as a matter of fact, one-half of the talented, one-half of the originals, come from the poor—will be a participant in a scheme which will be flexible, and adaptable not only to public-school education, but which will co-ordinate that with other organizations, with the end in view of educating the specially endowed, so that there can be secured the greatest strength from the strongest, and as well a wise conservation of the strength of the weakest.

It is not necessary to go into the dangers connected with such a policy. There are dangers attendant upon it, dangers that will first of all belong to or connect themselves with the child himself, but by judicious care those could be overcome; and, in fact, some such scheme has already been tried in two European cities with, on the whole, favorable results.

In conclusion it should be said that while this is probably a selfish motive on our part, it is a just one. If the child who is weakly endowed makes an appeal for assistance and social interest, and the child of mediocre ability requires help in the development of his powers to their best capacity, beyond all these, the child of superb intelligence calls loudly to civic pride and social interest for the development not only of the qualities that make for success in adult life, but of the qualities that make for success in childhood. Because his inherent possibilities and powers represent so much effort and achievement in the past, his future makes still greater appeal; and it is therefore not only desirable but highly urgent that the maximum of the influences of childhood may be brought to bear upon him, and the richness, the unfathomed richness of human nature, of which we have yet no conception, evoked and the strength of the exceptionally gifted conserved for human service.

THE NEED OF AN INSTITUTION FOR THE TREATMENT OF EPILEPTIC CHILDREN

HUGH T. PATRICK, M. D.

Professor of Nervous and Mental Diseases, Chicago Policlinic, and Northwestern University Medical School

First of all I shall state very briefly what epilepsy is. Epilepsy is a nervous disease that shows itself in the form of periodical attacks or seizures of various kinds. The typical attack is that of a general convulsion, in which the subject falls, loses consciousness for a rather short period, and gradually recovers. Then there are the little fits, the petit mal, or little-sickness attacks, in which the patient does not fall, does not have a general convulsion or spasm, but which recur at longer or more frequent intervals, and which are just about as hard to cure or control, as are the large attacks, and which have quite as bad an effect upon the individual. And the general tendency of this disease is to continue, to become chronic, gradually to become worse. It has a bad effect upon the individual, not only because the disease continues, but also because it tends to cause mental deterioration. In other words, the child instead of becoming more capable and developing mentally, progresses slowly, does not progress at all, or goes backward.

In the state of Illinois there are some 8,000 epileptics, perhaps more than half of them children. Concerning these four or five thousand children, three pertinent questions present themselves and may be briefly answered: (1) What is their present status? (2) What is being done for them? (3) What can be done for them?

To indicate the answer to the first question: A few, a very few, have ample means and every advantage, and are being well cared for, as well as possible. The unfortunates of this group constitute a portion grievously small, a quite negligible quantity. About five per cent are cured by medical treatment, and more, but a very indefinite and limited number if not cured, are relieved to such an extent that the disease constitutes no grave disability. This still leaves three thousand or thereabout to be dealt with. And what of these? Only after again and again listening to the anxious questions of fathers, the tearful pleadings of mothers, and after looking again and again into the wistful faces of little children; only after learning by heart the story of hopes shattered, plans frustrated, ambition abandoned, friendship cooled; only after watching over and over the physical, mental and moral deterioration of fellow-humans until death brings a kind release; only after all of this and more, can one have any idea of what these epileptic children mean in the community. Innocent victims of a dread disease, they and their friends are daily suffering the tortures of the damned. This is no exaggerated statement. To the confirmed epileptic are denied in large measure all the rights of man except mere life. Liberty he has none. At every step he is hemmed in, shoved back, bound down by his peculiar malady. The pursuit of happiness is not for him. If one thinks for a moment of the things that make life sweet—the right to love and the exercise of this right in marriage, motherhood and fatherhood; the privilege of activity, of education, of accomplishing something, of doing a piece of work well; the joy of sowing and tending the crop and reaping the harvest; the stimulus of ambition, the pleasure of anticipation, the planning of the future; and then adds to this the world of human associations with its wonderful metabolism of ideas and emotions, the soul chemistry of the social cosmos, he has about all there is in this life—except two elements only.

But all these rights and blessings are denied the epileptic. If one tries to conceive of his own lot with these things left out, he realizes what a dreary blank life would be. But two strands would be left to bind him to heaven and earth—religious faith and the devotion of family and friends. These the epileptic may have. But even the devotion of family is embittered by the knowledge that he is a burden, a care, a sorrow. His very presence stamps misfortune upon consciousness. Every moment his associates are anticipating the seizure and they are never free from the feeling that he is a pathological pariah. And he knows it. That is part of the bitterness. He has neither the callousness of the criminal nor the psychic oblivion of the insane, but is acutely conscious of his own condition and the suffering he innocently causes others. The more devoted the friends, the more he knows they suffer.

Everyone has had, I presume, at one time or another a frightful nightmare of falling—falling into some terrible abyss; or of feebly, impotently fighting a perfectly hopeless fight; or of vainly straining to flee from some relentless monster—until a troubled awakening brings grateful relief. What must it be to live, constantly to live the waking nightmare and only occasionally have a good dream of freedom and happiness and peace—to waken then to the hopeless battle and the hopeless flight!

Now what is being done for the epileptic children? What, indeed! Naturally one asks: What are physicians doing? What is modern science doing for epilepsy and epileptics? It can only be answered that they are striving. All over the world, in hospitals, dispensaries, asylums, laboratories, and private practice, medical men are unselfishly devoting their time and talents to investigation of the disease and efforts to relieve the sufferers. But after all is said and done, the medical treatment of epilepsy remains sorrowfully futile. Probably not more than five per cent of the patients are permanently cured, and a majority of the remainder go gradually or intermittently on from bad to worse, through invalidism and disability, to a kindly death. The causes of this great medical failure lie in technical details not germane to this discussion, but two difficulties may be mentioned. The first is the inherent difficulty of the disease; the cause of epilepsy is not known. In a few cases it may be known. For instance, an injury to the brain occurring at the time of birth, or a traumatism later in life, frequently causes these fits; but after all, it is not known why the injury causes the convulsions. But why an injury to the brain in some persons should cause these succeeding seizures, which come on time and time again in subsequent years, and why in other people a similar injury causes no epilepsy, is not known. Since the cause is unknown, it cannot be removed. In other words, the medical treatment of epilepsy is purely empiric. It is simply based on what has been learned from years of experience, and has no real logic. It has no real sense. It is only doing what one physician has learned to do from another, year after year.

Another difficulty is the impossibility of having all directions carefully and capably and continuously carried out. It is so difficult as to be almost impossible to convince patient and friends of the importance of a hundred details of living, of eating, sleeping, occupation and exercise; the abstinence from alcohol and tobacco and tea and coffee and all excesses; regulations as to fresh air and work and play, and so forth. And even when they are convinced that the physician is right about all these things, it is almost impossible to have all these things carried out for a sufficient length of time and in sufficient detail.

I had thought to relate some of the cases, to give you specific examples of child after child, out of my own experience, cases in which the friends, the parents, and even the patient co-operated, and we fought shoulder to shoulder and finally lost out. It is a very sad category. I do not need to relate it. Any one can go to a friendly doctor and hear the same story; how he has tried to cure the child, how he has tried to keep the child in school, or the young man in his business, or the young person in college, and how in a large number of cases he has finally had to give up, or if not give up, acknowledge a partial defeat, and how eventually the patient has drifted off to someone else. Is it any wonder, then, that the poor patient and his family finally become the pitiful dupes of the seductive vender of nostrums, the double victims of an implacable disease and a conscienceless charlatan? The desperate people cannot be blamed for catching at an elusive straw, but a merciless Hades contains no recess too hot for the abandoned miscreant who trades on the credulity of misfortune. There are hundreds of these designing rascals who are advertising in the daily press (which ought not to take their advertisements) the cure of epilepsy; "A Sure Cure of Epilepsy," "Epilepsy Cured," "Guaranteed to Cure Epilepsy," and the like. Every one of them is a lie; a deliberate, swindling lie, and the advertiser knows it.

To sum up, then, the answer to the second question, it may be said that patients, friends and physicians are doing the very best they can, but are accomplishing relatively little, and that the state is doing nothing. I do not wish to be misunderstood. I do not mean that medical treatment is useless or that every case is hopeless. On the contrary, there are few cases that cannot be helped, and some can be entirely cured. For an epileptic and his friends to give up hope simply because he has epilepsy is absolutely wrong. As I have said, some are cured, and more, though having an occasional seizure, continue to be happy, useful and long-lived citizens. And it is a well known fact that sometimes what seem to be the worst and most unpromising cases yield the most kindly to treatment.

Now, third, what can be done for them? The community can be protected from the numerous calamities arising from epilepsy, and, to a great extent, the patient can be protected from his disease. The commonwealth can be saved millions of dollars, and hundreds and thousands of hours now spent by anxious friends in watching and nursing their epileptic dependents can be saved each year for a normal and productive ability. To save many people from manifold cares and sorrows is public economy as well as obvious duty. What more can be done? The state can be protected against propagation by confirmed and hereditary epileptics, which would mean not only fewer epileptics in the future, but fewer criminals, fewer degenerates, fewer persons on the public charge.

And then what cannot be done for the epileptic himself? He can be given occupation and something to strive for. He can be given associates, occupation, and recreation. He can be given vastly better health, sometimes he can be cured, and the feeling can be eliminated that he is an outcast, something apart, to be looked at askance. In short, he can be given life, hope, a measure of liberty and the pursuit of happiness.

And how can all of these things be done? They can be done by having a liberally conceived, properly founded, well-organized, scientifically conducted state colony for epileptics. Perhaps it might be well just to indicate what is meant by liberally conceived, properly founded, well organized and scientifically conducted. Such an institution should be conceived as no temporary expedient, but as a monument to endure as long as epilepsy exists; conceived to meet requirements of the disease and of the patients in the fullest and best sense. In its conception should be seen the germ of development and the possibility of embodying all the best known features of such a place. Practically, this means, first of all, a large tract of well-watered land with good drainage. Less than one acre per patient should not be thought of (two would be better), and the land should be diversified so as to allow naturally a diversity of products and industries. It should be conceived as a rural village of largely agricultural population, but with all modern improvements and industrial possibilities. By a proper foundation is meant one devoid of embarrassing conditions, personal or political; a foundation in pure motives and high ideals.

A well-organized colony is one organized not for custodial care, not for the mere herding together of a couple of thousand sick unfortunates, but one organized so that it may be and must be scientifically conducted, in the highest sense of the word. And a scientifically conducted colony is one which will cure the greatest attainable number and develop the best possible physical, mental and moral state of the inmates; which will give them a real home, stimulating associations, satisfactory occupation, wholesome pleasures; which will give them the opportunity to teach and to be taught, to strive and to accomplish. Naturally, a scientific colony is absolutely divorced from political party, is run only for the public good and regardless of personal emoluments. Quite as naturally, it serves as a focus for the observation and investigation of epilepsy; a center where may be accumulated and whence may be promulgated knowledge of the disease—knowledge sorely needed; knowledge of its causes, its nature, its prevention; its symptoms, course, treatment and cure; knowledge which eventually will rid us of this monster, which respects neither age, sex nor condition, and now holds in its foul embrace more than two million of our brothers and sisters on this earth.

It is just possible that some one still may say: This sounds very well, but it is a fairy tale, a dream, a vision; at most it is transcendentalism and has nothing to do with statecraft or practical philanthropy. For such a one the answer is that actual demonstration has superseded theory. Founding a colony for epileptics no longer has the uncertainty and merit of pioneering. It is no bold venture of constructive statesmanship. We have but to imitate, and to the shame of Illinois be it said that we have been disgracefully slow in following good example. France opened the way in 1846, Germany followed in 1867, and England in 1888. Ohio led the states in 1890, but New York has eclipsed all with her splendid colony started in 1891. Other states have followed. Our predecessors have not only shown the feasibility of the colony plan, but have worked out many details as well.

The most skeptical could not visit the wonderful settlement at Bielefeld in Germany or the Craig Colony in New York without becoming an enthusiastic convert. There is not any manner of difference of opinion among those who know, those who have investigated this subject, those who have observed, those who are competent really to have an opinion. There is absolute unanimity as to what should be done. No one could visit one of these places without becoming a convert. Here is a busy, happy village life. There are schools for the different grades of intelligence, and industrial instruction for all. The boys are shoemakers, carpenters, machinists, designers, potters, draftsmen, blacksmiths, printers, bookbinders, gardeners, and farmers. The girls are tailors, seamstresses, cooks, and housekeepers. Each is an integral part and an active factor in this social community. Instruction is given and duties are assigned in accordance with the talents and capacity of the child, and the benefits of association, occupation, ambition and emulation are denied to none. The matters of diet, exercise, mental hygiene and medicinal treatment are easy to manage.

Time might be taken to answer some of the objections that have been made, objections that still occur to those beginning to consider the subject; but it is unnecessary. Proof has supplanted argument, facts have ousted theories. The epileptic colony is. It is a success. It has been shown to be a great public economy, the fruit of good statesmanship. Before a great while every state in the Union will have its colony or colonies. Illinois cannot be one of the leaders, but surely it need not be the very last.

It may by some be thought to be an unkindness to put so many epileptics together. One might think that an epileptic would suffer from the mere fact of being in an institution for epileptics; that it would be horrible for him to see others in seizures such as he has himself. Now quite the reverse is the case. Every asylum physician knows that the epileptic patients naturally gravitate together; very frequently two become inseparable chums. When one has a seizure it is his fellow sufferers who promptly and naturally go to his assistance and minister to his needs; that is a matter of everyday experience. At first thought it seems odd that an epileptic should be less shocked and distressed by the convulsion of another patient than is a normal person. On further consideration it is seen to be the natural and logical state of affairs, especially in a colony. To be an epileptic in such a colony is no more strange or abnormal than to be an Eskimo in an arctic village. If we were all epileptics, to have a fit would be as natural as to laugh or weep, and would occasion no more comment. But in this question as in so many matters pertaining to the colony plan, experience has removed doubt. For instance, if one should visit the great Bielefeld colony he would see several stretchers standing in the vestibule of their church. On inquiry he would learn that they are for the purpose of removing such patients as have seizures during service; and further he would be told that an epileptic attack in that congregation occasioned no more comment, distracted no more attention, than does the normal sleepy nod of the normal pewholder listening to the normal sermon in a normal congregation.

In conclusion, then, there is no single valid objection to a state colony for epileptics, while good statesmanship, good citizenship, public policy and private duty, the love of God and the brotherhood of man all point to it as the best solution of the desperate problem of the epileptic.

And was it not also of these poor little epileptics that the Master said: "Inasmuch as ye have done it unto one of the least of these my brethren, ye have done it unto me." Are such as these alone to be neglected among the countless homes, schools and churches of a happy people? Is their welfare alone to remain forever outside the legislative halls and sapient courts of a just people, and are they to fall forsaken while a merciful people build commodious refuges for the insane, and comfortable, busy prisons for the criminal? In the name of good statesmanship, of humanity, of love, of mercy, of progress and the higher life, let this happy and just and merciful people answer.

THE DEFECTIVE CHILD AND THE JUVENILE COURT

JULIA C. LATHROP
Hull-House, Chicago

There have been almost twenty years of futile effort in Illinois for a state colony for epileptics. The records at Springfield show bill after bill introduced session after session. One bill even became a law, but never became effective because no appropriation was made.

If it has not been possible to convince the whole state of the necessity for a colony, the children in the Chicago Juvenile Court for the last ten years may well have furnished an argument for this city for better care for epileptic and feeble-minded children.

The Juvenile Psychopathic Institute, of which Dr. William Healy is the head, has given new value to the court work for the last two years and a half, by examining, at the request of the presiding judge and parents, the cases of many hundred children. Nearly all of the cases examined have been those of repeaters or flagrant offenders.

Especially do the painstaking studies of Dr. Healy into the relation of physical defect to moral defect demonstrate the need of separate colony institutions under medical control, for many persons who would formerly have been classed as youthful offenders—responsible lawbreakers.

By the courtesy of Dr. Healy, I repeat briefly the histories of two children:

About a dozen years ago, a little boy was born in this town. His mother died at his birth. Afterward he had a good and faithful stepmother, who treated him as well as she treated her own growing brood of children, but he soon proved unmanageable. He would not go to school, he would run away. Until he was twelve years old, he ostensibly went to school, but he never got out of the first grade, though doubtless, as the family moved from place to place, he was in a great many first grades. It is not very strange that he found this everlasting first grade uninteresting and running away much more attractive.

At first running away or traveling is very satisfactory in itself, but after awhile a traveler begins to chaffer with dealers and pick up little things; and so, probably as innocently as the average traveler, this little traveler began to pick up things without stopping to chaffer. Of course he got into all sorts of trouble for pilfering, and finally, not very long ago, he was brought into court on the charge of stealing four pigeons from a neighbor's coop.

The police officers said he had been in and out of the police stations many times, he was always running away, he would not tell where he lived, the family were always chasing and hunting him, and the little boy was always being used as a "stool pigeon" by groups of cleverer lads. He had broken into freight cars and he had stolen the torpedoes off the back of the Pullman sleeper.

His accumulated offenses seemed to compel the judge to send him to the John Worthy School, but he was first examined by Dr. Healy with all the tests that have been so wonderfully worked out to determine natural ability. It was discovered that he was under-developed and under weight; that his mind could hardly be expected to discriminate between right and wrong when it could not discriminate between the letters of the alphabet and, therefore, he was sent to Lincoln as a feeble-minded child, and not to the John Worthy School as a responsible offender.

There was a girl born seventeen years ago in this town, who, from the time she was eight years old, could not be sent to school because she would not learn anything, and she would not go. She moved in the line of least resistance, and there was no sort of vicious company she did not keep, no sort of vileness of which she was not the tool and the partaker. Finally her decent parents, her brothers and sisters, humiliated beyond all expression, because they could not understand how this could be in a decent family, brought her into the Juvenile Court. Again it was shown, by the examination of the Psychopathic Institute, that she was an irresponsible, sick girl, not epileptic it is true, but having a feeble mind which could never grasp wise, clean thoughts; and the court sent her to Lincoln, instead of sending her to a reformatory.

Is it not good for the morals of all of us to know that such children as these are really helplessly sick, not wilfully bad?

Of over six hundred "repeaters," twenty-six per cent were found by Dr. Healy to be mentally defective, in various degrees, and over seven per cent to be epileptics.

A circular which has been issued as a part of the product of the Exhibit shows that in Chicago there are several thousand backward children, of various types of mental defect, for whom we are doing nothing, who go in and out of our schools, a trouble to the teachers, a detriment to the schools themselves, an annoyance and hindrance to the normal children. Out of this unhappy company, we are recruiting children for the throng of the Juvenile Court.

The Exhibit indicates the chief lines of further progress for normal children, and they will be followed. But in the interest of the normal and defective children alike, we must not fail to take hold with a new vigor of the problem of the child who cannot hold his own.

THE CLAIM OF THE COLORED CHILD

BOOKER T. WASHINGTON
Tuskegee Institute, Alabama

I know of no subject that carries with it a greater degree of importance at the present time in the life of our Republic and in the life of the race to which I belong, than the subject that is occupying the attention of this conference and that has brought out this very excellent and praiseworthy as well as instructive exhibition. For too long a period, it seems to me, we have neglected in our education to give attention to the ordinary things in life. For too long a period, I sometimes feel, we have neglected to apply education to the ordinary, everyday affairs of life.

For a number of years after starting to work at Tuskegee Institute, we used to have old-fashioned, artificial commencement exercises. People came to these exercises from all parts of the South; mothers came and fathers came; their friends and friends of the students came; and for a number of years on commencement day we used to have a boy come out on the platform and instruct the great audience on some such subject as "The Grandeur and Glory of the American Republic," or something like "After the Alps, then Italy." I stood that thing as long as I could, and after several years I called our teaching force together and said to them: "On commencement day there are thousands of people who come here hungering, thirsting for instruction, who want to know something, to be led into a better life. And the commencement exercises that we are now putting before them are a farce and do not mean a thing to these people. Let us change all this around." Now I have found by experience that in making changes it is always best to strike the point that will concern the greatest number of people, and so I said: "Suppose we make this change by beginning with the subject of preparing and serving food. Every family represented on commencement day is interested in having food prepared and served three times a day."

We called one of our brightest girls in the graduating class and said to her: "We want you to take for your commencement essay an illustrated description of the best method of preparing and serving a meal." And so we had on the commencement platform the stove and the table, and that girl went through the process of preparing a meal and setting the table, placing the different dishes in their proper places on the table, and ending by putting a beautiful, attractive bunch of flowers in the center of the table. That essay on preparing and serving food attracted ten times more attention from that audience than all the essays on "The Grandeur and Glory of the American Republic" or "After the Alps, then Italy"—more attention than we had ever had from the beginning of that institution.

Last commencement one of our young men took for his part a description of how he had planted and worked an acre of turnips. He described how he enriched the land, how he had worked the land, putting his knowledge of implements and of literature and of science into each operation. By his side upon the commencement platform was a table piled high with the most delicious and tempting turnips that one ever saw. And when at the close of his address he took up two of the largest and most tempting turnips and held them before the audience, the cheers that came back in answer proved the success of our experiment.

Now, at Tuskegee, we find that it is interesting, instructive and valuable to teach our people to apply their education on commencement day as well as every day in the year in our work and we find the kind of commencement oration I have described has two advantages: In the first place, the boy knows what he is talking about when he describes how he has done the thing. In the second place the audience knows what the boy is trying to say. And so throughout our work there we have tried and are trying not to confine education to the extraordinary things in life but to apply education to the ordinary things in life. In connection with this movement I am glad to see that, beginning in New York some months ago, for the first time so far as I know in the life of the nation, we are commencing to apply our knowledge to the practical, everyday well-being of the children of America.

A very large part of my work for a number of years has been in connection with teaching people how to farm. It is not agriculture that we teach at Tuskegee; just straight farming, working in the soil. And it is not domestic economy either that we teach down there; just cooking, straight cooking. I find that a lot of people get confused on this subject of domestic science and domestic art; but, when you talk to the average girl about cooking, she comes pretty near knowing what you are talking about.

When we first began our effort to teach farming at Tuskegee, I began to cast about to see where I could get the best and most up-to-date information on all subjects concerning farm life. I wrote to a number of places; among other places I wrote to Washington, and I found that if we wanted to get information on how to propagate plants of any character, how to grow peas, beets, turnips or corn, we got accurate and reliable information. If we wanted to find out how to grow a mule or a cow or a goat, how to grow a chicken or a goose, or how to propagate fish, we got accurate information.

After we had learned a good deal about the care of animals and birds and fish at Tuskegee, I said: "Now I think that we had better take up the subject of growing children." And so I wrote to Washington again, but could not get a scratch of a pen in the way of information on that subject. It is a curious fact, that we have so far failed to apply our education to the ordinary things of life that there is no—almost no—one central, dependable source in this nation where you can get information concerning the proper method of growing young human beings, the same as you could get information as to the proper method of growing young peas. I am glad to see that Miss Addams with her co-workers has begun here in the city of Chicago a revolution which I hope will not stop until it has become nation wide in its influence and in its work.

Just before leaving Tuskegee I sent to the head of our woman's department and told her I should like to tell the people in Chicago just what we are doing in teaching child-growing; and I am going to read the outlines of a course of study in child growth that we have been pursuing at Tuskegee for a number of years in connection with pig-growing and cow-growing and all the other matters. First there is a course in child nurture; the subject of food is considered, the nature of food, the wet nurse, artificial foods and their preparation, vessels used and their care, systematic nourishment, quality of nourishment; then babies' exercise in the house and outside the house, amount of sleep and sleeping-periods, the bathing-period, the infant's cry, treatment of the infant's fears, infants' diseases, infants' physical deformities—I shall not go through the whole process, but simply enough to show you that we have given some attention at Tuskegee to the matter of the growing of little human beings.

But my special object is to call the attention of this audience to the importance of the welfare of the Negro child in your community and in our nation. You have here in the city of Chicago colored people to the number of 90,000, and I rather think the number is increasing every year. You may not like to have them here in so large numbers, but in any case they are here, and I believe that they are going to stay here. You know that the Negro has the peculiar characteristic of going wherever the white man goes. And this American Negro is the only human being with a black skin, or with a dark skin, that you have ever permitted to live by your side for any length of time, look you in the eye and survive; we are the only fellows with a dark skin that have ever tried that experiment successfully. And so we are here in Chicago, 90,000 strong, and the question for you to answer is: Shall we be good citizens or poor citizens? Shall we pull down the civilization of Chicago, or shall we lend a mighty hand in lifting up the civilization of Chicago?

There are at least 15,000 Negro children in the city of Chicago. Now the greater proportion of the colored children in Chicago come here from our southern states; many of them are recent comers here. The question that they have to solve is that of adjusting their lives to the new conditions that they find surrounding them in a large city such as you have here. The average colored child or parent in Chicago comes from the rural districts of the South. They come from open country, where they have had, if nothing else, plenty of good, pure air and where in most cases, though it has been of a limited kind, they have had a fairly good quantity of fresh food. The other day I asked one farmer in Alabama how he was getting on, and he said he was selling a good deal of his produce. He said he had sold a good many eggs recently to the people of Atlanta, and I remarked, "I congratulate you on the fact that you are able to sell eggs; you must be very prosperous." "Well," the old fellow answered, "I don't sell the fresh eggs, I sell the city fellows the old eggs and I eat the fresh eggs myself." Many of these people have come from the country, where they have been eating fresh eggs and sending stale eggs to the city. But when these people get to the city they eat the stale eggs themselves. Food conditions are new, housing conditions are new, climatic conditions are new, labor conditions are new. Their entire life has to be readjusted within the space of a few years, or a few months in many cases.

It is difficult for 90,000 people to adjust themselves to these new conditions within a short period of time. And you have to be a little patient with the colored people while they are undergoing this process of adjusting themselves to their new life. To speak perfectly frankly, I know that you as white people have become impatient with my race because of our seeming backwardness, because of our slothfulness; but you must remember, my friends, when you become impatient with us because of our seemingly slow progress—you must remember that there are about ten million Negroes in America, who in the providence of God have been set right down here into your midst, and, naturally, unconsciously, you measure the Negro's progress by your own progress. You measure his growth by your growth, forgetting when you are doing this, that you are measuring the black man by a pretty stiff yardstick. If the Negro were living in the midst of an oriental people, if he were living in the midst of a Latin civilization, his effort to keep near those people would not be so great as to keep near you. I was down in southern Europe during the past summer and I saw a good many of the people there to whom I think the Negro could keep pretty near; some of those fellows in southern Europe are nearer to our gait than you are. But you must remember when you grow impatient with us that we are living in the midst of the most aggressive, the most pushing, and the highest civilization that the world has seen; and, when we catch up with the American white man, there will not be any other fellow ahead of us. If, then, you will remember these facts, my friends, you will be a little more patient, a little more long-suffering with us, when you make comparison between your degree of civilization and our degree of civilization.

The Negroes coming in so large numbers to a city like this find themselves at a disadvantage in housing conditions. They are not used to living in the cramped conditions of a large city. They have been living in a one-room cabin, perhaps, on a plantation in Alabama; but they have lived out of doors as much as they have lived indoors, and that one-room cabin with all of its disadvantages has this advantage, that it furnishes plenty of good, fresh air every day in the year. Bring these people to a city like Chicago, put them into cramped conditions —meaning high rents and poor air—and, my friends, you must not be very much surprised if a large number of the children living in such conditions early disappear by death. And in many cases, by reason of the poverty and often the ignorance of the colored family, they are not only compelled to live in cramped, unwholesome, insanitary quarters, but in too many cases they are forced to live near the worst districts morally. And that places the Negro child at another disadvantage.

What is the net result of all this? In the nation I find, for example, that within a given length of time thirteen white persons per thousand die and twenty-one colored persons per thousand. Coming more directly to the subject in hand, in Chicago, I find from statistics furnished me by Dr. George C. Hall, one of the colored physicians of your city, that while the death-rate for white children under the age of twelve months is fifteen per thousand a year, in the same length of time the death-rate for colored children under the age of twelve months is thirty-four per thousand.

But I have never found any special satisfaction in detailing difficulties and troubles. How can we get out of these conditions? In the first place, I believe that the American child will never come into his own until we have a more rational school in the rural districts. That will mean that a very much larger portion of the children will be kept in the country, on the soil, in the pure air, away from the temptations and complications of your large, complex city life. The average rural school means a little building out in an old field, having no likeness in its architectural form to any building in that community; a building in most cases without a tree, without a flower bed, without a piece of shrubbery, without anything near it; that is the picture of the average rural school. And when you get on the inside of that building, so far as anything being taught which actually concerns the life of the people in the community for whom the school exists, that school might as well be located a hundred miles away from that community.

Some years ago I said to our people at Tuskegee that we are going to reconstruct the rural school for the Negro children of those communities near us. And so we built, not a schoolhouse unlike anything in the community, but a cottage. I said: "We shall build a simple farmer's home; we shall have in that home a sitting-room, we shall have a bedroom, we shall have a kitchen, we shall have a dining-room, and the teacher will live there in a natural way. We shall have the children in this farming community come to this home, and the teacher will teach them how to live. And so this new type of school was built. The teacher lives in that cottage. The children from the surrounding community come here every morning. They are taught how to clean the sitting-room, how to clean the bedroom; how to cook the breakfast, a farmer's breakfast; how to set the table, a farmer's breakfast table. And then surrounding that schoolhouse is a garden, and then near the schoolhouse are the cow and the calf and the pigs and the chickens. The children are taught how to live a farmer's life, and the lessons gleaned in the cultivation of the garden, in the care of the pigs and the cows and the chickens are woven into their lessons in arithmetic in the schoolroom; and instead of that little schoolhouse being a foreign territory, it is a little green spot that is articulated in a perfectly natural way into the life of the people. And when we have schools of that character scattered all through this country, then conditions such as exist in the city of Chicago, in my opinion, are going to be changed so far as the life and happiness of the child are concerned.

We must make up our minds, in trying to remove such conditions as you have in Chicago, that disease draws no color line; disease draws no racial line;

filth draws no racial line. If, by reason of the Negro's ignorance, by reason of his unclean, unhealthy life, disease is propagated in the body or in the home of the Negro in Chicago, that same disease will spread to the body and to the home of the whitest family in the city of Chicago.

And your courts, in punishing crime growing out of ignorance, draw no color line. The ignorant Negro child is tried before the same judge, before the same jury, under the same laws, the same rules of evidence, that the whitest child in the city of Chicago is tried by and under.

Now another way to remedy this condition so far as your 90,000 colored people in Chicago are concerned, is for the best white people in Chicago to undertake the task of actually getting acquainted with the best type of colored people in Chicago. It is too often true that the worst class of white people in these large cities know more about the worst class of black people, than do the best class of white people about the best class of black people. My friends, you want to take enough time and interest actually to meet and talk with and understand some of the best Negro characters in Chicago. No one task that I have performed during my life is so inviting as the task of discovering black diamonds. And I find these black diamonds all over the country; men with black skins, who, in their thought, in their action, in their heart, are just as pure and high and noble as is any other human being under the sun. And you have those black diamonds, undiscovered black diamonds, by the thousands here in Chicago.

We sometimes have a prejudice against a race—we might just as well talk right open in meeting while we are at it—we sometimes have a prejudice against a race because we do not know that race. I went to Sicily last summer, and while I claim to be pretty free from racial prejudice, I confess that after I had read for years about crime in Sicily, about the Black Hand, about the Mafia, and all that, I went there fairly well prejudiced against the Sicilians. I stayed a week or more in Sicily, going into the rural districts, going to their farms, their sulphur mines, their vineyards. I went into their homes, I shook their hands, I talked with them, I got their point of view of life, and, my friends, instead of finding a people to detest, I found a people to love. And during all the time I was in Sicily, I never locked my satchel once, never locked my hotel door once, and felt perfectly sure that I could trust the honor and the goodness of heart of those simple-hearted country people. And I should add further that the country people in Sicily were the only people in all Europe that I found who would refuse to take money in the form of a tip when I offered it to them. And so I came out of Sicily, no longer hating the Sicilians, but loving, respecting, and honoring them because I had come in contact with them, had shaken hands with them. And so, my friends, if you in Chicago will take the pains to seek out some of the best colored people in Chicago, after you get into their life, get their point of view, you will be surprised at the fine, worthy, noble, unselfish characters among my race that there are in Chicago. They will be ready to work with you in all your efforts in civic betterment to make this a model, beautiful and healthy city.

In making a comparison between the death-rate of colored children in large cities of the North, I find this to be true: In the city of Washington the number of deaths in a year per thousand of population is twenty-six; in Baltimore twenty-eight; in Philadelphia thirty; in New York twenty-eight; in the city of Chicago I am glad to congratulate you on the fact that you have a death-rate of only twenty-one among the colored children. I find that comes about very largely by reason of the fact that you have an able health commissioner, who meets with the colored people, advises with them, co-operates with them, in bringing about more healthy conditions among the 90,000 colored people in Chicago. That shows what one competent official can do in lowering the death-rate by getting in touch with the Negro population of Chicago; and what he has done, others can do.

And then there is another point of encouragement. In an increasing degree each year we are turning out from our medical colleges a large number of Negro doctors. And in proportion, my friends, as the number of Negro doctors increase, the health conditions of the Negro race, of the Negro child, are going to improve, the death-rate is going to be lowered and the efficiency of the colored population thereby increased. Led on and guided by such characters as Dr. George C. Hall of this city and other Negro physicians who are doing the same kind of work in other large cities of this country, reaching colored children in a way no white physician can do or perhaps will do, the race will improve.

And along with the doctors who are being turned out, the Negro hospitals, the Provident Hospital and others in this city, are doing an excellent work in lowering the death-rate. And I will not and cannot withhold the praise that is due to the Negro nurse in lowering the rate among our people in Chicago and throughout this country. My friends, we ought to have five times as many Negro nurses in this country as we now have. In the South, alone, we can give employment to five times as many Negro nurses as we now have. And down there, you know, in that matter we do not draw any color line. The best white people in the South want the Negro nurses. In fact, the Negro never has much trouble anywhere in getting on with the best white people, North or South. It is the other kind with which he has trouble in most instances.

I know that the Negro as he touches your life, as you touch his life, as you observe him on the streets of your cities, sometimes tries you; and you sometimes think that you have a pretty difficult problem upon your hands. But we are improving year by year. You remember that it is sometimes with races as it is with individuals, they know more as they get older. You know a boy has to pass through his silly period in most cases. When a boy is about twelve or fourteen years of age, as a rule that boy is pretty wise; at that age he can give his father and mother instruction on most points as to how to run the household. You have to be patient with the boy when he is passing through his silly period.

I remember that when I was a young boy living in the hills of West Virginia I took it into my head one day to write a lecture, and after working on it for three or four weeks I finished it, and the subject of my lecture was "Family Government." I went through my county, delivering that lecture for a number of months, wherever I could get anybody to listen to me, and I kept on delivering that lecture on "Family Government." After a while I got married, and in the course of some years I not only had a wife but three children. Then I quit delivering that lecture; I knew more but I said less.

You must remember that the colored people twenty-five or thirty years ago were passing through a very silly period in many matters concerning American life. We are over that period now. We have grown into more rational and sensible ideas of life and action, and in proportion as you take an interest in us, as you are doing in connection with this Child Welfare Exhibit, and in connection with what you are doing through the Young Men's Christian Association of Chicago, in the same degree will the Negro get out of his silly period and settle down to the common-sense idea of rational living, not only in Chicago but elsewhere throughout this country.

You must remember that you owe us, as a race, a duty. We have never proved very much of a burden upon you, since we became a free people, so far as our personal living is concerned. When Mr. Lincoln freed my race or was contemplating the freedom of these millions of my race, a number of people said to Mr. Lincoln: "Don't free those black people; they will prove a burden upon the pocketbooks of the nation." Some people said: "These millions of colored people will die, because they cannot feed themselves; they will perish because they cannot clothe or shelter themselves." Do you realize that, during all the years that are past since the days of reconstruction, we as a race have never called upon the nation to appropriate a single dollar with which to provide food, clothing, or shelter for our race? Absolutely we have provided for our personal needs in the past, and mean to do so in all the future. It is seldom that you find a black hand reached out at the corner of a street anywhere in America, asking for anything. And we have gone a little distance, sometimes, in helping in some parts of the country to support some other people.

Some time ago, in Selma, Alabama, near where I live, the white people decided to hold a convention in the Court House. There was an old colored man, a janitor in the Court House, listening at the door, who got a few snatches of argument here and there, and he became a little excited as to what this convention meant. When it was over, he went to the president of the convention, the man who used to own him, and said to him: "Colonel Jones, what are the white people holding this meeting for? What are you up to now?" Colonel Jones replied: "Why, Uncle Sam, we are simply holding an immigration convention. We want to get more white people from the North and from Europe to come down here and settle in our county." The old colored man shook his head. "Why, lawsy, Colonel Jones," he said, "we niggers has got just as many white people down in this country now as we can support!"

When I was a young boy living in the hills of West Virginia I used to be a great fighter. In fact, I used to have a fight with some boy every day, but always whipped the boy. I was champion for my community, and held the championship longer than some of these fellows hold it now. But the people in my community did not know how I managed to be the champion fighter for so long a period. I shall tell you how I did it. I never fought a boy until I had the chance of examining that boy, and knew that the boy was younger than I was and smaller and weaker than I was, and after I informed myself concerning the boy in those three directions, then I was willing and anxious to fight the boy. In my youthful days I used to feel great delight in getting these little boys by the neck, I used to like to get them down in the ditch and hold them by the collar and listen to them holler. But, my friends, as I grew older and had more experience, I realized that I could not hold one of those little fellows down in the ditch without remaining right down in the ditch with him.

And so, thank God, throughout this country, North and South, we are all gradually learning that one man cannot hold another down in the ditch without remaining down in the ditch with him. One race cannot hold another race down in the ditch without being in the ditch with that race. One race cannot be surrounded by another race which, by reason of ignorance and poverty, is in the ditch of crime and filth without being itself in a degree in the ditch. The Negro children in Chicago, in the nation, cannot be in the ditch without the white children in a large degree being in the ditch with them. I thank God for this movement, a movement that means the lifting of all children of all races, of all colors, out of the ditch into the sweet, pure air of Heaven.

QUALIFICATIONS AND TRAINING FOR SERVICE WITH CHILDREN IN A CROWDED CITY NEIGHBORHOOD

LILLIAN D. WALD

Henry Street Settlement, New York

This discussion may well imply an obligation to consider the entire subject of child culture, the criticism of methods employed in the machinery of education, and may in turn bring forth a challenge to the settlements to show what they have to offer after twenty years' experience with the children.

As an educational expert I have little to contribute; for I know nothing of educational psychology apart from what the child himself has taught me. From psychology, as the child reveals it, I bring the conviction, which I believe almost all settlement people entertain, that where the school fails, it does so because it makes education a thing apart from the life of the child, separates its work from all that makes up his life outside of the classroom.

The people who know the child in a less formal relationship—that of neighbor and friend—have repeated experiences to impress that point upon them; and if anything has been contributed by them to thought or to method of education, it has been because of the reality of the child to them as a personality.

The Settlement Worker

The neighborhood worker associated with the settlement, as a usual thing, does not start out with any definite theories of education or club direction. He, in a way, reverses the plan of the school teacher who comes bristling with textbooks and methods. He seizes his opportunity for observation

IN NEED OF FRIENDS
We mix from many lands
We march for very far.
"And their fields are bleak and bare"
"And their ways are filled with thorns."
A City Playground
Waiting for Mother.

of the child and almost unconsciously, if at all, develops methods. In other words, he does not bring conditions or systems to fit the child; he meets conditions as they are and becomes critical of systems as they act and react upon the child, or fail to reach him at all.

The pioneers in settlements came to their neighborhoods without preconceived theories, and many good people are still coming to them with open-mindedness and a desire to learn. Perhaps not enough has been made of the rich accumulation of experiences they have had. Perhaps it may be charged against them, as has been charged against organized efforts for remedy, that they have not crystallized into definite form the protests that they make against society and their programs for improvement. If the "statesmanship of morals consists in bringing morals into action," they have failed to qualify as statesmen in this if the charge is justified.

The children in congested neighborhoods have no sequestered nursery life. They have little distinct provision made for them at any time, and they share, at a critically tender age, the experiences and the anxieties of the adult. Both adult and child in the immigrant neighborhood are being socialized on American soil, and the child is not always the one who loses in the process. Training for service with these children would include training for every phase of life. The families, the home, and indeed the Child Welfare Exhibit are a startling advertisement to the general public, not of what has been done, but of the children's needs, and incidentally show the pathos of the parents, the gaps of neglect and indifference—and how far from touching bottom we are after all.

However, the optimists are the people at work and they believe that society is moving and that things are measurably safe so long as there is search for light and a readiness to exhibit and confess the sin of inadequacy.

Technique

The technique of social work among children has hardly been worked out. Perhaps much of it does not admit of formal presentation, since the most valuable connections are possible in the settlement because of the flexibility of its organization. If, however, the technique of social work with children does take form, I for one pray that place will be left for the amateur of sympathy and culture and sincerity who brings freshness and sensibility and does not accept conditions that by too many are assumed to be unavoidable and incapable of change.

In a recent inquiry made of experienced people as to the qualifications they deemed essential for workers among children in order to apply some test of efficiency standards, there was unanimity on three distinct points:

(1) The desire for the big, indescribable personality which makes the children feel that "the King has arrived"; (2) a broad education and background of culture to enable the worker to see the child in a large perspective and to discern the subtle social bearings of the child's life; (3) some specific and specialized kind of skill or training.

Personality

"Personality" may mean a thousand different things—a democratic spirit; love for children, accompanied by tact and judgment; good looks; health; justice and humor—above all, humor. But it carries with it one fundamental essential, the power to affect individuals, and in the case of children to start them towards the major morals and to accustom them, through imitation perhaps, to habits of courtesy and good manners—those minor morals of right living. It means so much, this personality; it seems hardly definable, and yet its use is not misunderstood. It is what we try to measure in the "personal interview"—the attempt to establish in one's mind at least some test of standard.

I have no hesitation in giving "a chance" to young inexperienced persons, even when there is nothing very definite that they can offer, if the qualifications of character, or personality, and sincerity are there. Some of the finest spirits that have enriched the settlement and neighborhood have started with no more definite program than the sincere desire to be of service, and the subjective unrest that usually accompanies this desire to serve. There is carried with the acceptance of their co-operation, however, a good deal of responsibility to help these ardent young spirits to find themselves and also to be sure that the children are not practiced upon to the point of exploitation.

Settlement Program with Children

I speak more particularly today from the experiences gained in a settlement where much of the program with children is informal, but a good deal has grown into distinct specialization; and it may be simpler for the purpose of our discussion to separate the club work and home service, the social from the more definitely educational of school or classroom. The social or the informal work demands pre-eminently the quality of inspiring and effective personal influence.

The clubs with children present the most valuable medium for sustaining a connection with the leader, and I am inclined to be indifferent as to the specific program a club may carry out so long as the director has power to enter into the lives of the children to win them away from the limitations of their narrow and harsh world, and to lead them into poetry and culture outside of their rough environment; and, on the part of the leader herself, the sincerity of purpose will induce her to secure additional training to round out the experience secured by association with the children.

All of us have seen the curious effect of the transmission of distinct traits belonging to the club leader upon the children with whom she is brought in contact. I have known in a settlement where scores of clubs meet regularly, that one very well acquainted with the personality of the club leaders could almost tell to which club the young people belonged, because of their interest in subjects that were known to be distinctive of the leader, and even a curious suggestion of physical resemblance, resulting from the unconscious mimicry of manners, style of dress, arrangement of the hair, modulation of the voice; and this is not surprising, since, to the children, "the King has arrived."

Club Organization

The constitution and by-laws that every club, excepting those of the very youngest members, consider necessary for the preservation of their dignity, were worked out to meet the point of view of the boys, a good many years ago. Although constitutions seem to be almost uniform, with a wise non-aggressive club leader, they may be the means of bringing out points of wide educational and ethical value, such as co-operation, submission to the will of the majority, courtesy and the encouragement to express dissatisfaction with the things that shock the public sentiment of the club; or these same constitutions may be the source of endless wrangling and disorder. It depends entirely upon the club leader whether she has the ability to put the constitution to use or misuse.

The ability to organize is, in itself, very valuable—a talent almost essential unless intercourse with the children is limited to contact with the individual.

Civics for Children

It is not difficult to bring to even very small children some understanding of civic duty, by relating their experiences of life to the street and housing ordinances which they know something about. As the club leader watches the opportunities for development, almost endless occasions arise to bring the stimulus of civic responsibility to them. Sometimes there is conflict in the various appeals, and I recall a club organized for general purposes of culture and civics that took Hawthorne for their divinity. Later on, when the wise club leader wished to interest them in clean streets, they became so enthusiastic that a member rose to change the name of the club, saying, "What did Hawthorne ever do for clean streets?" Another club began, while very young, to study the lives of those men and women whom they voted to call heroes because of some contribution they had made towards American citizenship. The range was wide and care was taken not to have all their heroes dead ones. This naturally led the club to a bigger social outlook, and at the second anniversary of the club the chairman, in announcing the program for the ensuing year, said: "Having exhausted American heroes, we will now study civics."

The Definite Educational Work in the Settlement

For the more definite educational and administrative work it would be absurd to deny the need and value of education and specific training, when we demand more and more of the volunteer and the salaried instructors and when we expect concrete evidence of their ability to train and to hold the children. Some of the measures that have been pushed into the city departments through the knowledge and experience gained by those workers in the neighborhood have in turn placed upon the originators the obligation of training people to carry out the ideas originated there.

Schools for social workers that have been established in the several large cities seem to be more definitely directed towards equipping the institutional agent, and they are tremendously valuable in giving the students the conclusions of experts—the theory and the practice of social welfare movements. They furnish a short cut to knowledge that would take longer in acquiring when gained from personal experience, though the lesson learned cannot be as deeply bitten into the mind and the heart.

I might cite the fact that, although great emphasis is now laid upon personal oversight of the physical condition of the children from the time of their birth, through their school life, the inspiration of this extension of the "socialized parental control" came to the persons who knew the child first and departmental methods second.

The appointment of the first physician to the public schools of New York City was brought about almost entirely through a neighborhood worker's discovery of a child who was attending school while desquamating from scarlet fever—who did not stop with the mere discovery; and the present extension of medical inspection in New York City, which includes the trained nurse and makes possible the carrying out of the treatment prescribed by the school doctor, was also brought about because a worker in a crowded neighborhood discovered for herself that a child with a very small sore on his head could be excluded, on account of that sore, from participation in the educational provisions of the city.

Today we find educators who declare themselves ready to discard the instruction of books and to replace it by physical education, if both cannot be obtained. Knowledge of social conditions that environ a child, and affection and sympathy for him, would of necessity make the unclean head or the trachoma of vital consequence, even if the neighborhood worker who discovered these handicaps of the child had no genius for suggesting cure or relief. The chances are good that sympathy and sincerity and intelligence would induce her to inquire further and to direct thought to the matter.

Inspiration and Training for the Social Worker

To give inspiration and training to the social worker, the most potent method and the most effective influence is to surround him with people who have the power of interpretation and enough experience to influence the recruit to think, to read and to analyze. To accomplish this, I suppose there is nothing comparable to residence in the settlement house, where new members can begin to grasp the problems as a whole, and see the relation of the various divisions of helpful service among children.

Definite education for work such as I have alluded to seems to come best from hearing at first hand the stories and experiences of the older residents and of the visitors who come to the settlements. And yet one can easily conceive that even with personality and sincerity a man or woman might go in and out year after year, giving pleasure and fellowship to the children, but in no way relating them or his own experience to broad social bearings.

They must be shown how more directly valuable training and suggestion is brought about through the conferences of the leaders of the groups in a settlement or neighborhood house. One such group that meets in New York began without a definite program. It is composed of some of the most highly trained workers with children, on the east side, and they have in reality trained themselves, although they are in close relationship with the head resident of the settlement, to whose older judgment they are ready to defer. They come together regularly when their conferences take the form of experience meetings.

In a highly organized settlement it must be borne in mind that no single club or class can be conducted without the recognition of the inter-relationship of the groups to each other. The exchange of entertainment between clubs for the exercise of hospitality, dances with suitable partners provided, combinations and friendly competitions—all of these train the club leaders in an all-around way, while they cultivate the child.

Kindergarten Training of Value

Kindergarten training is perhaps the education of most definite value as a start to work with children. The kindergartner has obtained through training an important power, the facility to play with children, and has obtained a knowledge of philosophic experience out of which comes a point of view in helping her to understand them. Some of the value of kindergarten training comes from any definite training—from serious courses in gymnastics, from training in music and story telling.

I do not know whether anybody can be trained to tell stories; not to read them out of a book, but to be able to make the great characters live in the minds of children. That is a very great art indeed, and one often wonders why the story-telling gift and the humor (good American gifts) have not been more developed in our country.

Home Visiting

I cannot conceive of a sincere neighborhood worker who does not find knowledge of the home essential and no training good that does not recognize the necessity of taking the family with the child. And yet I think we ought to acknowledge that there may be too much visiting in the homes of the tenements if it leads to nothing but visiting.

We acknowledge the inability and the inefficiency of the parents and the home to control the fortunes of the child when we substitute for them the parental function of the government; nevertheless, the stronghold of education remains in the home, and the school and the settlement and the other agencies that hover over it cannot replace that home.

We speak of this as the child's era and while it is fundamentally the child's, it should be the parents' era also, and we must not detach the child from them or from the traditions which are his heritage. Even in small details which affect the child's welfare the parents should be consulted. This is not only just, but is wise from the point of view of the child's friend, and the failure to recognize parental responsibility to the child is unworthy, unless indeed the child belongs to the wholly inefficient or immoral parent, in which case cherishing the idea of filial piety and obedience can be overdone. Pieties can become conventions and we are not justified in ignoring the child's welfare, consequently the race's welfare, even for the most pious convention.

It is remarkable, however, how often one can secure intelligent co-operation from the most discouraging kind of a parent if an avenue of approach can be established. As an illustration of this, at the milk dispensary we have for years insisted upon the importance of modification of the milk in the homes, rather than at the milk station, because we recognize that there can be no hope of a permanent or widespread reduction of infant mortality unless the mothers are educated and unless they can be made to accept the co-operation of the outside expert. The nurse at this dispensary reports that she has never found a mother who could not be educated to modify the milk correctly and to keep the bottles clean for her child.

The visiting nurse's service in the homes is largely for the children, and it has seemed essential to add to the technical training of the hospital a social education or, more literally, a social interpretation of the conditions encountered.

A Spiritual Conception of the Nurse's Work Necessary

It would seem inevitable that an uninspired service would be offered by the school nurse or the school visitor, or the nurse assigned to infant work, if the significance and social importance of her services have not been presented to her. Our training schools for nurses practically ignore this new demand for the specially trained nurse. To start a nurse, bag in hand, with instructions to give treatment to her patients, would seem to invite the perfunctory or else the sentimental service that is deplored by all educational and social experts. It calls for something beyond and outside the nurse's daily routine to help carry the heavy bag up and down the tenement stairs, and the best spirits may be discouraged and lost to the cause if they see nothing in their toil but the relief to the individual, and that perhaps temporary. A hint that wages are below the possibility of maintaining a standard of cleanliness—that cleanliness is a modern luxury—a clue to the history of the races to the representatives of which the nurse is sent—all this is a kind of specialized training that makes it possible to give to the nurse a spiritual conception of her work.

It is the best trained nurses—those who have something valuable to give in addition to their hospital experience, who should be at work in the homes, for it is they who carry the responsibility of interpreting the outside world to the stay-at-homes and relating their experiences to those of society in general. We have, all of us, known of excellent service, faithful and loyal, given by men and women who saw nothing beyond the relief and help to the individual, but I take it that the efforts today have a wider significance.

Study-Room

The person who has charge of the study-room or the library of the settlement must bring to it, or secure for it, some knowledge of the life of the children, or she loses the opportunities in her work. As an illustration of what I mean, Miss Miller, who has charge of the study in the Henry Street Settlement in New York, places on her bulletin special reference to things that touch the students outside of school and in their homes.

Just now she has put before them the origin of the Jewish Pentecost that they may know the dignity of its origin, and not relegate it in their minds as a wornout tradition, part of the orthodoxy of their alien parents. Last March the legend of St. Patrick had its place, and in consequence, I think the day meant more to the children than the flying of green flags with no significance attached.

Festivals

In the festivals at the settlements where the gifted club leaders have worked out a poetical interpretation of the ceremonies cherished by the neighborhood, their success had been twofold—with the parents and with the child. There is a contrast between this inspiration and the exhibitions which work out a theme which has no direct appeal to the children or their parents. It has been possible, in a small way, to accomplish something with the colored children, and to glorify in a degree the songs associated with the painful experience of their race.

Vocational Training

In conclusion, I should like to lay emphasis on the necessity of directing workers among children to consideration of their occupations when the time comes for them to take upon their shoulders the economic burdens. Vocational direction has been in the minds of many social workers. It is inevitable that men and women, as they become acquainted with the fortunes of the children in an immigrant neighborhood, take a look ahead, and rebel at repeating in the lives of the next generation the misfortunes of the preceding.

Harvard College is about to establish a school to train vocation guiders; Mr. Snyder of Cincinnati has worked out a plan of part-time instruction and part-time employment; Munich has done well; and inquiries are being made and experiments tried out in other communities. It behooves us to work together to prolong the childhood so that the children of this generation may be more and more fitted to present a higher standard to the next.

THE PLACE OF THE IMMIGRANT CHILD IN THE SOCIAL PROGRAM

HENRY MOSKOWITZ
Down Town Ethical Society, New York

At the very outset of this discussion on the place of the immigrant child in a social program, I desire to emphasize in no uncertain terms that there can be no effective social program for the immigrant child without recognizing the need of a social program for his parents.

Any one-sided program directed exclusively toward the child carries a serious and dangerous implication—that the parents are a generation in the wilderness, for whom any program of Americanization is futile and that their ideas are fixed, their characters are set, and it is impossible to make them responsive to the influences of the new world. The adherents of a one-sided program resign themselves to what they regard as a basic fact and concentrate their energies upon the new generation exclusively.

Such an attitude, however, is fatal to parent and child alike. It omits the relation between the two. And the welfare of one is bound up in the influence of the other. This is especially true in an immigrant neighborhood, where the welfare of the child is determined by two important factors, the inner environment represented in the social world and religious traditions, the historical background brought over to the new country by his parents; and the outer environment expressed in the physical, social and economic conditions over which the parent has no control. So the problem of child welfare in an immigrant neighborhood may be formulated in this way. How can we reach a child who is influenced by ideas new and often alien to the parent, and who is affected by the outward surroundings more profoundly than his parents?

However, no one who has lived in immigrant neighborhoods and has studied immigrant conditions has adhered to the one-sided program very long; for slight familiarity with the immigrant's outer surroundings will convince even a surface observer of the dangers attending the entire community from the neglect of his outer environment. This neglect is one of the bitter fruits of the laissez faire policy concerning the adult immigrant. Until a comparatively few years ago, the attitude of the average American towards the immigrant was characterized by temperamental optimism. America has opened its doors and welcomed him to her shores, to the rich land of opportunities. All that is necessary, is to push him into the melting pot and let him boil. He and his children will boil into happy and prosperous Americans.

Now what is the nature of the pot in which the immigrant is permitted to boil? Let some facts in a report issued in February of this year, published by the New York City Commission on Congestion of Population, which was appointed by Mayor Gaynor, enlighten us as to New York conditions; and since congestion is not a local but a national condition in this city civilization of ours, these facts may have some bearing on the Chicago situation.

First, there is the economic fact that there are relatively few heads of families in New York City, even skilled mechanics, who are earning the minimum of $800 a year, which a Commission of the State Conference of Charities and Correction has reported to be essential to maintain a family on a reasonable basis, permitting no saving whatsoever and promising the utmost care and thrift on the part of the family. It is true, of course, that many families of the city have more than one worker, so that the total income of the family is greater than the figures given above, but the minimum of $800 provides for the support of three children under fourteen years of age and for the parents, while the expenses of children over fourteen years of age working are naturally greater than those of children under this age. This economic fact, namely, that the parent alone cannot be the chief breadwinner of the household and cannot sustain the family alone, has a direct bearing on the relations between parent and child; for where the parents are chiefly dependent upon their children who are more valuable economic assets of the new country than their parents, the sentiment of filial piety cannot survive. It is an abnormal relation sometimes resulting in an inverted moral order that the self-respecting parent accepts with resignation and says with a sigh, "Well, this is America!"

In this connection it is germane to refer to the influence of the trades-union movement upon the immigrant. It lays the right emphasis—a living wage and decent labor conditions for the parent. It enhances his self-respect as a worker and, if he is an immigrant worker, as a parent. The trades-union movement has emphasized the brotherhood of the races more effectively than any other social influence. For in their common devotion to an American standard of living, Jew and Gentile, Italian and Slav have discovered in each their common humanity. I shall never forget the sight on Rutger Square when the cloakmakers gathered there eager to hear the news that the strike had been won. In that square I saw Italian and Jew; and when the announcement came that they had won the strike, I saw a Jew and an Italian embrace each other for joy; and in that moment of joy the Jew was of the Italian a common brother, and the Italian of the Jew, and behind the strange tongue, behind the strange custom, behind these prejudices that divide, is just this humanity of the worker, which is emphasized by the trades-union movement.

The trades-union movement has a very vital connection with a social program in the interest of an immigrant child. Any such program means raising the standard of skill in industry, raising the working age, exacting a higher standard of equipment for the foreigner in industry. This means added burden to the parents, and drives us inevitably to recognize the need of a minimum wage, which will enable the parents to bear the burden. You cannot save the child by breaking the parent's back.

What the trades unions are demanding of employers, an enlightened social conscience confirms. The evil cannot be palliated by surface philanthropy. There are some employers who during a strike will create dissension among the organized workers by pitting race against race in the struggle for bread. They recognize the brotherhood of man as a Sunday church luxury perhaps. Tolstoi has flung the grim challenge in their teeth and said, "You are willing to do everything for the poor except get off his back."

Let us turn to some of the health conditions which have been reported by this Commission on Congestion of Population. There are nearly 10,000 deaths a year in the city of New York from tuberculosis and nearly 28,000 new cases of it every year. There are 25,000 to 30,000 deaths from preventable diseases. Of 125,000 babies born in New York annually, about 16,000, one in every eight, die. The death-rate in congested blocks and overcrowded rooms is much higher than among the same races and ages living in less crowded rooms. The economic waste from certain preventable diseases in the city, that is, loss of wages of men and women who die of these diseases in New York City, amounts to from $37,000,000 to $41,000,000 annually. Congestion of population is contributing very largely to the $10,000,000 a year that New York City spends annually on her departments of prevention and cure of diseases.

The Division of Child Hygiene, Department of Health, reports that for the school year, September 1908 to June 1909, 242,048 children out of 322,344 examined were found to need treatment; of these, 183,862 on account of defective teeth; 38,329 on account of defective vision; 73,058 on account of defective nasal breathing; 86,688 on account of hypertrophied tonsils. In view of the great efforts of the department to urge treatment, it is, therefore, probable that a greater number of effective treatments cannot be secured because of limitation of clinics and the economic inability of parents to pay doctors' fees. But I must not burden you with too many figures. I need only call attention to the 170,000 windowless rooms in our tenements and the 645,472 rooms that are inadequately lighted, according to the report of the Congestion Commission; I need only call attention to the fact that 13,500 licenses were issued by the State Labor Bureau, for tenement labor, permission to work in the tenements.

These are grim facts, facts which picture the outer environment, the melting pot into which the immigrant is drawn. Here is evidence enough to show that the physical environment endangers parent and child alike.

Now, what are some of the other influences affecting the parent, and indirectly affecting the child? Take the civic influences affecting the parent. In the congested neighborhoods where immigrants live, the parent often comes in touch with democracy at its worst. If he must bribe the policeman for the privilege of selling in the market or on the street, if he must tip the ash-remover for taking away refuse, if in his ignorance of city ordinances he is brought before the courts, where a shyster lawyer magnifies his misdemeanor to mulct him of a fat fee, if he must resort to a powerful individual for protection that a social or civic institution should give him, if he perceives the magic influence of "pull" in the poor man's courts, small wonder that he greets the enthusiast for American institutions with a smile of disillusionment born of bitter experience. But if the parent sees democracy at its worst, the child comes in touch with democracy at its best in the public schools. The basis of a social program for parent and child is clear; give them both common experiences; let the institutions that reach the child, direct the life of the parent too. No one who has looked into the eyes of the parents beaming with happiness at a graduation reception when they see their children receive the diploma, can fail to note the possibilities of the school in bringing democracy at its best, closer to the life of the parent. The organization of parents' meetings in the schools is also a step in the right direction.

The Independence Day celebrations for foreigners, planned by the Committee of One Hundred appointed by the mayor of New York to provide a safe and sane Fourth, illustrates what I mean by bringing the higher mood of democracy closer to the foreigner.

The play festivals, in which parents and children participate, developed by your city so elaborately, are a step in this direction.

Another constructive suggestion to interpret the finer side of democracy to the immigrant is the one submitted by Miss Wald, to permit voting in the public-school buildings and other semipublic institutions; whereas today the immigrant votes in barber shops and in groceries and in other places that are not calculated to dignify the function of voting. The immigrant's entrance into citizenship should be dignified by ceremony and celebration.

I remember a story that illustrates the rough and uncouth method by which the immigrants are naturalized. One of the immigrants was brought to the Federal Court for naturalization, and he was asked by the judge, "Who is the father of our country," and he replied "Tom Foley." Tom Foley was the district leader, who was very good to him.

We should make more serious efforts to counteract the experience of disillusionment, when the immigrant associates America only with money-making, and that commercialism which ruthlessly crushes the idealistic yearnings he experienced in the old home. The young Russian revolutionist whose soul was gripped by the cause of Russia's freedom, whose all was spent on his country's liberation should be made to feel that his devotion, enthusiasm, and powers of self-effacement are cherished and needed in the mission of America to realize a real government of, for, and by the people. We must hitch up this dynamo of spiritual energies for the new civic life of the new country.

A social program for the immigrant child must include a program for his parents. It must be based upon the recognition that the economic struggle, the congested environment, in addition to the parents' ignorance of our language and institutions, makes parental control difficult.

The problem of parental control is complicated even in a normal American home because of the complexity of modern life, because of the wealth of social appeal and the conflicting larger social claims, claims competing with the ancient sanctions of family life. No one has brought that out more eloquently than Miss Addams in her book, "Democracy and Social Ethics." In a congested environment, normal home life is not possible; the children and young people must perforce take their pleasures outside of the home. The dance hall and the recreation problems arise chiefly because the young people have neither the natural protecting influences of social convention nor the personal protection of the mother. The mother is a toiler; she is working; she is constantly subjected to drudgery. There is need, therefore, of an impersonal chaperon, through the protecting influences of a wholesome environment, where the spirit of youth can express its wholesome buoyancy. The socializing of our public schools, parks, and playgrounds is, therefore, an essential feature of a social program for the immigrant child.

We of the settlements who approach educational problems from actual experience with concrete maladjustments, which we trace back to the social or educational systems responsible for them, have noted these interesting facts regarding the education of the immigrant child. We have observed that the vast majority of immigrant children drop out at the end of the sixth year. What have the schools done for them? Examinations at the board of education are given to determine whether they have received a minimum of education without which they cannot begin their careers as breadwinners. The standard of this test must of necessity be low. Many have not mastered writing and reading elementary English; they know little about our history and our government; and many of them present the appearance of a forlorn army of prospective industrial misfits.

The immigrant child who must leave school at fourteen is fit for nothing. The curriculum was not designed to meet his needs. There is no curriculum especially adapted for him. He must face the world of industry without having received the slightest equipment imparting that minimum of capacity required for a beginner. Our democracy has been lavish in its expenditure of wealth on this undemocratic education. The tragedy of our educational system consists in the fact that it pours out of its schools hordes of helpless children to be tossed about in the whirlpool of industry, without guidance or a compass. They must get there in hit or miss fashion and find a nook of safety.

As a result of a curriculum unadapted to the needs of the immigrant child or of any working-child, these children are, after six years of schooling, unfit for the industrial struggle, and even if their parents can afford to give them the luxury of graduating they too must help in large measure to swell the legions of the industrial misfits. Graduation does not assist the children because the curriculum of the school prepares for the high school, which the vast majority cannot enter.

Our progressive City Superintendent, Mr. Maxwell, has begun to recognize this woeful stupidity of the grammar-school curriculum by establishing a few, two I believe, vocational schools for boys between the ages of twelve and fourteen years. The

Manhattan Trade School, a vocational trade school for girls, is now incorporated in the public-school system.

I do not want to be misunderstood; I do not want to be arguing for a materialistic system of education; I do not want to be arguing against culture. I believe though with Dr. Kerschensteiner, whose book on "Education for Citizenship" your Chicago Commercial Club has published, that the deepest and profoundest culture results when a man has centered his culture on his job; has prepared for his job; has received a thorough equipment for his job; and from his central vocational interest will emanate these higher values, which will have reality because they are connected with his vocation. And it is significant that Dr. Kerschensteiner's book on education is entitled "Education for Citizenship," because he conceives of civic education as beginning with vocational training.

The life of the immigrant child is one of instability, and the words "economic pressure" are written large on every tenement wall that shelters him. He is the victim of pressure. Pressure pushes him into preparatory schools or private vocational schools with low standards of scholarship but with an efficient machinery for turning out half-baked stenographers, bookkeepers, and candidates for professional schools, only to fill an overglutted labor market with incompetents. This results in a waste of efficiency and personal character, and in a social loss to the community.

Sometimes a study of a special problem, like this one of the education of the immigrant child, leads to a re-examination of the basis of our educational system and results in a sweeping general reform. This general school reform is one of the lessons of immigrant education.

Tenement life offers the girl no example of good housekeeping. Overcrowding and the physical surroundings of tenements make efficient home-making difficult. The vast majority of these girls cannot learn it from their toil-burdened mothers, who give them devotion and sacrifice but no notions of efficiency. It is too new and modern a conception to the parents; and even if they could be efficient housekeepers, it must be remembered that a minimum of economic security is needed before the gospel of efficiency in home-making can bear fruit. Before you can prevent waste, you must see that there is a little surplus of income to exercise your economy upon. Efficiency will find a barren field where there is a minimum of subsistence.

A course in home-making is especially needed among the daughters of the poor in large cities, who often live in homeless homes.

Thus far I have dwelt upon the problem of adjusting the parent and child to the outer environment. There is another aspect to the problem of the immigrant child, which has been so sympathetically discussed by Miss Addams in her illuminating writings. It is the old story of Turgeneff's "Fathers and Sons," the clashing of the generations; the painful throes of progress represented in those dissonances that precede a higher harmony.

The struggle is made more transparent and vivid by the outer surroundings of the strange new world with its powerful influences over which parents have no control. I have a faint recollection of the tearful partings of close relatives in the old world when they wrenched themselves from old friends, hallowed associations, and a life deeply rooted in an historic past. I have seen the dazed look of bewilderment in the eyes of immigrants when they land here. Wrenched from a stable environment they enter a land, often a city, and nearly always a neighborhood, characterized by instability and flux. I have tried to show how the experience of the adult is not such as to connect his ideals and his traditions with the ideals of the America he learns to know. He gets a second wrench in the new land, and when his children sometimes confound lawlessness with individualism, and lack of reverence with American freedom, he is wrenched again; and he suffers from a lonesomeness often more poignant than the lonesomeness of solitudes. He is a lonely person in a crowd.

The moral dangers to the child in a transitional period of rapid changes are serious because he can develop into a person devoid of deep loyalty. This is a serious danger of any environment in a constant state of flux. This is one of the threatening moral dangers of city life with its tenements and flats. Living in a flat not infrequently results in flat living; for we give ourselves so little time to strike root. Without rootage there is no moral advance. All the finer fruits of civilization have come from a people who have had time to anchor. We must prevent the child of the immigrant from becoming a moral nomad by connecting him with his parents' past; by inculcating in him a reverence and a loyalty for those fine social and moral traditions in his parents' heritage that have stood the test of time; and especially those moral and social ideals that counteract a too pronounced individualism in the younger generations and that give him, the younger generation, an atomic view of life. We must fill him with a mission to contribute the best of that heritage to the America of the future.

The parent, too, is not free from an obligation to recognize the new surroundings, the new world of ideas. His institutions, his churches and synagogues must translate the precious moral and spiritual traditions in terms of the child's experience. There are, happily, signs of such intelligent adaptability in church and synagogue. A new Talmud school of New York was recently opened, and it has a playground attached. And the Jewish Community of the city of New York is revising its system of religious instruction on a more modern basis. Ethical statesmanship demands that we make a connection between the precious traditions of the parent and the newer ideals of our young democracy. What we must do is to conceive of the future American as a blend, a fusion of the past civilizations of the old world with the finer fruits of our newer civilization. This is the challenge of the ethical statesmanship involved in the rearing of the immigrant child.

ideas. The institutions, the churches and synagogues must reemphasize the precious moral and spiritual traditions in terms of the child's experience. There are hopeful signs of such [illegible] ability in church and synagogue. A new [illegible] School of New York was recently opened, and it has a playground attached. And the Jewish Community of the city of New York is renewing its support of religious instruction on a more modern [illegible] statesmanship demands that we make a connection between the precious traditions of the [illegible] and the newer ideals of our young [illegible]. What we must do is to conserve out of the future, not as a blank, a fusion of the past [illegible] of the old world with the finer [illegible] of our newer civilization. This is the challenge of the ethical statesmanship involved in the rearing of the immigrant child.

PART FIVE

THE WORKING CHILD

"For Oh," say the children, "we are weary"

THE STANDARD FOR FACTORY INSPECTION IN ILLINOIS

MARY E. McDOWELL

Chairman, Illinois Federation of Woman's Clubs Committee on Industrial and Social Conditions

John Dewey in School and Society says, "What the wisest parent wants or desires for his children, that the State must want for her children." That seems to me the only standard to set up; what the wisest parent wants for boys and girls between fourteen and sixteen years of age, that the state must want for children of the same age. If that is the standard that we want to think about this morning, I think none of us here would want any child to go to work in a factory or store or shop between fourteen and sixteen. I think everyone of us here would want these years to be kept for education. We might want that education to be different education from that now given, a vocational education, for example more working with the hand and not so much with the book; certainly I think we should want during these especially critical years to protect the boys and girls.

On the way downtown I have to pass a factory. It is a rather good looking building from the outside; it looks as if it were well built, but there is a very pathetic sign out there every few days, and this is the sign, "Small girls wanted." I must say it goes into my heart and almost strikes terror when I think of it. It is very close to the vice district, in the Twenty-second Street neighborhood. "Small girls wanted!" When you think of the care and protection we had and how everything was arranged with reference to our lives between fourteen and sixteen years, and then think of this constant bid for small girls in a factory, and small boys, you shudder. I do not know whether they mean that they actually want them to be small for some purpose in the factory, or whether it is just young girls, or what it is they mean. It may be some dainty work that they have that requires daintiness, but it is something that ought to appall us that industry should want small girls; that is something that should stir us.

Now, that means that girls at this critical age, and boys, are put out of the home into a public place. The mother cannot follow them. The mother cannot follow the young girl as she goes down to the State Street store or into this factory where the small girl is wanted. The little girl has to take care of herself, or we have to have such factory inspection that we may feel sure that the child is safe, physically and morally. It seems to me that that is the standard I must set, and that every thoughtful person in the state of Illinois must reach that standard. If we must still have children between fourteen and sixteen working away from home, there must be mothering and fathering in the factory. Every industry we see organized today is so immense and enormous, and the men who determine its policies and are therefore responsible for it, are so far away from it that we have to depend upon this artificial care of the factory inspector.

Since 1907 we have had seven new laws passed demanding factory inspection in the state of Illinois. We have 10,000 children working in the state of Illinois, as nearly as I can learn. We are the third largest manufacturing state in the United States. At this last legislature we got something. We asked that the factory inspector should be put upon the merit system, under the civil service sys-

HOME WORK

Child Labor in the home is not prohibited by Illinois Law

When Everybody Works but Father they earn

35¢ a day 75¢ a day

Nut Picking

Finishing Pants

The Illinois Law provides that no room shall be used for the manufacture of clothing, flowers, cigars, Etc. except by the Immediate members of the family.

This means that clothing is manufactured Without regulation or inspection.

tem. That has been passed. July first, the factory inspectors now employed will be put on the merit system, and after that all who come in will have to pass an examination.

Mr. Edgar T. Davis, the chief factory inspector, asked for thirty-five inspectors. He got five. Remember, there are seven laws that demand factory inspection, but no proportionate increase in appropriation. The office force was, on the contrary, cut by almost half, two years ago.

That shows that the state of Illinois does not yet appreciate the importance of this subject. How can we make the public feel such a sense of responsibility that the children will be protected morally and physically? The ten-hour law has been extended so that the factory inspection will have to go out into a larger field than before. The Occupational Diseases Bill has become a law. We cannot, of course, inspect factories for occupational diseases unless we have assistance; we must have sanitary experts and physicians, who will know lead poisoning when they meet it. We must have such agents as they have in England, prepared to recognize the prohibited conditions when they find them. So far we have not such agents. Many in the community are working hard to get laws passed; and laws are being passed so fast that we are not keeping pace in the inspection force. It is a very serious thing. It might be a good thing to stop getting labor laws for a couple of years and simply construct and educate the force of inspection so we could be sure that these laws would be enforced; if they are not enforced, then we have tremendously failed.

We have not even begun to make conditions safe: when in a shirtwaist factory there are 156 little girls burned—and the report is that they were very little girls, little Italian and Jewish girls—that fact brings home to many people this need of protection. It is not only protection from accident by machinery, but from fire as well. We must see to it that somebody is responsible for protecting the little girls who work on the third and fourth floors in our factories. I do not believe it is the factory inspector's business to do that. It is, in my judgment, the fire department's business. As it is now, we divide this responsibility. If the factory inspector finds wrong conditions he reports to the building department; the precinct fire captain inspects only three times a year; the building department in Illinois inspects only once a year. You see what can happen between those periods of inadequate inspection. Recall the catastrophe in the Fish building on State Street. The fire department official warned the manager of that establishment two or three times, warned the people who owned the building, and report was made to the building department. Nothing was done and within thirty days after that warning the girls were burned in the building. Now for this sort of carelessness and irresponsibility you have to hold three people, and you can fasten responsibility on none. We should have one department, and I think the logical department to look after protection from fire is the fire department. All experts who have studied the question have put the responsibility on the fire department—I understand that in New York an effort is being made to put the responsibility on the fire department. The Woman's Trades Union League committee in Chicago has seen this need and is trying to find out whether or not we shall have this fire protection put into the hands of the fire department or whether it shall still be left with the building department.

It is interesting to note that in the case of this disaster the building was a fireproof building. Firemen walked across the floors an hour and a half after the fire, and they were intact, but no one had made the manager clear the way to the fire escape. No one compelled him to have a fire drill so that those little children, little girls, who would naturally be frightened and excited in time of panic, could be led out as the public-school children are under like circumstances.

EFFICIENCY IN FACTORY INSPECTION

FLORENCE KELLEY

Secretary, National Consumers' League

There is no greater injustice than that which is done to the officials who have the duty of inspecting factories when they are burdened with a great variety of activities, left without money wherewith to get necessary help and do necessary traveling, left without preliminary training before their appointment, without enlightened public opinion to judge them justly.

When I was factory inspector of Illinois, our laws sweepingly said that children should not work in factories or workshops (and afterwards added stores) until they were fourteen years of age. Every time that a deputy found a child under the age of fourteen years illegally at work, we had to spend time on that child, and that was an outrage upon us. With only twelve inspectors, we ought never to have found children under the age of fourteen years at work. The schools ought to have looked after the children under that age. Every inspection department that has an age limit to enforce has also a compulsory education law reinforcing it, and it is the grossest injustice to the factory inspection department to saddle upon it the work that ought to be done by the schools and school attendance officers.

The state of New York recognizes that and draws a sharp distinction as to the responsibility for the children. It establishes a divided responsibility, and we enforce that upon the people to whom it is apportioned. It is the duty of the schools to keep children in school until they have finished the work of the fifth grade. And whenever a factory inspector finds a child at work who has not finished the work of the fifth grade, the labor commissioner reports that fact to the superintendent of schools and to volunteer societies which interest themselves in the children, and life is made as bitter as two energetic societies can conveniently make it for whatever school authority let that child out of school. That ought to be done in every community. It is an injustice to an undermanned body of factory inspectors to foist upon them a task that belongs to the schools.

The state of New York has made another division of duties. The working papers of children in New York have to be issued by co-operative efforts of the local board of health and local school authorities.

Our limit for beginning work in New York is constantly approaching sixteen years because of the red tape tied around the children for the purpose of keeping them under the control of the health authorities and the school authorities. Before Simon Solomonski can leave school and go to work, he must first send to Russia and get a birth-certificate. Seventy-five per cent of all the children at work in the city of New York have their birth-certificates on file at the department of health. There is no serious difficulty in getting a birth-certificate for any child who was born abroad; it is only our American child who knows nothing about his birth-register. Foreign children can get their birth-certificates unless they have come from massacre regions of Russia where many Jewish birth-certificates have been burned, or unless they come from earthquake regions of Italy, where many birth-records have been swallowed up; unless revolution or oppression or the forces of nature have destroyed the records, the civilized part of the world has records of the births of its children. So three-fourths of all our working-children in New York City before they leave school show their proper birth-certificates. Then before they can leave they have to pass a special examination in school to make quite sure that they will pass when they go to the department of health, and the examiner learns whether they are ready to be sent out under the care of the factory inspectors. The children pass one examination in school, and then they go to the department of health and pass a revising examination.

On the day I left New York there was a meeting of the Child Labor Committee at luncheon at the Mid-day Club. The central decoration was a little iron anvil and a large collection of nails, great long spikes. The policeman who weighs the children as they arrive at the department of health had weighed a little boy about three weeks before and sent him away because he weighed only sixty pounds, and it is thought by the department that a boy who weighs only sixty pounds is not fit to go into industry; he must come up to eighty-five pounds. After three weeks this little boy came back and said to the policeman, "Do you see how fat I am? I don't think you even need to put me on the scales; I weigh so much." Then the policeman took the little fellow up by his heels and emptied his pockets of the anvil and nails, over seven pounds of them. The children must come up to eighty-five pounds without the help of extraneous substances. They must read fluently, write legibly, answer a dozen questions intelligently, and do a problem in simple arithmetic.

By this method we are bringing up the age-limit from the fourteenth birthday towards the sixteenth birthday. And feeble-minded children and subnormal children, who used to be shooed out of school early on the ground that they were filling school seats that should be filled by children who were brighter, that they were obviously learning nothing —those children, 2,000 of them, we are deliberately keeping in school until they are sixteen years old, partly on the ground that they are not fit to be entrusted to the care of officials so overworked as the factory inspectors.

A great burden, which is placed on the factory inspectors in most of the other states, is thus taken from them in New York; for the great majority of children who work are over fifteen years old. And this burden has been further reduced by our much more rigid eight-hour law. We have the most rigid eight-hour law in the world for children, the only law which provides that every child under sixteen years of age working in a factory or workshop must go home when the clock strikes five in the afternoon.

A manufacturer does not like to have in the factory children who have to go home at five o'clock, because it suggests to everybody else the great desirability of going home at five; thus he does not willingly take on children under the age of sixteen years. So the law which provides that children must go home at five o'clock has banished from industry in the city of New York more children under the age of sixteen years than all other provisions of our law taken together. There was a great reduction in employment of children after that law took effect, more sweeping, more permanent than all the gradual reductions gained before. In the whole city of New York, covering factories and stores as our inspectors now do, they found at work last year approximately only 10,000 children among 5,000,000 people. That we believe is more due to going home at five o'clock than to all other provisions of the statute.

Our American states place unjust burdens upon the factory-inspection departments. Even fire risks are placed in part upon the factory inspector. Our new buildings in New York are steel and concrete, they are built like Dutch ovens, warranted to burn to ashes anything within them and remain intact themselves, and they are built without adequate exits. The fire expert, Mr. Porter, has recently stated that in many new buildings he, as an honest fire engineer, could not undertake to empty the buildings in case of fire with the present exits, even if he had had weekly fire drills for a year. How murderous are the narrow stairs, the insufficient fire escapes, the absence of fire walls!

Nothing could be more unjust than to put even a share of the duty of seeing to the fire safety of the people working in the loft buildings of New York on the factory-inspection department. We have a million and a half people coming within the provisions of the law required to be enforced by factory inspectors who have to enforce the eight-hour law for men employed by the city, county and state; who have to enforce the laws in regard to the men working on the new canal. On these inspectors, already overburdened, it is proposed to place the responsibility for the safety of the lives of people in buildings that from the day they are built make safety impossible.

Now, suppose we keep our children in school, suppose we make the fire department take every precaution to prevent fires, so that our buildings become safe, suppose that the work placed on the factory-inspection department is only that which we should reasonably place upon it, how unjust still are the demands made upon the factory-inspection department in every state. In Germany, in order to be a humble beginner in the Germany factory-inspection service, even in a little place like Wurtemburg, even in the most non-industrial German provinces, the candidate must be a graduate of a technical school or a university, having heard special lectures arranged for the education of factory inspectors. Who has heard of such a requirement in the United States? I did once know of a Cornell graduate fitting herself to become a factory inspector, but she died before her name ever came up for consideration for such an appointment, because she had no political pull.

We do not prepare or train our candidates; we do not even offer courses for training or preparing candidates. Any inspector is liable to have my experience, when I was called to the telephone at eleven o'clock at night by a newspaper reporter who asked me to tell him what I knew about my successor. "Why," I said, "I am my own successor." "Oh," he said, "your successor has been appointed and will be in your office tomorrow morning." Every factory inspector in the United States outside Massachusetts is liable to that insult. We all perhaps do not know these things when we criticise the work of the factory inspectors as though they were highly experienced surgeons, or members of the Supreme Court of the United States. They have a burden of responsibility for the life and health of the oncoming generations, and the Supreme Court of the United States has no more important task than that.

In spite of all the disadvantages, in spite of the lack of tenure of office in which to acquire experience, in spite of lack of previous training, or of recognized responsibility on the part of the community, factory inspectors have worked out for themselves in the last thirty years certain objective tests.

The first test of efficiency of a factory-inspection department is the record of its successful prosecution of important employers. If an important employer is held to exactly the same responsibility as the most trivial sweater, and if both are prosecuted for every ascertained violation of law, then that department is in a high degree efficient, and its efficiency diminishes just in proportion to the diminution in the number of successful prosecutions. Where factory-inspection departments are so small as they are in all American states, they must, to be of value, be first and last and all the time efficient prosecuting bodies. They are not instructors, they are not supposed to teach the law to willing learners, they are prosecuting officials charged with the duty of collecting fines or assuring the enforcement of prison sentences on employers who break the law. That is what they are for, and just in proportion as they do that are they valuable; just in proportion as they do not do it, they are worse than nothing, they are actively injurious because they teach lawlessness to the children who know the law, they teach lawlessness to the employer who knows the law, they teach lawlessness to the parents who know and break the law. And, in general, in the whole outside public, in the employes in our factories, they intensify that corroding American state of mind which believes that all officials do not enforce the law.

The prosecution of offenders in New York by the department of labor is such that employers have come to look on the department with respect. It has the respect of the voluntary associations that have to do with its work. The New York Association for Labor Legislation, the New York Child Labor Committee, and the Consumers' League were asked by Governor Dix about a possible successor to the present commissioner of labor. These three associations unanimously, upon his record of honest prosecutions of big and little violators of the law, urged his reappointment as long as he may care to keep his office and maintain his present policy of efficient prosecution.

We have once in a while a magistrate who will not convict, and, of course, we have to make allowance for that. But the inspection department gives full publicity—this is the second test of efficiency—the department takes the public absolutely into its confidence and keeps its records as public records, open at all times to the public and perfectly easy of access and comprehension; it gets out reports on the days on which the reports are due, gives the bulk of the reports to the press even though the public printer may delay publishing anything put into his hands. The public need not be kept without the news because the printer delays. If the department tells the truth that Magistrate Smith refused to hold all defendants, and Magistrate Jones decided differently on different occasions, although the cases were alike, sooner or later Magistrate Smith and Magistrate Jones will come to know the law, and respect and obey it. That is the second test of efficiency of the work of the department.

The third test is the success of the department in its co-operation with school and health authorities. It is not so easy for the public to judge that, as to judge whether reports are full and clear and honest, or whether prosecutions are efficient and uniform, but the third test of the work of the department is the manner in which the department and the health and educational authorities are co-operating.

It is an injustice to judge the department as to its efficiency as tested in this way when the numbers of inspectors are so meager as they are throughout our Republic. We must make these demands and we ought to remember that these tests can be applied, but we ought perhaps to apply them with justice tempered not only with mercy but with a high degree of shame and humiliation on the part of the public.

THE ILLINOIS DEPARTMENT OF FACTORY INSPECTION

EDGAR T. DAVIES

Chief Factory Inspector of Illinois

I do not quite agree with Mrs. Kelley's idea that prosecution is the standard of efficiency by which the department of factory inspection should be judged. I have had some experience, having convicted over eight thousand people for violating the law, and I find that we can obtain greater results by explaining the law and winning the co-operation and the support of the employer, showing him that there is no desire on the part of the state to pick him up for every little technical violation. We frequently find a child employed who is under age, or who has not a certificate. The certificate can be obtained easily. If there has been a previous violation in the establishment, or carelessness, and there is no excuse or a change in management, these violations may occur. For such cases we have a card system, so that the offender may admit a violation and have his admission go into the record. If the same kind of violation occurs again, we can spring that on him. Of course, prosecutions are necessary and they should be carried on honestly, regardless of who the accused may be, whether he is running a store or a shop, whether a large employer or a small. Moreover, the public are entitled to know exactly what is being done by any department. Under the present system of financing the department in Illinois that is impossible.

In 1907 the appropriation set apart for the Illinois Department of Factory Inspection was cut in two, in order to influence certain prosecutions and for other political reasons. We had to make a reduction in the office staff. Since that date, too, the legislature passed the most comprehensive factory inspection law in the United States. It is known as the Health, Safety and Comfort Law, and contains thirty-two provisions requiring inspection of plants, some requiring the inspection of machinery and of the general hygiene of the establishment. A law has been passed requiring us to inspect the building of bridges and viaducts; we must also see that in certain establishments the machinery is protected in certain ways.

There is an efficient way of enforcing the law and there is an efficient way of defeating it. It is very easy for the legislators to respond to the public clamor for the passage of a very necessary law, but there is another way of defeating it. They furnish the law but refuse to furnish us the coal and oil and fuel to put the machinery into operation. We have been unable to publish an annual report since 1907. It is contrary to the statutes and I should be subject to removal from office or imprisonment if under the present law I diverted the funds appropriated for another purpose to pay a typist or to secure clerical help for tabulating the report. Of course, I have not the time to get out this report and I have no contingent funds out of which to pay five typists for four months to catalogue and type the report.

We have no statistician in the office; we have very few clerks, eight less than have been employed for the last four years, so it can be seen how impossible it is to get out a report of that kind. We asked for thirty-five deputy inspectors, a corps of engineering inspectors, an electrical engineer, a mechanical engineer, a practical builder, a chemist, and a bacteriologist, one who would be especially familiar with industrial poisoning. We had the open opposition of only one individual; but we had the secret opposition of many others, members of the House. That one man, whose name is Smythe, who lives in the strongest sweatshop district in the state and who charged me with prosecuting his friends, was able to dictate to one hundred and fifty-two members of the House what should and what should not be allowed for my department. It is true I prosecuted his friends; but they deserved it, and I shall still continue to prosecute them if they violate the law.

We have in many factories to go into the engineering department, to be pretty good machinists, pretty good engineers, to be practically everything that is required. The work of the department covers every phase of industrial life from child labor to home industry, from machinery and pulleys to the general hygiene and industrial poisoning. We have therefore a pretty difficult task, and all that we can do in our humble way is to ask for your co-operation.

THE STREET TRADER UNDER ILLINOIS LAW

FLORENCE KELLEY

Secretary, National Consumers' League

Nine years ago, in 1902, the General Federation of Women's Clubs created for the first time in its history a committee to deal with children who work. And the first task of that committee was to publish a four-page leaflet, into which it was perfectly easy to crowd the headings of all the child-labor laws that there were in existence in the United States at that time. We could not give the text of all the statutes, but we called the roll of the statutes in the space of four pages.

The national movement in this country for the protection of children from overwork dates back no earlier than 1902, although there were here and there experimental laws before that date. In Massachusetts, in New York, in Ohio, in Illinois, and in Pennsylvania there were experimental laws, but there was no systematic effort to provide legislative protection for all the children who worked in all the states of this union until nine years ago.

Since then, however, there has grown up the National Child Labor Committee, which has co-operated admirably with the Federation of Women's Clubs and the Consumers' League and many other organizations striving to mend the situation as well as can be done under our crazy-quilt provision of statutes in forty-six states.

But now at the end of nine years, there is still one large body of children who are omitted in many states from that effort to provide legislative protection for all the children who work—the children who work in the streets. And the illogical nature of our legislation is nowhere so glaring as in the case of

STREET TRADES

These are the only workers not protected by law.

A group of children found selling in one city block. April 3, 1911.

Bootblacking, selling gum and papers leads to

?

Truancy
Low Vitality
Ill Health — Dullness
Irresponsibility — Careless Habits.

Breaking down of parental control. Five cent show habits — Petty thievery. Children on the street at all hours of the night.

Ruin for the boys and girls

those children. In many cities, even in the state of New York, where we have had the so-called street-traders law for five years, we find children vending in the streets. Not a fortnight ago I saw in the capital city, in Albany, a little child five years old selling papers late at night near the railway station. And within three weeks, in violation of our New York City ordinance and of our New York State law, I saw a little boy, a very ill-fed, wretched, shabby little boy, offering papers for sale at a quarter to twelve o'clock, midnight, at the door of the women's hotel, the Martha Washington Hotel. He seemed to be speculating on the pity of women who might be coming home late from theater or opera to that hotel. He was dressed for his part rather more than the boys are who sell papers by day in the streets of New York.

At one end of the scale, we have a little chap five years old selling papers in the capital city of the state; we have hundreds and hundreds of little fellows ten years old selling papers hither and yonder with no effective restriction on their work. And at the other end, we have an unusually rigid provision for the protection of boys, namely, a provision that no boy under the age of sixteen years shall be employed after 7 p. m. in delivering messages or telegrams or merchandise; and no boy under twenty-one years of age shall be so employed between the hours of ten at night and five in the morning.

The legislature of the state of New York two years ago affirmed the principle that a boy is a child until he is twenty-one years old. The night-messenger statute is a part of the labor law under the general heading of child labor. The legislature discussed the use of the word "child" in that connection and deliberately kept it, saying that in New York an infant cannot sell real estate until the infant is twenty-one years of age and that, if an infant remained an infant until twenty-one years of age in relation to land, surely a child remained a child until twenty-one years of age in relation to work at midnight. So boys engaged in the delivery of messages and merchandise in the state of New York are today infants, children, under the protection of the Department of Labor and the statute law. Their employers are threatened with prosecution, with a fine of $20 for the first offense for letting a boy carry a message or merchandise at five minutes past ten at night; a fine rising to $50, and then to $100, followed by imprisonment, in case of continued violation.

This stringent regulation in New York of one form of child labor at night is the result of a study made by the National Child Labor Committee of the experiences of boys at night in the messenger service in a number of cities. The typewritten record of that investigation could not be sent through the mails; it could not be printed. It was not read by all the members of the National Child Labor Committee. Some of the men and women who recognized it as their duty to read that report before it should be submitted to the legislature found themselves incapable of finishing it. I was one of those shirking members. It was carried by the investigator and by the secretary of the National Child Labor Committee to the legislature; it was submitted to the necessary committees of the legislature behind closed doors. Those committees heard as much of it as they could endure; and they unanimously reported, without an adverse vote in either committee, in favor of prohibiting the work of boys below the age of twenty-one years between the hours of ten at night and five in the morning in the delivery of messages and merchandise in the larger cities of New York State. The legislature passed that sweeping measure unanimously, and Governor Hughes signed it within an hour of its reaching him. I believe that it is obeyed. I have never seen such an astounding change in the personnel of any occupation as the change from the slow, shuffling, shabby, irresponsible, little twelve-year-old boys sent to my office a dozen years ago when I rang for a messenger, and the somewhat shabby, stooping, but alert and eager white-haired men who come now to my office either by day or by night when I ring for a messenger. The pay is so poor that men of adult years do not willingly take it. Only the aged, and the irresponsible youth are to be had for the money that these corporations pay. Our messages go very much more rapidly than they used to go, and nothing like so many are lost between the telegraph office and the suburban home. The work is better done than it used to be, although it has been suggested by a light-minded member of the Child Labor Committee that soon we should need protection for messengers in their second childhood!

But why should we draw so sharp a line between boys employed in the service of companies that can be located and held to their responsibility and prosecuted, and boys who, under the fiction that they are merchants working on their own responsibility, offer papers in the street? And why should Chicago have girls, as merchants on their own responsibility, selling in the streets? Bad as we are in New York, I have seen in twelve years only six different girls offering anything for sale in the streets of New York who could be imagined to be below the age of sixteen years. We have aged grandmothers who conduct little stalls, little booths with a cover over them, where they sell papers, just as women on the streets of Paris sell papers. But little girls prowling about on the sidewalks, offering chewing-gum or papers or pencils, or practicing the kinds of beggary that children practice who are nominally trying to sell things on the sidewalk, we do not have, although certainly the poverty in New York affords as good an excuse as poverty could afford anywhere in this country. We owe the removal of the peddling girls from the sidewalks to the Society for the Prevention of Cruelty to Children, which years ago made itself responsible for clearing from the sidewalks little girls selling and peddling. Why are girls in New York more carefully protected than girls here? I ask myself that question every time I come to Chicago.

But in the matter of the boys, we do very badly. We have a sham law which provides that they shall not sell papers until they are ten years old; and that between ten and fourteen years they shall not sell after ten o'clock at night. Every little boy selling papers is presumed to be a schoolboy permitted to sell papers because he is doing well in school. It is presumed to be a premium on his school work that, as a capable boy, he has a badge given him free of charge by the board of education and is then allowed to sell papers. Nominally he must obey these slight restrictions: he must be ten years of age, and must not work after ten o'clock at night. But what happens is that boys of any age sell papers, at any hour, in any place, with or without badges.

At first we thought that the disregard of this law was due to the fact that it was left to the police department and that uniformed police were ashamed to engage in foot races with little urchins who could always beat them. So the police were re-enforced by a special group of truant officers assigned to follow up newsboys and see that they obey the law.

But, while the uniformed police are unwilling to arrest newsboys, they arrested last year eight thousand other boys not newsboys, some thousands of them for playing ball—that was the charge against them in court. It seems strange that a newsboy violating the terms of his license should be an unworthy object, beneath the attention of the police, but that any little chap eight, nine or ten years old playing ball should be worth arresting and bringing into court. But it has been an unwritten law of the police department of the city of New York that promotions are made, not according to the good order in a policeman's precinct, not according to the convictions following arrests, but according to the number of arrests. A person arrested and entered on the books of the precinct stands to the credit of the policeman for promotion; and little boys playing ball are valuable for the promotion of policemen. But why are newsboys not valuable? A newsboy breaking the newsboy law, it would seem, would answer every purpose for promotion quite as well as another boy. And yet newsboys are rarely arrested.

It seems unreasonable that newsboys should be sleeping on the gratings of buildings through the inclement winter of New York. They are found occasionally asleep on the steps of the elevated railway stations and in hallways and in empty boxes that happen to be outside a wholesale warehouse. Why is a boy who may be engaged in delivering merchandise and messages more precious than these little boys? One explanation which has been suggested is this: that public opinion in New York has been mis-educated with regard to newsboys by a philanthropic tradition. About forty years ago a man started a lodging-house for them. He assumed that there would always be newsboys, and he got a permanent endowment, which exists today and probably will exist for a long time to come. He made heroes of newsboys, and people wrote novels about them. I remember when I was a little girl reading novels of which the heroes were newsboys. And the public assumed apparently that the newsboy was to be a merchant or a railroad director or a general, or President of the United States; all that was necessary was to start as a newsboy. That old tradition, perverting our minds, lingers to this day; whereas when we learn of the evil experiences of messenger boys, having no such poisonous traditions concerning them, our minds are free to enable us to get whatever protective legislation they need. But having this poisonous old tradition that newsboys must be encouraged, we cannot even get the police to do the things that the law requires them to do in the way of checking and restricting overwork and too early work of the newsboys of the streets.

Nothing could be worse than the experience of those boys, physically, mentally, morally. The contact of the newsboy is certainly as bad as that of the messenger boy. There is nothing in the city of New York that remains unknown to a ten-year-old newsboy who has sold papers for six weeks—no evil whatever. There is not only all the evil that is recorded in the papers he sells—and he shrieks the most evil thing that he can find in a headline as an enticement to people to buy his wares—but there is a tradition among the boys themselves that in order to be a "wise guy" he must know the greatest possible amount of evil, and what he does not know he must invent; and he must tell the last newcomer everything he knows or can invent.

Nothing could be worse than the conversation of newsboys at the street corners; nothing could be worse than their experience. Why do we put up with it? Why do we go to the roof, into the cellar, searching the empty packing-boxes and sugar barrels of the factories to pull the youngsters out of their hiding holes? Why do we do all this and then walk up State Street and Wabash Avenue and across Lake and Randolph and see this army of children on the streets and encourage them and think that we are starting young merchants on the commercial road? I do not know why we do it except that as a nation we are a little insane on the subject of legal fictions. We say that the little fellow who sells papers is not employed. We think he is a merchant and we all go mad and forget that he is a little boy, that he is some mother's son; that he ought to be in school; that he is going to be a citizen with the rest of us; that he ought to be treated exactly like all the other children. We forget these perfectly obvious things which are before our eyes and, because of this legal fiction that we cannot legislate for a child who is employing himself, but can legislate for a child who is employed, we leave everything as it is. There is no sane explanation for what we do.

Some years ago, there died a woman who had been interested in newsboys. They were much on her mind, and she left a fund to be spent for wooden legs for them because she had been interested in certain boys who had been run over by horse cars. In the days of the horse cars no one had yet invented papier mâché legs; there were only wooden legs. And that money has to be spent for wooden legs; but the boys do not want wooden legs, which interfere with their appeal to pity. A little fellow who has had the luck to lose a leg appeals thereby to this same maudlin sympathy; and he appeals much more if he has a crutch and one leg than if he has sound limbs. They do not like having wooden legs, but there is the will and it records public opinion very fairly. I think that is just about where we are: instead of seeing that the little boys keep their legs, we still let them lose their legs and then give them legs that are of no use to them. That might be taken as a type of the intelligence with which we deal with children in street occupations. It is as true of Chicago, although there may not be a wooden-leg fund here.

It is also characteristic of our nation that, before all the boys employed by one company can be protected against work between ten at night and five in the morning, although the boys are of the same age and have the same needs, we shall have to have forty-six state laws enacted. I think that we have three of those laws already. I think that we have one in Wisconsin and one in New Jersey; but I think that there are still forty-three states in which the same nauseous investigations will have to be made, the same unmailable records will have to be written; the same secretary will have to carry those unmailable and unprintable records to the legislature before the bills can be passed; and forty-three governors will have to read and sign those bills. It does not seem reasonable when it is all one company employing the children and when the children are as much alike as children are alike in Maine and in California. Although the messenger-boy problem is the same in all the states, the law for the suppression of the evil conditions has to be enacted forty-six times.

In England they pass one law and leave it to the cities to enforce. And in Germany they pass one imperial law and leave it to the different kingdoms and principalities to enforce. But in the United States we have this strange, lingering preference for doing everything by way of protection for employers once through Congress, but for the children in forty-six fragments.

It is getting away a little from the street trades to compare the experience of boys who work for the Western Union Telegraph or the Postal Telegraph Company with the children of the cotton industry; but the principle involved is the same. The cotton lobby is at work at this moment, and I hear from Washington that it is successfully arranging to continue to be subsidized by the federal government as a unit, keeping its cotton schedules in the tariff as a unit. But when we try to protect the children in the cotton industry, we have to go to sixteen legislatures and sixteen governors.

It is the same unreasonable thing when we try to deal with the street trades by city ordinance. Then instead of going to forty-six legislatures and governors, we have to go to hundreds of city councils and mayors; and the ordinance is usually less efficient than the statute and vastly less efficient than the cotton schedules for the protection of the great unified industry that employs the mill children.

The street children are almost the last body of children to receive legislative protection. The others have been covered in some way, except the children who work under the eyes of their parents in the tenement houses or on the farms. We are doing as ill about the tenement children as we are about the street children; and we do not realize that they are commonly one and the same.

For instance, a little boy sold papers at the Brooklyn bridge when the weather was good. The tiny fellow suffered from tuberculosis; his left elbow and left knee had been surgically reduced because of it. When the weather was bad and there were not many purchasers for papers, he stayed at home and cracked nuts; for he and his tuberculous father had a nut-cracking business. The boy sold papers in the streets, the father, propped on pillows in bed, cracked nuts at home. With his crutch the boy fetched and carried his nuts between the health-food factory and the bed of the tuberculous father, who coughed as he cracked the nuts and picked the kernels out of the shells. That little fellow was both a tenement-house worker and a street worker. He obeyed all the law there was. He was ten years old and more, and he had his badge. The house in which the father lay dying as he worked, or working as he died, was licensed properly as being sanitary and in suitable condition to have work done in it. They both obeyed all the law there was, and they came on rather badly; they were really supported by charity but they kept selling papers and cracking nuts to prove to the society which helped them that they were worthy and ought not to be sent to the poorhouse.

It is an interchangeable crowd very largely, the tenement-house children and the street children; and we are equally unreasonable in both cases. And in both cases it is largely due to this insanity that obsesses us with regard to legal fictions. We have a legal fiction that a man's house is his castle. It may be the sixth-story rear of a tenement house, but it is his castle, and you cannot tell him sweepingly what he shall not do in it. If you found him beating his children in a public place, the Society for the Prevention of Cruelty to Children would interfere with him; but if he is overworking his children, having them make willow plumes or artificial flowers or tie strings for tags, or make paper bags, or do any of the innumerable things that children do in tenements (so that a little girl ten years of age works ten hours besides going to school and her able-bodied father has elected to retire from work) then we do nothing. Italian men have told me that, though they were not yet forty, they had retired when their children were old enough to work. It is quite possible for a man to retire and live on the work of his children, while they both go to school and work in the tenement. But because his house is his castle and because he does not beat them, he is not a subject for the Society for the Prevention of Cruelty to Children. He is simply using his parental right to have his child do what he chooses to have him do in his home, and his home is his castle; and that is our insanity. I think that we shall have to get well of it, as we have recovered from so many obsessions during these last nine years.

We know now that the entire working class no longer consists of widows who are being supported by their young children. It used to seem to me that the American people believed that the working class consisted of widows. We now know that that is not true. We have a great many working-children with perfectly able fathers, who ought to be made to support them. The men ought to be made to demand wages sufficient to support their children, if they do not do it voluntarily. The street trades ought to be reserved for the tuberculous and the handicapped adults.

THE ARTIST CHILD

S. H. CLARK

Professor of Public Speaking, The University of Chicago

The function of this meeting, as I understand it, is to focus public opinion on the victory that has been achieved through the admirable work of Miss Addams and those who have co-operated with her. It is understood in this discussion that we are not opposed to the stage, as such, and that this splendid social factor is one which Miss Addams recognizes by encouraging dramatics at Hull-House.

At the beginning it must be admitted that there are two sides to this question. It should not be forgotten that there are such men as Dr. Slicer and Mr. Frohman, and such women as Mrs. Fiske, Maude Adams, Miss Barrymore, and several others on the opposing side; it must not be forgotten that they are honestly and not merely for selfish financial reasons in favor of allowing the child to go on the stage. They are undoubtedly just as honest in their desire to set aside the Illinois law as the people of Illinois are determined that the law shall not be set aside.

It is also obvious that exaggeration is of no value. No one should for a moment contend that the woman of sixty can adequately take the part of Juliet, as has been alleged, nor can she take the part of the baby in "Madam Butterfly." It should be conceded that a woman of forty has no power to play the part of a child of six and that we lose our point entirely by making any such claim. No cause is furthered by holding that stage children have miserable surroundings, that they wake up in the early morning with rings around their eyes, that they are half-starved and all the rest of it, for as a matter of fact I know a great many whose lives are simply a paradise compared with what those lives were before the children had the chance to go on the stage. Too much may in fact be claimed for either side. Our friends claim a good deal when they cite such a list as they have put out giving the names of actors who began in childhood. They have published a pamphlet in which there are some ten, twenty, fifty, one hundred, or one hundred and fifty names, swelled by innumerable musicians. Now the fact that Mozart began to play in public when he was six is not any argument that Molly Gray will be able to play Lady Macbeth when she grows up because she goes on the stage at seven. The value of the list as testimony is greatly reduced by such exaggeration.

Let us take up and answer some of the arguments advanced by the other side and touched upon in this pamphlet, and look at both sides of the question.

One of the great claims made by the other side is that Miss Adams and Miss Barrymore and many of the other great actors began their stage life early. I am willing to concede that this early experience was very helpful; but we cannot close our eyes to the thousands of lives that have been spoiled by that same enterprise. We must not ignore the thousands and tens of thousands of children who, if the law be set aside, would be allowed to appear in every theater in the state, of good repute or bad repute, of high repute or low repute. I will grant you that we can conceive surroundings so beautiful, so highly educative, that it would be a positive benediction to have part in them, but we are dealing with conditions today. When the Ideal Theater has been established, I grant you that our Miss

Addams will be the first one to permit the child to take part in plays produced on that stage and under supervised arrangements. But the circuit court judge is not constituted by training, or profession, or natural competency, to pass judgment on whether my child or any other child shall take part in "Four-fingered Jack or the Pirate of the Gulf" or "The Midnight Escape." I should rather lose a genius than spoil ten thousand children or even one thousand children by their contact with that form of art, with that form of theater.

There are a thousand unfit places in this state, and how are we possibly going to keep the children out of them, if we allow this amendment to get into the bill which we have with such patience and with such energy constructed? I grant you, too, that many have survived those evil influences of which we have just heard from the lips of our specialist. I do not think it is even quite fair to the other side to compare the midnight labor with the eight or nine hour labor, or the nurse in the hospital with the three or four hours, or two hours which the child spends on the stage at night. The comparison is a little bit too favorable for us; but the point I make is that while many have survived and are pointed out to us, hundreds and thousands have perished.

Now to take up in detail and rapidly some of the claims of the other side. Apparently unconsciously the writers of this pamphlet issued by a committee representing those favoring the amendment—you must remember that this is their argument—the writers of this pamphlet consider every child a genius. They say that we should not cramp the "child genius," we must not keep the "dramatic genius" from the stage. Well, if we were certain that every child who went upon the stage was going to become a great artist we might concede their argument; but ninety-nine out of every hundred that go on the stage are better off away from the stage because they have no genius nor talent nor aptitude for it. I should not take the chance of creating one genius at the risk, morally, physically, and intellectually of spoiling thousands of others. I claim the game is not worth the candle. It is unfair to say that we are keeping the "child genius" off the stage because he may have shown ability to take a small part in "The Blue Bird."

Furthermore, it is held, if we do not give the "child genius" the chance to grow and develop in the earliest period, we may lose it. I shall grant you that the person who does not have the opportunity of expressing himself freely and largely in early life is likely to come to his adult years awkward and self-conscious. But we have the playground, and the school, and the club, and the college, where there is an opportunity for the freest expression; and if they want to prevent the genius from shriveling up there is the opportunity.

And again, if early training is absolutely necessary why not establish schools for young children, where they may be taught and trained under the direction of competent teachers and in an environment suited to childhood and youth. It is ridiculous to claim that the theatrical training can only be secured on the professional stage! I shall agree with you that you need the audience in order to train the child. Well, get the audience. They do not have any trouble getting an audience at Hull-House; they do not have any trouble getting an audience at the Northwestern Settlement. So far as those arguments go, then, there need be no difficulty in developing the artist and we need not lose a single dramatic genius.

Now what are the objectionable things in early stage experience for children? I make no charge, be it understood, of immorality against the stage. The stage is neither better nor worse than the community out of which the actors come, and that statement is based on intimate knowledge of many actors and actresses. But on the other hand the atmosphere of the stage is affectation from beginning to end; the atmosphere of the stage is false, artistically false, if you will. There is a glamour and an attractiveness about it that is a bane for young minds; and my judgment is that constantly dealing in fictitious emotions before life habits are formed, is pernicious. I believe that acting should be undertaken only by those whose moral habits have been already formed, because the environment of the stage is not conducive in young people to the formation of good habits. Note, I say, in "young" people. We should keep the child off the stage because it deals with aspects of life with which he has no capacity to deal and on which he has no capacity to express any judgment.

They say that it is not necessary to keep the child off the stage in order to keep it away from bad environment, but that it is a positive godsend to give him a chance to go on the stage in order that he should develop in some way or other. My answer to that again is that we must not take the chance of losing one hundred children, for the sake of making one genius, because I believe that the genius somehow or other will make himself.

Nor is the precocious beginning of the actor's child any argument. The actor says, "My child has been on the stage all her life; you are separating her from her inheritance." Well, a great many of these children who have been on the stage from their fourth or fifth year—and I want to say it sub rosa—are not altogether the crowning glory of dramatic art. Some of them have made pretty good bookkeepers, and I know some that would have made expert ironers and others good floor-walkers. I shall never forget a letter in the *Dramatic Mirror,* edited by Harrison Gray Fiske, to a young lady who had written concerning an engagement to go on the stage, and this expert woman—I cannot think of her name—who knew the stage and stage-life as few people know it, said to the little girl, "Do not go on the stage unless you can't possibly keep off, until you have exhausted every test to prove that you are not better off elsewhere. It is far better to be a successful typewriter or bookkeeper or shop-keeper and have a few people say, 'What an actress you would have been!' than to have the world say of you as an actress, 'What a fine housekeeper she would have made!' "

Now let us consider the argument that if children are not allowed to take part, we shall be deprived of great plays. Let us consider that many plays which are produced today are not particularly worthy. The fact that they require children in certain parts does not necessarily mean that they are good plays. In fact children could gain nothing by appearing in them. I am willing to concede again that under our present law we must give up the pleasure of seeing the charming Piper and the glorious Blue Bird. But I would give up even more than that to keep young children off the stage of a thousand cheap theaters, and out of a hundred cheap plays where they would surely go if we put into effect the proposed amendment.

Further, our opponents, perhaps unconsciously, leave the impression that we shall be deprived of a great many plays unless children participate. Let us examine this claim. First, there are few plays of consequence in which young children from one to four could not be suggested by dolls carefully handled. Again, there are many actresses who could take the part of children from twelve or thirteen years of age. What then do we miss? Actors for parts between four and twelve. Well, what really great plays must we omit? I grant there are a few; but as I have said so many times, we must sacrifice them to keep the children out of cheap theaters, cheap plays, vaudeville houses and worse.

Ellen Terry began at six, and says, "If I had begun later I should not have acquired the place which I have in this work."

Miss Barrymore began at an early age and she says that her success is due to that. And there is other similar testimony. They say it is an injustice to the child who is clever, to the child who has some dramatic genius to keep him from the stage. Is it quite fair they claim to such a child to say you must not appear upon the stage? I repeat if it were absolutely certain that that child would be lost to us—some great actress perhaps to take great parts in the greatest plays and make them live before us—I might be willing if it were possible to open a little breach in this law; but as to those thousands of children I will take no chances on them in the presence of the false, affected, unreal atmosphere of the theater today.

Let us concede then we shall lose some good plays, some very good plays, by keeping our present law as it is; but it is a question of compensation, and I am convinced that to permit children to go on the stage under the conditions proposed in this amendment will be a bane and harm that can in no way be compensated for by the pleasure good plays would give an audience, by the encouragement the performances of such plays would be to authors, nor by the training the child would get in preparation for an acting career.

The benefit derived from going on the stage at an early age is the development of freedom and of unconsciousness. This can be obtained just as well in the school of dramatic art, in the public school, or under church auspices, or in the settlements, or in the playground, and so we shall be able to save the child genius for the stage—and incidentally save the ten thousand other children from the stage.

THE EFFECT OF IRREGULAR HOURS UPON THE CHILD'S HEALTH

F. S. CHURCHILL, M. D.
Attending Physician, Children's Memorial Hospital, Chicago

Much of the discussion in which such interest has been aroused, has to do purely with the effect upon the child's physical health, of working at abnormal, irregular and unusual hours and also of sleeping and resting at abnormal, irregular and unusual hours.

I want to speak very briefly of the effects of such a mode of life upon the physical health of the child. Now I take it that we are all agreed that there is nothing pertaining to our children so important as blooming good health. Good physical health is the foundation of all things for them. Then how are we going to preserve this abounding good health in our children?

Perhaps if we take the time to make a résumé of the child's life, we should see that regularity of hours is the most necessary thing in his daily life, and that regularity should apply to everything that the child does. He should eat regularly, he should play regularly, he should bathe regularly—very often perhaps—and he should above all things work regularly. He should go to bed at regular hours and get up at regular hours, and he should have a definite and regular way of sleeping—and plenty of sleep. So regularity in the child's life perhaps is the most important thing that we can insist upon in the guiding and bring up of our children.

But the advocates of this law who wish to put children on the stage may reply: "Oh! our children will work 'regularly'; they will be on the stage 'regularly' from eight to eleven, six nights in the week and perhaps seven nights in the week." Of course, that is regularity; we shall have to agree that that is one kind of regularity but it is not the kind of regularity which we like for our children. We should apply not only the principle of regularity but we should stick to natural hours in our regularity. For countless ages the young of all animals have naturally slept and rested at night. They have not been careering around cities and careering around the stage at night. The natural and logical thing for them to do is to get their rest and their sleep at night, and in the early hours of the night as much as in the late hours of the night.

This system of having our children live this regular life, especially as concerns hours of sleep, is not pure theory. Any physician who has practiced in a city as big as this one for a matter of twenty years, who has devoted most of his time to the study of children and infants, knows the effect upon their lives of regular hours, the effect of not being out late at night, not working at night. He sees in such children the bloom of health. But on the other hand when he goes into another part of the city and finds children who are working at night, what does he see? Going into their homes, he finds that these children are poorly nourished, that they are undersized, that they are weak and sickly. That is the condition of many of these children who are forced to do this sort of labor and to keep late, unseasonable hours, who are insufficiently nourished, who are living the terribly sad and pathetic life that so many of these youngsters have to lead. That is one effect then of the carrying out of a law such as these New York theater people wish to put on the Illinois statute books; that is the effect it would have upon large numbers of our children.

Moreover, those children who are working in that way during the night time are not nearly so keen either physically or intellectually as the other group of children who are sent to bed early and have properly regulated lives. They are very much like the nurse in a hospital. The superintendent of any training-school for nurses will tell you that while the nurses are on night duty, even though they may have the same amount of rest—and, of course, they do have the same number of hours of rest as when they are on day duty—they are not nearly so keen intellectually and they cannot do their work nearly so well, as when they are on day duty. They never can do their work so well because they are not physically and mentally in so good condition as when they are doing their work in the daytime. Of course with them night work is an absolute necessity, though fortunately only a temporary one. They have their night turns in short periods of time throughout the year. It is the same way with children forced to work at night, only still more so.

If in considering this question one could keep in mind constantly the question: Would I want this for my child? Would I allow my child to do this? Would I allow my baby boy, my little girl, to go on the stage or into the street to appear or to sell? If our representatives and senators would ask themselves this question, our laws would be better and we should not have to fight to get good child-labor laws or to keep them after we got them on our statute books.

PART SIX

THE LAW AND THE CHILD

"What shall repay for waste of life?
What shall repay for pain?
O what shall give the land its food
If the young wheat have no rain?"

THE JUVENILE COURT

MERRITT W. PINCKNEY
Judge of the Juvenile Court of Cook County, Illinois

The first decade of the twentieth century should be known in American history as the children's era. Since July 1, 1899, when Illinois made the first great contribution to the welfare of children, the progress of events has been steady and pronounced. Chicago, from which came the impulse that culminated in the enactment of the Juvenile Law of Illinois and the establishment of the Juvenile Court, has reason to be proud of her handiwork.

From the enactment of the Juvenile Law to the present time is a little over a decade, and yet in that short space of time the Juvenile Court has become a distinct, a permanent institution, which, under the law as amended in 1907, has changed the practice of centuries, has made the citizens of Chicago acquainted with her boys and girls of tender years, and has brought her to a realization of her shortcomings and her future opportunities in the care, education, training, and control of her children.

Prior to July 1, 1899, little if anything had been done by any state in the Union toward improving the condition of the delinquent children of the state, as distinguished from the dependent children. Illinois was the first to awake to a realization that a great wrong was being done these children. Credit must be given to some good women of Chicago for starting the crusade. From the time of mother Eve down to the present day, there have been thrust upon women many burdens which the men have shirked, and of these, the care, education, training, and control of the children are neither the lightest nor the least important. The men of Chicago, our business and professional men, had not the time, were too busy to give their attention to the child problem, and so it fell to the lot of the women of our city to discover the direful conditions existing on the criminal side of our child life in Chicago; to awaken the public conscience to the almost inhuman treatment, under sanction of the law, of our boys and girls of tender years; and in the name of humanity and justice to bring about a reform.

I desire to emphasize the fact that in so far as the Juvenile Court has to do with dependent children there is nothing fundamentally new about it, and that the only underlying new thought which has come to our jurisprudence through the Juvenile Law and the Juvenile Court is in the care, training, custody, and control of the delinquent children of the state, as distinguished from the dependent children. There are, however, in the Juvenile Court several important and distinctive features, such as the machinery, or working force, the pleading and the practice, and the simplicity of the trial, distinguishing it from the other courts of record.

First, a few words are to be said in regard to the working force of the Juvenile Court. In addition to the usual bailiff and clerk that you find in every court of record, we have over in the Juvenile Court, sixty-three other officers called probation officers. Of that number some thirty are city policemen, who travel the districts to which they are assigned in citizen's clothes and are paid by the city of Chicago. Of the remaining thirty-three, all but three are women, in the pay of the county of Cook and under civil service.

In the talks that I have given to various organizations in the city of Chicago, I have frequently said that it has never been my good fortune to meet a more earnest, capable and industrious group of men and women than the probation officers of the Juvenile Court. With no guile nor attempt at flattery, I say now that without the help of that magnificent body of men and women under the efficient and capable leadership of Mr. John Witter, the Juvenile Court could not do the successful and effective work that it is credited with doing, that whatever of credit, whatever of honor has come to that court must be shared with the probation force of the Juvenile Court. And if perchance any criticism should be incurred, they will have to help bear the blame. It is the duty of the probation department of the Juvenile Court to furnish to the judge the history of the child, of the parents, of the environment, indeed all the facts upon which the judge of the Juvenile Court determines the entry of the order of parole or commitment, as the case may be. Therefore it will be readily understood that if these facts are incomplete, hastily gathered, founded on hearsay or biased by the undisclosed prejudice of witnesses, the order of the court must necessarily fail to meet the needs of the case. Nor does their work end with the entry of the order. With the boy on parole their work has only just begun. Here their vigilance must be redoubled; for this is the turning point in the life of the boy. A helping hand is needed now, more than ever before, to keep the lad in the straight path. My observation teaches me that when men and women, boys and girls, are on the downhill road, everything in life seems to be greased for the occasion. It is so easy to slide, so hard to climb. Whether the boy on parole climbs or not depends more upon the work of the probation officer than upon the judge. The court only stops the descent, points out the chasm just ahead, faces the lad in the right direction, bids him walk in the sunlight and not in the shadow, and then turns him over to the probation officer, who by conscientious thought and labor, carries on the good work and saves the child. Again I say the ultimate success of the work for the children on parole depends chiefly on the probation officers of the Juvenile Court.

Just a word on the pleading and the practice of the court. So far as the child or children, the father, mother, guardian or custodian is concerned, no formal pleadings are required. Any reputable citizen can file a petition in that court, containing the facts required by the statute to give the court jurisdiction. If the defendants are residents, then a summons is issued, and service is had under the rules of our chancery practice. If the defendants are non-residents, jurisdiction is obtained for the purpose of commitment by publication notice, as provided by our statute. So that, so far as the pleadings are concerned, without cost, without expense, any reputable citizen can obtain relief in that court either for one child or for all the children of any one family.

The simplicity of the hearing or trial is attractive to all those who are familiar with the technicalities that hedge about the trials of common law cases in our courts of record. In the Juvenile Court, all technicality, all formality, and indeed most of the dignity of the court is sacrificed in order to get at the facts, the truth. It may take more than one hearing to accomplish this, but in the end the truth is revealed. This cannot always be said about the other courts of record. We strive in the other courts to obtain this same result, but I sometimes feel that we signally fail.

I recall asking the attorney in the Circuit Court in the trial of a common law case about a year ago, whether he thought his action in the case at bar

EVOLUTION OF DETENTION HOME

Who is the Criminal – the State or Child?
A law prohibits the confinement of minors and adults in same quarters.
Revised Statutes 1845.

Boy offenders and adult criminals in common pen at jail. Expert criminals tell alluring tales to youthful ears. Detained for months awaiting trial.

Conditions in Cook County Jail prior to enactment of Juvenile Court Law July 1, 1899

1705 Boys in Cook County jail for 3 years ending July 1st 1899.
During first two years Juvenile Court Law was in force – 24.

Conditions to day in many County jails

MADISON COUNTY

Massac County

Williams County

Jackson County

Dawn of the New Way

Cook County Jail school. Time – 1895. Occupation and training take place of idleness and harmful association.

was fair and just to the parties litigant. "It may not be justice," he replied, "but it is the law." I told him that in whatever I could control, justice and the law stood for the same thing. In the other courts we try to bring about this result, but with a jury to deal with, with the technicalities of the common law to hamper and bind us, we often do not attain the result that I feel we always attain in the Juvenile Court.

In the same building where the Juvenile Court is located we have a detention home, and in that home we have several young women who are devoting their lives to children. If ever I am at loss to know whether a child is telling the truth, I continue the case, send the lad or the lass upstairs, and get one of our school teachers to turn the powers of her mind upon that particular child; and she seldom fails to get a good result. You see even over there I have the assistance of women in the trial of cases, and that is another reason why we are so successful.

In the three years that I have been working in the Juvenile Court, I think it is safe to say that there have been before the court, before me personally, at least ten thousand children. In passing upon these cases, I naturally have come to form impressions as to the work done and to be done; have come to recognize to a certain extent the causes which lead to the dependency and delinquency of these children and to realize the limitations of the law and the limitations of the court, if you please, under the law, in taking care of these children, especially the delinquent children.

To my mind, society and the state of Illinois have never been quite fair in the treatment of the delinquent children of the state, as distinguished from the dependent children of the state. I find this especially true, as I have often said, in regard to the semi-delinquent boys and girls who come before me in the Juvenile Court—the so-called semi-delinquent boys and girls. My observation has taught me that many good men and women in this community interested in social betterment and in child-saving turn away from the delinquent boy and girl while they readily open their arms and their purses for the dependent child. The work of the Juvenile Court is hampered today by this sentiment. The needs of the semi-delinquent boy standing midway between the boy on parole and the boy at St. Charles or the John Worthy School are not met. We have no place for this lad. This is also equally true of the semi-delinquent girl. This child, delinquent for the first time mayhap, is given the same treatment as are habitual offenders and is mingled with them. In the name of justice should we not as good citizens provide for these unfortunate children a way station midway between the girl at home and the girl in Geneva or the Chicago Refuge? Surely we must, if we would do our duty by them, if we would make it easier and not harder for them to return to a moral and upright life.

The state provides two institutions for delinquent children and society provides in Chicago and the county of Cook three more, so that we have in all five institutions where delinquent boys and girls can be taken care of, while thirteen associations, societies and institutions stand ready to care for Chicago's dependent children. Of these five institutions for delinquent children, the capacity of three is wholly inadequate. So I repeat, the delinquent child is not as fairly treated or as well provided for as the dependent child.

Let us go a little further with regard to the delinquent child. I have spoken of the semi-delinquent.

Let us take the habitually delinquent child, the girl. In 1910, in one year, there came to the Juvenile Court of Chicago, while I was there, over 4,100 children. Over 2,500 of this number were delinquent. After eliminating the delinquent cases that were continued or dismissed for some good reason, there remained 1,161 delinquent boys and 475 delinquent girls to be provided for, to be cared for. What became of them? I shall not discuss the boys because I want to call your attention especially to the girls. Of the 475 girls, habitually delinquent, needing institutional and custodial care, 131 being Catholics went to the House of the Good Shepherd; 77 Protestant girls went to the Chicago Refuge in this city. How many, then, do you think the state of Illinois provided for, out of the 475 girls? It cared for 35 girls out of 475. The great commonwealth of Illinois took care of 35 girls sent from the Juvenile Court, while there were 232 delinquent girls needing the institutional care, knocking at the doors of that institution with the doors closed against them—asking the state for help with no help given.

What is the Juvenile Court to do under such conditions? The only thing that I could do was to send those 232 girls back to the same old environment, back to the same bad associates, to travel the downward path to ruin, many of them eventually ending their careers in the red-light district, dragging with them innocent girls and boys with whom they associate. And yet, notwithstanding this attitude of the state of Illinois, which seemed to me almost criminal, because every one of those children was a violator of the state law and therefore should have been taken care of by the state, I could not get the state board of administration even to reply to a letter I wrote them six months ago;

not even a reply from this great, magnificent commonwealth of Illinois. The state of Illinois under its administration, past and present, takes better care of the rabbits than it does of the delinquent girls of Illinois. You can go to the legislature at Springfield and talk your head off and you get no attention; and these girls are allowed to gravitate to their ruin. That is another reason why I say that the state and society have never been fair in their treatment of the delinquent children of the state.

I shall say just a word here concerning the care provided for the dependent child; it is also entirely inadequate. Poverty, poverty alone should never be a sufficient cause for separating parent and child. And yet under the limitations of the Juvenile Law there is no provision made for the care of a child, whose father is dead and whose mother is too poor to keep him at home. The only financial aid given for such children is when they receive institutional care. The child or children are kept at home with their mother, and no aid is furnished. It has been my effort, during the three years that I have been in the Juvenile Court, to preserve the home intact, to keep the family circle unbroken; and, when that is impossible owing to the death of the mother or to her conceded unfitness, to substitute another family circle with the motherly love of another good woman. To my mind there is no love like a mother's love, and next to that, comes the individual care and affection of some good woman. Fortunate, indeed, are children so placed although necessarily dependent upon the charity of strangers, since under the Industrial School Acts no provision is made for the payment of any money to that motherly woman who takes care of such dependent children. An amount of money equal to that paid for institutional care would take care of those children with the mother at home, or with another womanly woman in a private family, not only helping the children, but helping the families of good, honest American citizens who have love enough in their hearts to take care of homeless waifs. I do not say this to belittle the great and good work done by the institutions of our city and of our county. There are many of these institutions and they are all doing great and good work, and the aid which they receive from the state or county has been too little for the work that they have done. But what I do mean to say is this: that the plan of providing a home for the child with the mother or with a motherly woman is better than the plan of providing institutional care for that child, however excellent such care may be. And I will say further that when a child is kept at home with the mother, the state of Illinois ought to give the same financial assistance for the support and maintenance of the child that it does when the child is sent to an institution.

However, a bill remedying this defect has passed the Senate at Springfield. I hope that, notwithstanding the confusion at Springfield, the House will not fail to pass that bill. The speaker of the House and influential members of that body have been written to and urged to put that bill through and send it to the governor for signature. If it does go through, then we shall be able to keep the mother and the child together, instead of separating them. Then, to my mind, the Juvenile Court will be accomplishing one great thing that it now, under the limitations of the law, is unable to accomplish.

In studying the influences that lead to the delinquency and the dependency of the child, especially to the delinquency, I have been impressed with one thought that I want to submit for your consideration. It seems to me that there has been a falling off of parental authority. I do not refer to the modern method of many parents of sparing the rod and the bed slat, but what I refer to is the total want of obedience, respect, and reverence on the part of these delinquent children for their fathers and mothers. It may be that I am too sensitive on this subject. The recollections of my own childhood are always with me. Obedience, respect, and reverence for father and mother grew among the children of our family as we grew from babyhood to girlhood and boyhood, permeating our whole beings. I say there is a falling off, a decay in that respect, as regards many of our children. It is said that Diogenes struck the father when the son swore. I have often wondered what that ancient philosopher would say and do if he were living today and in the Juvenile Court. I am sure that he would be kept very busy, although I am not certain as to the language he would use. I want to give renewed emphasis to this one thought, the falling off of reverence and respect on the part of children for their parents. In my opinion, parental neglect and incompetency are causes that lead to the delinquency of at least 70 per cent of Chicago's delinquent children.

Before closing, I want to say a word in behalf of the delinquent children. These children are most of them sick; they need a doctor. I do not mean by that that they need medicine to be taken internally, but I mean to say that they are not healthy. Some of them are mentally weak though physically strong; others physically weak though mentally well. Then again, we have some physically strong and mentally well but morally and spiritually deformed. That is what I mean by saying that they need a doctor.

There is one fact which may not be generally known about the Juvenile Court. In addition to the services of Dr. Britton, who looks after the physical condition of the child, we have over there a noted neurologist, psychologist and physician, Dr. Healy. He is at the head of the psychopathic institute, which public-spirited citizens were good enough to provide for the Juvenile Court. For two years he has given to the study of the psychological side of the children of Chicago his entire thought and attention. He told me the other day that he had made a careful scientific research into the mental and physical characteristics of some 620 habitually delinquent children. He has studied carefully the history of the child, of the parents of the child, and often of the grandparents. He has studied the environment. He has left nothing undone that will enable him to get at the causes of the child's physical, mental and moral attitude or condition. He tells me that of the children he has examined 7 per cent are epileptic and that probably not more than 25 per cent are normal.

Now, in all charity to these unfortunate children, ought we not to be very good to them? Ought we not to use every effort to see that they get a doctor and the right kind of doctor and the right kind of care?

In the Juvenile Court we are fighting these conditions that lead to the delinquency of our children and we are making headway slowly. We are lightening the burdens of many, we are accomplishing I believe some good. We are optimistic over there, for the man and woman who is not optimistic will never last long in the juvenile work. We do not expect the millennium next month, next year, possibly not in the next generation, but sooner or later the people of this and all communities throughout the state and the nation will rise en masse and wipe out these miserable conditions that speak for the downfall of our children, of our boys and our girls of today, the men and women of tomorrow. They will unfurl the standard which will stand for the purity of our daughters and the sanctity of our homes.

The final word I have to say on this subject is to urge the need of studying and eradicating the influences that lead to the dependency and delinquency of our children. In this study, preventive and curative work must go hand in hand, with stress laid upon the preventive work.

We have a plan here in Chicago for a "City Beautiful"—broad boulevards east and west, a new civic center, artistic and unique; public and private buildings, imposing and ornate, and a harbor rivaling the haven of the mariner's dream. But to me, higher and above all this material and artistic perfection is the plan that will give to the city of Chicago a purer body politic and a better citizenship; and the culmination and success of this plan depends—bear it in mind—upon the rearing of happy, healthy and moral children.

On one of the screens in the exhibit across the way is this sentiment: "The city that takes the best care of its children will be the best city, the greatest city." I say yea and amen, not only the best and the greatest city, but, above all and beyond all, the "City Beautiful."

THE MUNICIPAL COURT AND THE CHILD

HARRY OLSON
Judge of the Municipal Court of Chicago

The city of Chicago has made another departure besides the Juvenile Court. It abolished its abominable justice of the peace system a few years ago and established in its place a new court different from other courts in the land, known least of all at home. I suppose our own people know less about the court and what it does, than people outside. The court has larger powers than those usually given to courts; that is the judges have the power of a board of directors of a corporation to manage its business. The executive officer has large powers in making the calendars, in assigning those calendars to different judges, and in assigning judges in the court. And in view of those powers the court is able without legislation to do many things which in other states require legislation. For example, in the state of New York, it was necessary to go to the legislature to establish in New York City a court of domestic relations, which has a very limited jurisdiction and which is therefore not very useful. But in Chicago with the larger jurisdiction of the Municipal Court, we were able without legislation to create by a court order a court of domestic relations, which, as the name implies, concerns matters affecting the husband and the wife, and principally cases growing out of the circumstances likely to give rise to delinquency in children. While the Juvenile Court looks after the delinquent child, the Domestic Relations Court looks after the people who make the child delinquent. We think it is a departure that is significant. More than that, when the courts were scattered about in different parts of the city, these cases were handled in an indifferent way, occasionally by the police and occasionally by the courts. By creating one central court where all the cases of that nature affecting the women and children come, it is possible to get uniform action in those cases. Among other matters on the same line, the court has interested itself in an adult probation law. It sought to get power from the legislature to permit first offenders for certain minor offenses to go, pending good behavior.

The science or the psychology of youth has not been very well understood. Professor G. Stanley Hall's work on "Adolescence," written not over seven or eight years ago, was the first comprehensive treatment of the psychology of youth. We had known of course that the criminal statistics showed that nearly 75 per cent of the offenders under the law, those that were called criminals, were adolescent; they were under twenty-two years of age. That of itself was a startling thing, and when we became familiar with Dr. Hall's work, we saw that this as a period in life where the individual needs all the safeguards that can be thrown around him; that the growing-age is one in which it is easy to get into trouble so that very good boys and girls who in after life become magnificent men and women, do some things that bring them within the strictures of the law and are called crime. The result of the wider recognition of those facts was that an effort was made to pass an adult probation law. We have been working on it through many discouragements until this year, when the legislature in both houses passed the Adult Probation Bill that now awaits the signature of the governor.

The judges of the Municipal Court drafted the bill. The judges of that court also had something to do with the establishment of the Juvenile Court, as members of the legislature. Judge Newcomer introduced the Juvenile Court Bill, and Judge Goodnow and Judge Beitler were members of the legislature and of the Juvenile Court Committee and worked for its passage.

THE CHICAGO COURT OF DOMESTIC RELATIONS

CHARLES N. GOODNOW
Judge of the Chicago Court of Domestic Relations

It has often been said that there is nothing new in the world; that each new invention is only the application of a new idea to an old principle. That may be true in some respects; still, we who are engaged in the everyday affairs of life know that business methods are changing, new ideas are being introduced, and, consequently, new changes are being made. The science of the law, perhaps, is the last business to change, because the law is hedged about with constitutions, statutes, and so forth, and is circumscribed by decisions that are blindly followed from year to year. But the law at last and finally has to make changes in the modus operandi, or method of handling litigation that comes before it.

The courts of this country were divided first into chancery, or equity courts, and common law courts. But in the large cities, where there was a large volume of business, it was soon found that it would be necessary to specialize and to make subdivisions to deal with certain phases of litigation. And now the city of Chicago has the Circuit and Superior Courts with both common law and chancery jurisdiction, the County Court, the Probate Court, the Criminal Court, the Juvenile Court, and the Municipal Court.

The Municipal Court, like the individual who finds it necessary to specialize along some line, has specialized in various branches of the law. Under the Municipal Court Act, one of the powers of the chief justice is to prepare calendars and classify the cases. The result is that there is in the Municipal

Court the classification of judges into certain branches. The latest branch of the Municipal Court to be created is the Court of Domestic Relations.

In the large majority of cases of delinquency in children, and in every case of dependency, there is some adult responsible for that delinquency or dependency. The Juvenile Court of this state was organized upon the theory of taking care of the delinquent and dependent children, and that was the first step towards specializing a court to deal with a certain condition. The Juvenile Court, however, reaches the child only after he has become a delinquent or a dependent, but the creation of the Court of Domestic Relations is the most important step in specialization of courts, because instead of reaching the effect—which is the child after he has become a dependent or a delinquent—it seeks to reach the cause which makes that child a dependent or delinquent; it seeks to decrease the number of children going through the Juvenile Court every year.

The activities of this court are not restricted alone to reaching adults who cause delinquencies or dependencies of children, but reach all those who commit an offense or a crime against a woman or a child, in which the municipal court has final jurisdiction. It covers a large classification of cases, for instance: The sale of cigarettes and tobaccos to minors; the sale of intoxicating liquor to minors; gambling by minors in saloons, and violations of other city ordinances affecting the child; abandonment of wife or child; contributing to the dependency or delinquency of children; cases of illegitimate children; violation of all laws relating to child labor; violations of all laws relating to compulsory education and truancy; and, in fact, all state laws dealing with women and children exclusively.

A little statistical history of conditions will show why the judges of the Municipal Court of Chicago decided to create this new court. As a rule, courts are not given to going outside of the plain beaten path as laid down by precedents. The court has seldom gone beyond the cold facts and strict application of the law to those facts. But modern thought and the advance in the study of criminology, the reasoning of effect back to cause, has demonstrated that in dealing with these social problems we have heretofore dealt only with effects and not paid enough attention to the cause.

In all delinquencies of children, in all dependencies of children, in all desertions of wife or child, in all betrayals of girls, it must be recognized that these are only the innocent victims—the effect—and for every delinquency, for every dependency, for every desertion, for every betrayal, there must be some cause. It is to reach this cause, to dig down deep into the conditions and environments surrounding each case, to find out the reasons and suggest a remedy, that this court is organized. The humanitarian side of the law is here exhibited in its bright light.

The close analytical study and figuring that is necessary to solve these riddles of modern society can be appreciated as well as the great effort necessary to get at the real foundations of these sins of society, so called, and build up a new method wherein the errors of weak men and women might not only be rectified, but eliminated—for in this elimination the greatest results are accomplished.

The organization of the Municipal Court of Chicago was the opening of a new era in court proceedings; old methods were put aside, new and progressive ideas were placed in operation, and this court, instead of traveling in the old ruts, cut a new path in the method of handling crime; prosecution followed swiftly upon the commission of an offense; to offend against the law meant to start at once towards the jail or house of correction. There were no more delays until facts were forgotten or witnesses had died, moved away or been tampered with. Its effect was to decrease crime in a marked degree. This was true, however, only in certain classes of crime; in others it apparently increased it. By that I do not mean that there was more crime of that class, but that the new method of handling those cases caused more of those who heretofore suffered in silence to bring their troubles to the attention of the court that gave them instantaneous relief.

This fact is borne out by the following figures: The records of the Criminal Court for the three years immediately preceding the organization of the Municipal Court show an average of 313 abandonment and 98 bastardy cases docketed each year. In the Municipal Court during the past year, 1910, 1,548 abandonment of wife and child, 540 bastardy and 634 contributing to the dependency or delinquency of children, were disposed of. The large volume of this kind of cases caused the chief justice to inquire as to the cause: and in that court to meet a problem is to work out its solution.

Thus this court was organized to solve these vexing questions. It is a court that deals with the family, that considers the family the unit around which all that is good for the nation must be built. It stands as a friend of the man or woman in trouble; a counsellor in time of need; a protector to the delinquent or homeless child; a doctor to the young girl who has been unwittingly wronged; a mentor for both husband and wife when their misunderstandings have reached the breaking point. You ask why?

There are many reasons why, but one in particular. For the sake of the child; for there are children concerned—vitally concerned—in the majority of cases which come within the jurisdiction of this new court; little, helpless, innocent infants who otherwise are doomed to suffer for the indiscretions of their parents and to go through life with an overwhelming handicap for which they are in no way responsible.

The future business men and women, the coming workers and breadwinners, finally the fathers and mothers of tomorrow, are the principal objects of our consideration, although we sometimes reach them only in an indirect way. Is it worth striving for? Do the care and protection of the child mean the care and protection of the race? Do we believe that the home is the unit of society, and that all must be well in the home before we can say, all's well with society?

It is a fairly well established fact that our courts deal too much with cold facts and administer the law with a view more to punish than to prevent. There is little time to study conditions or environments. There is small chance to learn the causes, especially if those causes have led to troubles in the family, between the father and mother.

It was with the idea of getting away from this condition in the courts that the branch, Domestic Relations, was established. This branch seeks to wipe away the clouds of doubt, jealousy and misunderstanding by teaching the individuals their reciprocal rights and privileges; by defining to them their legal and moral duties to one another and to the public; by inspiring in them the desire to meet those duties like real men and women; by inducing them cheerfully to assume the burdens falling to their lot and to strive for their children's sake once more to make home what it should be—a haven of rest, peace, comfort and happiness.

Another important reason for this court's organization was found in the theory upon which the Juvenile Court was founded: that of removing the child from the evil influences and environments of the police courts. The failure, however, in the Juvenile Court was that, while the child was removed from this contaminating influence by being taken to the Juvenile Court when he became the offender, he was still forced to go to the Criminal or Police Court, as a witness, when a crime or an offense was committed against him. By the organization of this court we have succeeded in meeting almost completely the object sought.

This new court not only removes the child from this influence, but serves equally well in protecting women from the same evil influences. For many years little was thought of this influence upon women and children by being brought into contact with the motley crowd of law-breakers—the usual adjunct of any police court. So women and children were forced against their wishes to mingle with robbers, thieves, pickpockets, drunkards, lewd women and foul-mouthed men, their misery made twofold by this degrading environment thrust upon them before their wants were known and their needs looked after. It was a humiliation and an indignity which every self-respecting woman would resent if she only could, and a position in which no child should be placed.

In many of these cases the persons arrested or summoned into court are not hardened criminals. It is often their first offense, in many instances arising from misunderstandings and ignorance. Even these people, being brought into personal contact with this usual Criminal Court crowd, felt humiliated and degraded, and their moral conception at least was contaminated and changed in many respects; and instead of bettering them, instead of being able to reach their inner conscience and arouse their better nature, instead of being able to advise and suggest a remedy to correct the evil complained of, the court maddened and embittered them by this humiliating experience so that the end sought was harder to reach.

Many of these cases, before justice can be done, require a most thorough investigation. Many are based upon trivial complaints regarded as mountains by those connected with them, but in reality only mole hills of misunderstanding. All these require careful attention, investigation, and advice, and in many instances they are amicably adjusted by the parties themselves out of court. Under the past arrangement, owing to the large volume of business thrown upon the criminal branches, it was found practically impossible to give to each individual case the time necessary to determine what really should be done. Heretofore it was only one of a large number passing daily in review before the judges, who, while giving it as much attention as was possible, still recognized that they were falling short in accomplishing desired results. Hence the concentration of all cases of this kind in one central court, whose duty it is to give each individual case all the time which that case requires to effect results, to preserve the home, to bring the parties to a better understanding of their own duties, rights and privileges.

These troubles vary in their character, and the extent to which they have gone determines the amount of patient work that must be given each case to readjust the domestic machinery. They grow out of many trivial causes. These usually arise from ignorance and a misconception of the marital relations. The most frequent causes are drunkenness, laziness and their results; poverty, early marriages, and dissatisfaction with conditions and surroundings, too much interference by near relatives or meddling friends, a scolding tongue, ill health, immorality and often pure cussedness, form the basis of friction and frequently of desertion and delinquency and ultimately of dependency.

Why do these things exist? What mental and moral teaching has been lacking in the early training of these offenders? I should answer: In youth we are not taught the power of self-restraint; in youth we are not taught to discipline the passions and desires of our mental and physical make-up to follow out that God-given precept: "Do unto others as you would they should do unto you;" selfishness, envy, jealousy, hatred, cupidity and greed become the dominant characteristics of our minds; so few mothers and fathers ever become confidential enough with their daughters and sons to teach them the true object of their existence on earth; so many young men and young women are never taught to know or understand the seriousness of the marriage vow; they enter into that state with the idea that life forever after will be one long day of joy and bliss, until stern reality, adversity or sickness dispels the glamour.

To my mind the wonder is that there are not more cases of this kind in our courts, when one considers that for each delinquent or dependent child there is some adult offender, some adult guilty of and responsible for that child's condition. The logic of reasoning from cause to effect, and from effect back to cause, applies in crime as well as in any other phase of life; and when one considers that the records of the Juvenile Court show that between three thousand and four thousand children pass through the Juvenile Court of the city each year, and that about eleven thousand other young persons between the ages of sixteen and twenty years pass through the other courts each year, all these succeeded the following year by another fifteen thousand children, inheriting the same tendencies, exposed to the same temptations, surrounded by the same careless, neglectful and even criminal environments, often physically and mentally enfeebled as the result of neglect, carelessness and ignorance of parents, and with vicious and evil home conditions, is it to be wondered that the Court of Domestic Relations is working overtime? And are not these facts in themselves sufficient cause for its organization?

Is it not about time that more attention should be paid to the cause of all this trouble, and the effect should be eliminated by reaching the cause?

Would it not be better, if we are concerned in the welfare of the children, the future men and women of this country, to reach out and with a firm grip check the cause? Would it not be better to use formative rather than reformative measures?

It is an old saying that "as the twig is bent so will the tree incline," and this is true of human beings; as the child is taught, so will the man teach. The condition in a man's home is sure to reflect some phase of his own early training; that early training is in the hands of his parents and teachers, as they are alive to all his wants and needs, as they meet their responsibility and perform their full duty intelligently and faithfully, so will he in after life follow their teachings and reap his full measure of happiness. But so long as they fail to understand him, so long as they neglect the duty imposed upon them, so long as they fail to teach that power of self-restraint—so long will he bring unhappiness to himself and sorrow to others.

During 1910 some 4,100 children were brought into the Juvenile Court, of whom 1,161 boys and 475 girls were delinquent. And yet in Cook County in 1910 only 640 adults were prosecuted for causing the delinquency or dependency of children. What became of the others? There is something radically wrong in the make-up of our law or in its enforcement, when only 640 adults were tried in our police courts; for the large majority of cases of delinquency in children can be traced primarily to the door of the parents or the party who has the child under his care and control.

During the first month of the Court of Domestic Relations—the first twenty-one or twenty-two days—over 450 people were interviewed; in 219 cases warrants were issued. The rest of the cases, however, were referred in various ways to different institutions for investigation; some eighteen cases of destitution, to the United Charities; non-support cases to the County Court; cases where prosecutions for felony should be had, to the State's Attorney; some cases in which lost persons had to be traced, to the Detective Bureau; and some seventy-eight cases were referred to the Juvenile Protective Association. Since the court has been open, it has been one continual stream of misery, you might say, from the people coming in.

The Court of Domestic Relations, in my opinion, will be successful along the lines that have been mapped out for it, and to the extent of the cases which we are handling. But if we expect to have the success, the general, broad success that will take in everything touching the home, it simply means that instead of making a record for the boy as a juvenile delinquent, we must bring the case against the adult offender who causes the delinquency. Start the case against the cause that is making the boy a criminal. Go out and reach the causes of the delinquency. When the parents of this community know that if they permit their children to become delinquent or dependent they themselves are going to be dealt with, that the punishment is going to reach them, there will not be half so much dependency or half so much delinquency as there is today.

My dream for the future is that the Juvenile Court cases, the Court of Domestic Relations cases, the poor people's support cases, in fact every character of case that deals with the home will all be in one court under one jurisdiction; at the same time no record will be made of the child, but the record will be made against the adult. I am one of those who believe that no boy, the ward of the state, should have a record made against him in any court; that he should be dealt with in a different way. I do not believe in giving the boy a past. What he wants is a future; and the brighter the future he can be given, the better.

THE PRESENTATION OF THE CASE

ROGER N. BALDWIN
Civic League of St. Louis

I want to say a few elementary things and to picture the situation as it exists today in the juvenile courts of the United States as a whole, particularly in regard to presenting a case in court, coupled with the preliminary investigation which is so important a part of the presentation of the case in court.

If there is one thing in the whole Juvenile Court system that is the least satisfactory, it is, perhaps, the usual inadequacy of the information on which the judge bases his decisions. That is true in practically every city of the United States. The situation in the smaller cities of Illinois and the counties away from the larger cities is quite as bad as anywhere in the country. Certainly it is, in that portion of Illinois which is close to St. Louis.

The reason that social investigations by the Juvenile Court have been so poor when in the same states there have been excellent investigations by charitable associations, is found in two or three facts. First, because in many communities the judge, who is the arbiter of all investigations, is not trained to know a good investigation from a bad one. He is inclined to look at the offense rather than at the offender; at the facts of the offense rather than at the life and the surroundings of the child, and to make his decisions accordingly.

Then, second, while charitable organizations are able to make an investigation covering perhaps a week, two weeks, or even longer, becoming intimately acquainted with the facts, the Juvenile Court must have the case heard within two or three days, or a week at the outside. The officers must get the most conspicuous facts quickly and bring them to the court's attention. And furthermore—and it seems a very peculiar thing—the relation between the workers in the charitable organizations and the social workers in the juvenile court, is not nearly so close or intimate as might well be expected from the similarity of their work. Charitable organization methods, therefore, have not been transplanted into the field of the Juvenile Court, except in rare instances. In Juvenile Court work, we have no precedents to follow; no standards in thorough and efficient investigation.

To that end the National Probation Officers' Association about a year ago appointed a special committee composed of some of the best-known people in Juvenile Court work from all over the country, and that committee is now engaged in getting up a two or three hundred page report on every phase of Juvenile Court work, describing the conditions in the different states in the country and the general results of the experience of the last ten years. It is going to be a sort of cook-book for probation officers, who may turn to any particular subject and get their recipe.

Every investigation made by probation officers, or by other social workers, among delinquent and neglected children, is either a preliminary investigation before court hearing, or what may be called a supplementary investigation, dealing with the facts necessary, for instance, for releasing a child from an institution or changing the custody of a child from one foster-home to another. Every one of the Juvenile Court investigations fall under those two groups.

Delinquent children are investigated chiefly by our police officers, truant officers of the public schools, or by the probation officers, and, in some cases, by representatives of children's societies. In the case of neglected children the probation officers and children's societies do a great deal more of the investigating than the police and attendance officers.

Therefore at once is presented the problem of a multiplicity of investigating agents. For the presentation of a case in court you may have Mr. Police Officer, Mr. Probation Officer, maybe one or two representatives of societies, all coming in and laying their facts before the court. There is also often the prosecuting witness. The judge is put in the trying position of depending on these diverse sources for information, and he must judge of the efficiency of each one of these departments in their investigations. I think it is readily seen that these first investigations are far and away the most important part of the presentation of a case in court.

To face that chaotic situation leads one naturally to the conclusion that with so many different agencies presenting the cases in court, standardization is needed, one responsible agent is needed, who shall pass upon every investigation brought to the court. That agent naturally should be the probation officer of the court. If the case has had careful investigation by an assistant probation officer, the chief probation officer should review it before it is presented to the court. If the truant officer, or any other agent, brings a case into court, as he does in all our juvenile courts, it should be the policy of the judge to require the probation officer to review every one of the cases so brought. If not, the various children brought before the court will not get the benefit of equally efficient treatment. It is impossible to get uniform efficiency from our various agencies, without some central supervision. Therefore I think the conclusion would be that whoever makes the investigation for the court and whoever presents the case in court, the methods of getting the facts which comprise the investigation should be supervised by the chief probation officer.

The investigation preliminary to the presentation of the case in court involves two very distinct factors. It involves securing the facts regarding the cause of complaint—that is, the offense in the case of the delinquent child, or the situation at home in the case of the neglected child—and then securing the facts regarding his life and his home. We are obliged to separate the causes of the appearance of the child in court more or less from the social factors behind the situation. A great many judges will simply look at the offense, examine its details and discount the social factors. It is not in just a few instances that the judge so makes his decisions, but in a great many more than one would believe, and this is due in part to the indefiniteness and irregularity of the social investigations. Not nearly enough attention has been given the character of the social investigation. There should be a very thorough investigation of the child's life, as it has everything to do with the case. Even the most trivial facts may contribute to the delinquency of the child and necessarily have a bearing upon the child's future life, because very often it may be possible to bring about a child's reclamation by using the "leads" furnished by insignificant details.

Now, I want to say just a word about the necessity of making as direct and personal an investigation as possible regarding the offense and the offender in every case which is brought before the court. There are some who say that it is wrong to talk to the child about his offense and his life before he comes into court; that the constitutional guarantee to the defendant that he shall not be required to incriminate himself prohibits the probation officer from inquiring of a child as to his offense, and as to the social factors of his life. The questioning of a child is actually prohibited on that ground in some juvenile courts today.

The natural result of this, of course, is that when the child comes to the court his case is presented as in a regular criminal trial. The judge hears the stories of the witnesses, the prosecuting witness, and the police officers, and finally, after them always, comes along the youngster and his father and mother. They are naturally on the defensive, for it is to their interest to dispute as much of the evidence as they can. They think the prosecuting officers and the court are trying to "get something on them," a perfectly natural feeling under that method. They could not be persuaded that those things are done for the protection of the child.

Now, in many other courts before the cases come up for a hearing, the judge requires that the probation officer should actually see the child before anyone else does, and get from him his own story of the offense and of his life at home. In addition, he should visit the home and get the facts direct from the father or mother or both. In as many cases as possible father, as well as mother, should be interviewed, as a very large proportion of the trouble is in the home, and it is necessary to get all the facts possible from there. If the investigation has thoroughly covered the child and his home from direct examination, and the facts are fairly presented in court by the probation officer, then that investigation is going to be worth something.

Moreover, it is essential under this method that the judge should hear the testimony first from the youngster, and from the others afterwards. By that manner of approach one will come nearer getting the real truth out of the situation, than if the judge insists upon the procedure of the criminal court, by hearing first the prosecuting witness and then the boy in his defense.

The judge should examine the legal papers to see that they are in proper form, and should review the probation officer's written investigation. After he has thus secured a general idea of the case, then let him call Johnny and go to the bottom directly by some such question as, "Johnny, you tell me what is the reason you are here; what is this all about, anyway?" He has the boy's confidence right at the beginning, and he gets many facts truthfully that could not be had any other way. It makes the boy and his parents feel that the judge is interested in him and that the court is there to help, not to punish.

It seems to me that that method of presentation, the entirely informal way around the judge's desk, with the child only a few feet away from the judge, doing away with all the formalities of swearing witnesses—or as I saw in one court, of reading aloud the legal indictment—is the sane and rational method to secure real justice.

The Committee of the National Probation Officers' Association, in making out the report for the standardization of methods, has determined that every case that comes into court should be passed upon by some one agent, the information being written on forms in every case. Many of our investigations in the juvenile court are fragmentary, written often on little pieces of paper. A policeman comes to court, reaches under the rim of his hat and takes out a memorandum about the case and presents it orally to the court. Unless a stenographer is present—and this is usually an unnecessary and useless expense—those facts are lost for future record. It is becoming recognized more and more that the less information the investigator carries in his head, the more information he reduces to paper, the better the case is going to be handled.

Another difficulty is the presentation of opinions instead of facts as evidence. We all know the prosecuting witness, common in court, who states his conclusions and opinions as to what the boy has done, how bad he is, and what he needs for punishment. And probation officers too are not always clear on the distinction between conclusions and facts.

We know how many times cases are heard in court in a prejudiced way, either through the omission of important facts, because somebody perhaps did not think them really necessary, or through misplacing emphasis on certain facts. We know the probation officer with the theory, who always discovers adenoids, or something of that sort, as one of the contributing factors in the case and recommends their removal as the proper disposition. It may be that the adenoids have nothing to do at all with the bringing of the child into the Juvenile Court. It may not be so in every instance, but it very often occurs in the presentation of the case in court that a personal statement from memory takes the place of a written collection of all the facts.

There is another aspect of extremes in investigation. That is the over-zealous investigator who takes on the spirit and attitude of the detective. That is particularly true under the old criminal court system, but is decreasing where there are special investigating officers to handle children's cases. I have seen a whole neighborhood so stirred up over just one investigation by injudicious methods—talking to neighbors, to shop-keepers, to police officers and others—that the probation officer was brought into disrepute in the neighborhood and was unable to do anything with any case in that district thereafter.

Uniform courtesy is the only successful method in these investigations. That spirit in investigation and in the presentation of the case makes the parents feel that the Juvenile Court is an agency to help them when they cannot help themselves.

It is quite necessary, I think, that everyone who does investigating should have more or less of the same philosophy in regard to what the court is trying to do. The attendance officers in a great many of our American cities today, have absolutely foreign ideas from those of the probation officers about handling cases. The attendance officers very largely have been adjusting their cases regardless of the underlying social conditions in the home. That difference in method should be wiped out. It is essential not only that all the attendance officers, but also the police officers, and every person who has to deal with children, should do so from a similar social viewpoint.

There are two principles to be recognized in all this work. First, the investigators must maintain friendly relations with parents and children, first, last and all the time, so that their work may command the confidence and support of the people it aids. Second, the principle of protection of the child from any evil influence, together with positive constructive education, should underlie everything that the court does from the moment the child is brought into custody, until the time he is finally discharged from the process of the court. Now, if we have that attitude, if we can inculcate that simple, human principle in our police officers, our attendance officers, and our probation officers all over the country, we will have solved a large portion of the cases in the community before they go so far as to need the Juvenile Court.

THE DELINQUENT GIRL AND THE JUVENILE COURT

MERRITT W. PINCKNEY

Judge of the Juvenile Court of Cook County, Illinois

To my mind the delinquent girl is the most neglected, the most important, and apparently the least understood factor of the delinquent problem. During the three years that I have presided in the Juvenile Court of Chicago, the problem of the delinquent girl requiring custodial care has seemed to me to grow more serious with each passing year. The better acquainted I have become with this wayward child, the more familiar I am with the causes which lead to her delinquency, the more convinced I am that we do not meet her needs and that we fall short of a correct solution of her life's problem.

During the time I have spent in the Juvenile Court, I naturally have been led to study the causes of delinquency among children. And from my standpoint, I have grouped the delinquent girls into three classes. In the first class I have grouped those who have become delinquent because of parental neglect and incompetency; in the second, those who have become delinquent because of environment and bad associates; and in the third, those who have become delinquent because of temptation.

In the year 1910, more than 4,100 children came before me personally in the Juvenile Court on Ewing Street, and over three-fifths of this number were delinquent. After eliminating the delinquent cases that were continued and dismissed, there remained 1,161 delinquent boys and 475 delinquent girls to be provided for. Of these 475 girls—passing the boys since the subject of discussion is the delinquent girl—the great majority of them from my standpoint were delinquent because of parental neglect and incompetency. The parents of this class of delinquent girls are either dishonest, intemperate, shiftless, or immoral. Then, too, such parents have little, if any, conception of the duty they owe to their children.

Let me give one case that came to the Juvenile Court, as illustrating what I mean. Two of these girls, the older only sixteen years old and the younger fifteen, were seen at twelve o'clock at night in company with a Chinaman coming out of a chop suey joint down near the red-light district. The sight attracted the attention of one of our probation officers traveling in citizen's clothes; so he eyed the girls very closely. As they approached him, one turned to him and flippantly remarked: "I hope you will know us the next time you see us." He said: "For fear I may not, I will take you into custody now." And so these two girls came to the Juvenile Court. On the day of the trial their mothers appeared, representing and speaking for the girls. The way in which the girls were dressed, their powdered and painted faces, the slang and language which they used, clearly showed that they were on the downward path to ruin. I tried to point this out to the mothers, but the one speaking for both resented every suggestion that I made. Finally I said to her: "Madam, do you think and say that it was right for your daughter to be in company with a Chinaman coming out of a chop suey joint in a disreputable district of Chicago at twelve o'clock at night?" "Well," she replied, "I knew where she had gone, and she was getting her dinner for nothing." "Nothing!" I said. "Madam, it seems to me that your price, a mother's price, for that dinner was a human soul.'' That is what I mean by parental neglect and incompetency.

That may not be quite a typical case, but there are hundreds of them that come to the court which can easily be identified with this class.

As to the second class of girls, those who are delinquent because of environment and bad associates, it is hardly necessary to say that these forces figure very largely in the delinquency of girls.

Mr. Bodine, the superintendent of the Compulsory Education Department of the city of Chicago, in his census report of 1910, reported several blocks in the city of Chicago having over 900 children, and one block in the Sixteenth Ward of Chicago having 1,125 boys and girls—that block a congested tenement district where there was no place for legitimate, honest pleasure or amusement, where the case was almost hopeless for a girl or boy with any of the red blood of childhood and youth, desirous of pleasure, where the opportunities and inducements for leading an honest and moral life were few indeed. That is what I mean when I say that so many children come to the Juvenile Court and are delinquent because of environment.

A word of the children who become delinquent because of temptation. Children as well as adults become delinquent because of temptation; it is attractive to the children, naturally, and it is also attractive to the adults. These children who yield to temptation do not all come from the lower classes, though very many of them do. I have had fathers and mothers of the upper classes, very much surprised, come to the court and beg me to help save a girl or a boy who has yielded.

One case I desire to mention on the question of temptation, which has somewhat to do with our industrial problem, is the case of a girl whom we shall call Hattie. The necessity of working for her own and her father's and mother's support forced her to leave school when she was in the second year at high school and take employment in a department store. She had worked something over a year. She had risen from the ordinary salesgirl to an inspector of sales, in which position she had a certain department under her control. She was required to dress up to a certain standard. Her hours of employment were from 8 a. m. ordinarily, sometimes earlier, until 6 p. m. Saturdays she worked until 9 p. m. taking stock after the store closed to customers. She lived in the northwest part of the city and paid sixty cents each week for her carfare. Now and then she spent a little money for lunch. How much was she paid? After working a year or more for this department store, she received the magnificent salary of $4 a week. Is it any wonder she yielded to temptation? Is it any wonder that poor child, required to dress up to a certain standard and turning in almost every cent that she earned to father and mother to help support the family, stole a few trinkets of her employer and was brought into the Juvenile Court? When I found out what she was paid, the beggarly compensation accorded a girl of sufficient ability to be an inspector of girls, I told her to go home. And I said to her employer, or rather to the man who represented the big institution that divides a million and a half and more per year as profits among those who own the institition: "You are responsible, sir, for the condition of this girl today, and she can go home; no order of delinquency will be entered against her, if you please." That is what I mean by temptation.

While there are numerous minor causes which lead girls to do wrong and become delinquent, yet to me 95 per cent of these unfortunate girls can be grouped under these three heads, namely: parental neglect and incompetency, environment and bad associates, and temptation.

So much for the causes that lead to delinquency—now as to the delinquents, what do we do for them? To my mind society and the state of Illinois have never done their duty and are not now doing their duty for these unfortunate children. What did we do for the 475 delinquent girls who came to the Juvenile Court in 1910? Of that number, 131, who were Catholic, were taken care of by the House of the Good Shepherd. Of the others, who were Protestant, the Chicago Refuge on the South Side filled their institution to the doors in providing for 77. How many did the state of Illinois then take out of 475 children? It took 35 in the year 1910, leaving 232 children unprovided for, 232 delinquent girls who needed custodial care. These girls, the Juvenile Court was obliged to send back to the old environment and the old associates, to travel the downward path to ruin, dragging with them innocent girls and boys. Here in Chicago we have about half the population of the state. Why should we not have better provision made for our delinquent girls than was made by the state during the year 1910?

What I have said in no way reflects upon any official of any institution, but upon the state, which fails to provide him the necessary facilities for taking care of the delinquent children of Illinois who are in need of institutional care.

Moreover, society—leave the state out of consideration—society never has treated the delinquent girl fairly, the semi-delinquent girl. Let us throw out of consideration the girl who has been repeatedly delinquent, and turn our attention to the semi-delinquent girl. My observation teaches me that many good men and women interested in the social problem stand aloof or draw their skirts about them in the presence of the delinquent girl or semi-delinquent girl, delinquent for the first time perhaps, while they open their arms and their purses for the dependent children. The Juvenile Court is hampered today by the prevalence of this sentiment. Shame, I say, to the community, because it is the community who is the real party in interest. The community should make it a study, in justice to this girl, to furnish her some station midway between the home and the Chicago Refuge, where she may be taken care of. If we do our duty, we shall do this, and by doing so we shall make it easier, and not harder for her to return to an honest and an upright life.

PROBATION AND INSTITUTIONAL CARE OF GIRLS

MARY W. DEWSON

Superintendent of Probationers, Massachusetts Industrial School for Girls

There are two kinds of delinquency. First, there is the delinquency that can be uprooted by training, the right environment, and a strong personal appeal. Second, there is the delinquency that has its root in mental defect and that is incurable and permanent.

Because the difference between these two kinds of delinquency has not been understood, reformatory work with delinquents and criminals has progressed slowly. For some years in Massachusetts we have tried systematically to educate public opinion concerning the relation of mental defectiveness to delinquency. Thorough after-care of the girls from the State Industrial School gave us data on the menace of the mental defective to herself and to the community. Until an active parole department was established in the State School, we had not clearly recognized that every girl of this kind was doomed to failure, no matter what efforts were made to save her. Interest was aroused among the various social agencies of the state. At a hearing before the legislature this spring, the heads of all the leading penal, reformatory, protective, charitable, and social agencies in the state asked that custodial care be given to the "defective delinquent," in addition to the feeble minded, the epileptic, and the insane.

The Committee on Legal Affairs seemed to be much impressed by the far-sighted and vital report of the commission appointed to investigate the question of the increase of criminals, mental defectives, epileptics and degenerates. It is to be hoped that the bill drafted by Dr. Walter E. Fernald of the School for the Feeble Minded, which is now in the hands of the committee, will be passed at this session.*

The chief points of the bill are as follows:

1. It gives the power of the court to commit to departments for the defective delinquent all offenders who on medical examination prove to be defective and who would otherwise be committed to our reformatory institutions, prisons, jails, houses of correction, truant schools, and the State Board of Charity.

2. It gives power to commit to such an institution those who are not doing well at the various reformatory institutions, or when on parole from the same, are defective.

3. It gives the power of probationary release after a hearing in court of any inmate of the institution for defective delinquents if it is judged to be for the welfare of both the inmate and the community.

4. It provides for the maintenance of departments for the same in existing institutions.

In a farm colony defective delinquents would be happy among their equals, leading a routine life where there was no temptation and where many simple pleasures might be provided. Both the men and the girls would be happy when working in market gardens or dairies, or when raising chickens, and they would be practically self-supporting. I am proud of the forward step that Massachusetts has taken in defining this class and planning for its wise and humane care, but I wish to discuss espe-

---

*The bill is now Chapter 595, Massachusetts, Acts of 1911.

cially the girl who is the genuine delinquent, the girl who can be helped by training, the right environment, and a strong personal appeal

I have only one thing to say, although I shall say it over and over again, and that is, how much a young girl in leaving an institution needs a friend—not a casual friend, but the kind of a friend that we should want ourselves if we were to go a stranger among people who lived and thought in unaccustomed ways.

What girl between the ages of fifteen and twenty-one in any walk of life does not need a friend to steer her through the years so difficult and hazardous to every girl? She needs someone to inspire and encourage her, someone who cares about her success or failure. She needs someone to guide her and to show her what is practicable for her. Every young girl has day dreams, or she should have them. She needs someone to set her on the road toward realizing her dreams or toward realizing some more feasible substitute. She needs someone to arrange for her to have the right sort of pleasure and suitable companions.

If the girl had a wise mother and if she could be with her under the right environment, she would have in her mother the friend that she needs. But the wayward girl has no such good fortune. The employer, when the girl is placed out from the institution to do housework, cannot take the place of this friend. However kind and well-intentioned the employer is, she is not sufficiently wise or experienced in the problem of the wayward girl to serve the best interests of the girl. "Big sisters" are useful with the kind of girls sent out from our Massachusetts institution only when they are carefully selected and when they are closely guided by a trained and experienced visitor.

In Massachusetts we are fortunate to have established a careful system of after-visiting for our girls on parole from the industrial school. We are no longer in the stage of bewailing the lack of after-care for the girls or the lack of opportunity for the school officers to judge of the effectiveness of their methods of training at the industrial school because the girls are not followed up. We are in the practical stage of befriending our three hundred girls who are on parole. To carry out this work we have besides the superintendent, a bookkeeper, a stenographer and eight visitors, and also an office in our railway center, Boston.

Each visitor has about thirty-five girls as her special responsibility. The visitor is also constantly investigating applications from private families for girls to do housework. We do not take a girl to a place that we have not previously been to personally. We consider it essential to find out the character of the employers, as far as may be, from reliable persons who know them. The visitor also gets acquainted with the parents of as many of the newly-committed girls as are assigned to her. She goes to see the parents as soon as the girl is sent to Lancaster. She relieves the minds of the parents about the school and she hears their story about their daughter. She finds out what the parents are like and the reasons why they could not control their daughter. In short, she learns the conditions under which the girl has been living; she gets at the inwardness of the girl's waywardness. Moreover, she finds out from the local registration bureau whether any other society, church, or philanthropic individual is interested in the girl or in her people. She consults with these friends of the girl, with the police, and with other persons who can tell her the real character of the parents. The girls whose homes she investigates she sees from time to time on her visits to the school where she goes to talk over the girls with the officers and to keep in touch with the school. Some out-of-date social workers may claim that they can size up people in an interview, but, after all, such an estimate is only guesswork. And the character of the parents is too important a question for guesswork. Few men and women are so obscure that some responsible person does not know about them.

The course at the industrial school is definite, but the length of time that it takes for the individual girl to complete it depends on her ability and conduct. On the average, however, it takes about a year and a half. A much longer stay would of course tend to institutionalize the girl; for no institutional training beyond a certain point could make up for the time spent during these young and impressionable years in an institution where initiative, resourcefulness, and self-dependence cannot be taught. And the persons who get on best in the world seem to be those who have the most initiative, resourcefulness, and self-dependence. At the school the girl has gained what is for her the most crying need at the time that she is sent there, that is, the right spirit, experience in obeying, a pleasure in a well-ordered, disciplined life, and the power to make herself useful.

When a girl has finished the course of industrial training at the school and has shown a steady desire to do her best, her name is given to the probation department for placing, or in the rarer cases, she is sent directly home to her own family. For a year or two, perhaps three, the girl has been shut off from the excitement of the mill, the streets at evening, the theaters, and her old companions. The busy life at school with its new interests and ambitions has filled her mind; she has forgotten the fascination of the old way. She believes in her untried strength. Nearly every girl thinks that if she went straight home, she could stop a father from drinking, bring together a disrupted family, or save a sister from the streets. Experience has taught us that success is too unlikely to make it wise to risk such a test. It is usually not wise to send her even to well-meaning parents. The previous lack of control and of patience on the part of the parents, and of respect and of obedience on the part of the child continue to exist.

For instance, we have just tried a girl at home who had done well in a private family. Her own family were respectable and they co-operated with us. The father was a railroad conductor and a good man. He had, however, a quick temper and no patience, tact or judgment. Within a few weeks he began to scold his daughter for little acts of disobedience or thoughtlessness. The crisis soon came and the daughter is now back in a place, happy and satisfactory. Some persons are good but without the gift of teaching others how to be good.

There are many other reasons why it is not wise to send a girl directly back to her people. There are no better opportunities for interesting, healthful work or wholesome fun than there were before she was sent to school. She has been given a higher standard of living conditions at the school, and the sudden change to home conditions is discouraging to her, As yet she is not strong enough to improve the home conditions. Frequently old companions, the neighbors, the relatives, and even her own family taunt her with having been at school. Moreover, a strong objection to her going directly to her home from the school is that almost every girl is excited by her release from the confinement of the school. The period of transition is difficult. She must make new friends and new interests. She must learn what she must be and do to hold work, friends, and later on—it is true—a husband.

If the girl does go home, the visitor must gain the confidence of the parents; she must suggest and advise. The parents will need her. She will help find the girl suitable work. She will tell the girl about the chances for desirable social life in the locality and she will start her at the settlement club or at the young people's meeting at the church. She will know the educational opportunities at hand. She may interest persons in her, possibly the girl's better relatives who have been outraged by her conduct. And she will look after the girl physically. But above all, she will help the parents and the daughter to understand each other. She will be on the spot to secure for the girl a chance elsewhere if the trial at home is a failure, and before it is too wretched a failure.

The advantage of placing a girl in a private family to help with the housework over sending her to her own home is that in a private family she will have some one to control her whom she respects. She will have a wiser person to guide her than her father or mother. The whole situation is one with which she is not familiar, and it will tend to hold her old spirit in check. In a new place she will be taken at her apparent value, as her past is unknown. She will find interesting work, a happy family of which she is a part, and wholesome pleasure. The unfortunate and unhappy experiences of girls at housework in the families of unvisited employers furnish no criterion as to the possibilities of housework where the employers are under the stimulus and guidance of a good visitor.

In determining whether a place is suitable, we consider first the character of the family as estimated by outside reliable citizens. Second, we consider the personality of the woman. Will she be forceful and warm hearted enough to hold a girl, wise enough to guide her, ingenious enough to fill her life full of wholesome absorbing interests and friends? Third, we consider the social opportunity in a place, whether the family is simple enough to share their good times, to take her to church with them, and make her life a part of theirs.

Of course, we endeavor to fit each girl to the right place. If she likes children she must go where there are children. If she likes out-of-door life, we send her to a home where there are chickens and a garden. But we avoid hired men as much as possible. Moreover, we do not place girls where there are sons from fifteen to twenty-three years of age.

When the girl is satisfactory it becomes a question as to how often she should be visited. No one can befriend a girl whom she rarely sees. The girl needs her visitor often, because, if the girl is going to like the visitor, the visitor must not come in a perfunctory way at a stated time to get reports. When an employer says to a girl, "If you will do better, I shall not report you to your visitor," it is the beginning of trouble. There must be a vital, intimate connection. I know a visiting force whose visitors speak of visitations about once in three months, and I fancy that both the girl and the employer gives a sigh of relief when the visitation is over. A visitor cannot rely much on letters. Letters are splendid when they keep the touch close between visits but letters alone serve to lull an unwary guardian into a false security.

The efficient visitor will keep the girl's ambition aroused. It is for the visitor to show her girl how she can realize her heart's desires and how she is working toward them. It is for the visitor to interpret life to her girl. If a girl wishes to be a nurse, the first steps are to get character and robust health, to master cooking, and to study enough to be accepted in the hospital training-school. The girl can do this most successfully in a private family. In few desirable occupations possible for our girls would technical training alone be enough for success. The girl must have character; she must be faithful and attentive.

The visitor gives the girl courage because someone cares, someone is interested and believes in her. She helps her to be patient over small troubles. The value of praise when earned and judiciously given cannot be over-estimated. The visitor is the girl's safety valve. The visitor sees that the girl's health is protected and that she has proper medical care when it is needed; she looks after the girl's teeth. The visitor encourages the employer when she is ready to give up; she makes the employer see what a big opportunity for helpfulness she has, and that while it is hers, it is open to no one else; and she makes the employer more sympathetic. She removes friction between the girl and the employer. She helps the employer by bracing up the girl at some irritating point in her work or in her manners. Sometimes when a girl is upset, it is wise to see her every two or three days. A visitor rarely likes to let over a month go by without seeing her girls. A shopping excursion, an hour at the Art Museum, a trip with a girl to her home, perhaps to a funeral, a day of hunting work together, the going to a hospital, doctor or dentist, even a call at our office, may be the equivalent of a visit.

The story of Mary Brown will show what a visitor did with one of our girls who had to be wound up most frequently, although in later years many of the visits were made in the evening by the girl at the visitor's near-by home. Mary was committed at thirteen for being around at all hours with young boys. Her father was an aged man and her mother had no control over her; neither spoke much English. Sixteen months later the superintendent said of her, "She is a very incapable girl and very irresponsible; it is a question whether she should ever be placed in a family." Mary was then paroled to good cousins, with whom she did well for six months, until they gave up housekeeping. Within two months at her own home she went to pieces, and was sent back to the school and later to the State Hospital. Tried in families, inside of three months she exhausted as many places, and ran to her married sister, with whom she was allowed to stay. She went into a cigar shop, where five months afterwards the proprietor struck her; and her cousin sued him. After a short trial again at housework, she became an attendant for six months in an insane asylum. She left in a fit of despondency over a quarrel with her family and married sisters, which was a matter of frequent occurrence, and went for a few weeks to the beach. She admitted wrong-doing when she voluntarily came back to her visitor. Then followed a year and a half of living sometimes at home and most of the time in approved boarding-places, and working in cigar factories when there was work and elsewhere when there was not. Love affairs under such conditions are full of danger. The visitor saved her from the worst. When a month pregnant she married a steady, capable young man of her own nationality. It has been a happy marriage. She still consults us about her baby, her housekeeping and her other problems. Her husband says the most interesting book he has ever read is one that we suggested, Holt's "Care and Feeding of Children." During the four years and five months she was on probation, the dates of at least one hundred and sixteen times when she was seen were jotted down. After they were married they saved $700 in three years and invested in a small delicatessen store to take up Mary's spare time. They moved to a better district. Mary's last call was to consult about a mortgage on one of their three pieces of real estate, as it was a dull season in the store and they had spread out too much. They have had a second baby and Mary has mothered a younger sister of her own.

There are lessons that a girl can learn in a place that she cannot learn in an institution. She can learn to distinguish who are suitable companions, what is the right way to conduct herself toward young men, and how to bear herself to keep others' respect. She never thought of these things when she was living with her own people and she could get no experience of them in an institution.

I have spoken especially of the girl on parole from an industrial school. Everything that I have said applies to the girl on probation from the juvenile court. There may be more of the girls from the juvenile court than from the school who are tried at home with their parents, but in any case a large number of the girls who have gone wrong sexually have to be placed with private families, away from the former temptations and comrades and the alternately overstrict and too lax control of their parents. A probation officer of the St. Louis Juvenile Court told me last year that the greater number of their girls on probation were placed away from their families. I asked how long they kept their girls on probation. She answered that they were kept on probation until they were strong enough in character to be able to get on without a probation officer's visiting, but that so far, since the court was started, no girls had been released from probation.

It is a mistake to give a girl a trial on probation when she will only get deeper into trouble and when she should be sent to an institution at the start. If it seems wise to take the risk of trying a girl on probation, there is, however, under adequate probation, the safeguard that the girl cannot slip back without her danger coming to the knowledge of the probation officer. When the girl in a private family does continue to slip back, when she does not respond to the interest of wise friendly persons and the stimulus of the new life and the new environment, the probation officer should send her to the institution and should send her before it is too late. Institutions are an absolute necessity to start some girls in the right path. Girls should be sent to them who should not be allowed to stay at home, who would run away from a good private family or who are so uncivilized in their manner and habits that no private family would tolerate them. Because institutions have been regarded as the only resource in the past, and because as a consequence many girls have been sent to them unwisely, is no excuse for not sending girls to the institutions today before it is too late to give the institution half a chance to help them.

One type of girl should rarely be sent to an institution. She is the high-tempered girl who cannot stand the routine of an institution. It is against her nature to do things in unison with twenty other girls. The little rules and regulations that are necessary where twenty-five people live together under the same roof, tantalize her. She is always in trouble. I have seen girl after girl of this type make a failure at our school, but on probation, freed from rigid routine, yet guided wisely by a private family, turn out splendidly.

For example, Jennie was sent to our school because her undisciplined high spirits led her into all sorts of trouble except that of immorality. If her probation officer had been a woman of more patience, understanding, and resource, or if she had had more time to give to Jennie, she would never have sent her to the school. I thought that Jennie would never get out on probation. She was continually doing some little thing that set her back until she lost her self-confidence and her courage. Then no one at the school could do anything for her. When she had been there three years, twice as long as the average girl, her matron and I worked a little scheme. I encouraged Jennie by promising to get her a chance to go to high school if she would be obedient and self-controlled enough for the other girls to think it was just for her to have a chance on probation, and the matron aided by being conveniently blind and deaf and by giving her a course of Chautauqua reading to keep up her interest. Once on probation, with many jerks and hitches, Jennie finished a year or two at high school, while practically supporting herself by earning her board in the family where she lived. She was rather old for school, however, and as she grew restless, we suggested that she should go to work in one of the departments of the Women's Educational and Industrial Union. The discipline of work is more powerful than the discipline of school life. There is a reality about work in an organized business that holds a half-tamed spirit, and by this time Jennie was half tamed. We prevented her from getting discharged once or twice, but gradually things went more and more smoothly. Last summer, after four years of work, she left her position a sensible, attractive girl to marry a good, hard-working young man.

Since we demand for adequate visiting a close personal relation between the visitor and the girl, it goes without saying that the girl should have the same visitor from the time she leaves the school until she is twenty-one. The girl may be changed from one private family to another; for a provoking girl is bound to wear out the patience of a series of families. But a girl should never be changed from one visitor to another for convenience's sake—just because a visitor can look after more girls when they are in one locality. The relationship between the visitor and her girl should be genuine and helpful and too valuable to be broken by a change of the girl's locality. "It is not wise to swap horses when crossing a stream." The girl cannot have much respect for the relation if it is lightly cast aside. A regular siege has to be laid to capture the girl's better nature and to defeat her faults, and she suffers from a change of generals. No one point in organizing a probation department is more important than the permanency of each girl's visitor. Incidentally, it is stimulating to the employer to have a change of visitors when she has a change of girls. It prevents the employer from getting into ruts in handling girls.

Preventing the employers from falling into ruts is a real part of the visitor's work. There is a tendency among the employers not well visited to think that because Mary was so and so, Jennie will be the same. The employer is apt to generalize from two or three girls as she has known them and to expect any new girl to fit the stock idea. Nothing is more irritating to an individual than to be treated as one of a class. No school teacher, minister, lawyer, or Yankee wants to be considered like the stock idea of a school teacher, minister, lawyer, or Yankee. In fact, the spot in which to reach any person is in her variation from the stock idea—in what makes her an individual. So we try not to use stock phrases ourselves. We discourage persons who say, "Can't Mary have some time off?" "When is her time up?" "She is a state girl." "When will you make your next visitation?" etc.

There should be certain laws enacted in every state in regard to delinquent girls. The age of consent for a girl should not be less than sixteen years. This is a very important law. It should be enforced and the young girls protected. If the man was in doubt as to the truth of a girl's statement as to her age, it would encourage him to look for an older woman.

All girls whom it is necessary to put in charge of the state should be committed for their minority, that is until they are twenty-one years of age. The years from eighteen to twenty-one are dangerous and vital years when a young girl greatly needs mothering care.

Another essential law is that marriage should not end the guardianship of the state, but that the care of the state should continue until the girl is twenty-one. Theoretically it seems as though a girl should be entirely free at her marriage. But practically it works that without such a law a girl on the impulse of the moment when she is tired of wholesome control, will recklessly marry anyone in order to get rid of the state. That is not a wise way to marry and the results of such marriages are very sad. It is equally intelligent to have a law that a husband may be fined for marrying a girl from the industrial school without the consent of the trustees, since the lack of consent does not invalidate the marriage. If a married girl is still in the care of the state, the visitor, who is the girl's friend before her marriage, can help to make the marriage successful in a hundred ways without lessening the husband's responsibility. The husbands of our girls often come to us for advice as to the best way to handle the girl who was a problem to us and who is a problem to them.

I have said but one thing and I have said it over and over again because it is the secret of successful parole work, it is the keystone without which the arch of probation falls. Parole and probation are successful through adequate visiting alone. Anyone who thinks otherwise has allowed himself to be deceived by a weak optimism that is not based on facts. If you think deeply about human nature and what human nature needs to develop it to its highest possibilities, you will believe in the parole system, but that parole system must be built around a wise, strong, sympathetic visitor caring for a limited number of girls.

PART SEVEN

LIBRARIES AND MUSEUMS

"One whose child feet chanced to walk green paths of fairy land"

THE CHILD'S WORLD OF BOOKS

W. N. C. CARLTON

Librarian, The Newberry Library

As I looked through the Child Welfare Exhibit the other afternoon, I was impressed by the number of things which properly preceded the book and which very properly should be cared for before the libraries and educational workers could take the child in hand; and I saw very vividly how necessary all those other operations were, before we could enter upon the stage and take up our part of the work. Unless a child is healthful, unless he is free from illness and disease, mental deficiency, eye difficulty, or any other ills which are here shown as preventable, unless a child comes to the school or the library fit and well, how little after all it is that we can do.

But conceding that there are many things which precede the book in the child's welfare and the child's development, I want to say that it would have been difficult if not impossible for anyone twenty-five years ago to prophesy with any accuracy the rapid and great changes that have taken place in the libraries in their work for children. I use the words twenty-five years because it is just twenty-five years ago that I first began my library work, and there was not then for the children in the libraries I knew, one single thing that we have today. There was no children's librarian, no school for the training of children's librarians, no special furniture for the special use of children, there were no children's rooms in libraries, no story hours, no branch libraries, there was no special, organized relation between the libraries and the schools. Everything that you see in the adjoining building relating to libraries has come, and come very fast indeed, within the last quarter of a century. And as I saw those dear little children the other afternoon in the Library booth at the Exhibit looking so eagerly and so interestedly at the books shown there in the excellent selection from the municipal library, in those comfortable little chairs adjusted to their height, with the tables adjusted to the height of the chairs, I could not help remembering by contrast how in my early library days I had placed two big folios on chairs in order that some little fellows might be able to reach the reading-table.

An incident that occurred the other afternoon shows how strikingly this Exhibit is going straight to the people whom it most concerns. I was standing with a friend of mine, a well-known novelist of this city, in front of the graphic representation showing the deaths of children in the various wards from preventable diseases, when a little shock-headed fellow, who looked about seven or eight, but was probably a few years older, rushed between us and studied the chart with the same interest with which we were studying it, apparently searching for the number of his ward. After studying it a little while he turned around to my friend and said: "Say, Mister, can you tell me what diseases it is that babies die of in that ward? That is where I live, and I want to know." It seemed to me that if that was an indication of the way in which those graphic exhibits were going to the hearts and minds of the people, its value to this community both now and in the future will be incalculable. I doubt not, that from the library and museum exhibit similar striking truths and matters of interest were going home, and being deeply impressed on the boys and girls I saw sitting there.

BOOKS AND STORY TELLING

Reconnoitering

Favorite pictures are loaned

Helped with lessons.

This is how in ancient
ages
Children grew to saints
and sages.

Cooperation with
Public Library.

Roof Library

Sing a song of seasons
Something bright for all
Flowers in the summer
Fires in the fall.

The Child's World of Books

The child's world of books is a very large and wide field. As I have disclaimed any authority to speak as an expert upon it, I shall not discuss it at length. The child's world of books may be a very beautiful, a very helpful, a very civilizing world, or it may be exactly the opposite. It may be a world of beauty or of ugliness, or of opportunity for the taking in and absorbing of noble, high ideals of conduct and of life, or exactly the reverse. Left to themselves, I need not say how many, many of the children of the city are more than likely to drift toward the ugly world. But the municipal library and its adjunct, the branch library, stand always as beacon lights and beacon fires to point the children to the world of beauty which is in books. It begins with the child as early as he is able to reach the library—at the story hour; and even after he has passed all the grades at school, it is still with him as an adult, to be the means of intellectual and spiritual enlargement and enrichment, and of great vocational assistance through his life. If we start, as I know we are doing, tens of thousands of these children in the right direction toward the world of useful and beautiful books, that is a service which will deserve well not only of this individual community but of the republic of our day and generation.

CHILDREN'S READING AND MUNICIPAL LIBRARIES

CHARLES H. JUDD

Director of the University of Chicago School of Education

The only justification for my being here is that the library and the school do co-operate and are likely to co-operate more fully in the future in preparing the children to use books and in putting into their hands the kind of books that they should have. Attention has already been drawn to the fact that the world of books is divided. There are some books to which it is not advantageous to introduce the children. There are, on the other hand, and in growing numbers, large groups of books to which it is very desirable to introduce the children.

Those books which children should read, books that are supplied in our public libraries and are being made accessible by all of the different devices of distribution that industrious librarians work out—I say these books which children are to read can be read only by children who are qualified to read them. The part of the school in co-operating with the library becomes immediately obvious, because the supply which the library places in the hands of these children calls constantly for that kind of training in ability to read which shall make the children eager and able to take advantage of the opportunities offered in the libraries. This is the justification for the discussion of the subject by one who is primarily interested in education.

Within the last twenty-five years there has been an enormous change in the libraries with regard to their attitude to children and their ability to provide for children. The same remarks might be repeated in regard to the literature for children;

such literature hardly existed twenty-five years ago. Twenty-five years ago one came into the school and found there nothing but a series of textbooks; and these books contained nothing but predigested literary material. They were written in short paragraphs, and these short paragraphs were assigned and recited. There was a reading-lesson in the first few grades, and this reading-lesson was formal in its character. It was succeeded in the upper grades by more formal reading, which ultimately ended in declamation of some kind or elocutionary effort.

Even the books intended to give information were formal. The book in geography, for example, was a single textbook; it was well prepared, carefully predigested again, and assigned in small sections. The same thing was true of history. The same thing was true, so far as there was any science work in the schools, of all the science work. Therefore, in the schools twenty-five years ago formalism was the typical descriptive term to be used for the reading that was undertaken in those schools.

The schools have broken away from all this formalism and broken away very rapidly. Whether it is the influence of the library, the influence of the writer of children's books, the enlarging view of education, I am not able to say. Perhaps it is the co-operation of all of these. But at any rate we have had a great impulse in this generation in the direction of reading that is not formal in its character. Children are now sent to look up whole books, to look up topics. If one should run through the various items of school training, for example in history, he would find that it is no longer the digestion of a single textbook; children are now asked to go somewhere and look up all that is to be found upon a certain topic. It is called the source method in history and that source method has been introduced into the lower schools and into the higher schools. Children are asked in other words to get and read material on every subject and to make for themselves the abstracts which used to be made for them, and which used to be put into the book that was assigned as a textbook. The same thing is being done in geography. Lists of books known as supplementary readers are used in geography and nature-study. What does it mean? It means that the school is interested in having the children do reading for themselves; in giving them the material on which the earlier writers of textbooks used to base their few extracts, for it is quite impossible to determine in this day and generation of many interests where a child's largest interest will be, and reliance cannot be placed upon a single textbook to select those geographical facts that will attract the attention and interest of a given boy or girl; the boy and the girl must be put in contact with the material itself; and so the device of supplementary readers is employed.

The school, therefore, is no longer a place where a few textbooks are read and where mere formal reading in the lower grades is succeeded by more formal reading in the upper grades. The school is coming to be a place where children are taught to read and to read widely. I said a moment ago that I am not sure whether that is the result of the library's influence or whether it is the result of better views in regard to the needs of children, but I am perfectly certain that all kinds of forces are operating in the same direction. They are also operating to destroy the ugly type of reading which is obviously undesirable. In the earlier generations there appeared from time to time some boy who was eager to know the world more fully than he found it in the textbooks; and he would get surreptitiously some exciting literature furnished by those who were wiser in their day and generation than the teachers. He would read these stories of the larger world supposed to exist on the western plains or in the Rocky Mountains with the greatest avidity because he was eager to know that world; and he had now gained a sufficient mastery of the art of reading so that he could turn himself loose, so that he could find these larger worlds and find them easily.

This larger world has now been opened up in the school; and just in so far as there can be offered to the children good literature when they come to the age at which they can read, they will be found reading with avidity the supplementary books in geography and history and nature-study. They are found reading biography, reading that good literature of fiction which furnishes the necessary recreation even in the child's life and which will lay the foundation for an appreciation of all good literature.

There must be an enlarged supply to satisfy this demand which is created, and that enlarged supply must be made very accessible. Furthermore the process of education must go forward so as to improve and enlarge the taste in order that the adult may ultimately be in a position to aid himself. In short, school and library must co-operate in making readers independent. The business of the school is to prepare the child to go on without the school. The business of the school is to give the child that sort of training which will make it possible for him to pursue his own education independently when the school no longer has oversight over him. We did not have that view twenty-five years ago. Twenty-five years ago there was a certain training given to the child, and when he was sent from school it was supposed that his training in the lines which were cultivated by the school was completed and finished. Today we say to ourselves: "These children ought to be given some taste for literature, they ought to be given some taste for history and science and geography, and then they ought to be sent out into the world with the possibilities of directing their own reading." One cannot be sure that the school does all that it might. It is certain that, with our best endeavors, children go into the world unqualified to direct their own reading, needing further assistance. They need a different type of assistance, however, than that which they have had in the schools. In the school they need to learn how to read correctly and carefully, how to reproduce the information that they have been getting; they need to learn something about the use of books. In the later day when they have gone away from school, they need to be guided to books with some degree of precision but not with that exact aid that they get in the school when they are given single books or when they are given limited collections of books. Because in this larger world, when one boy is going into some sort of occupation that leads him in the direction of the literature on metallurgy, another boy is going into some occupation that leads him toward the literature that deals with importation of some sort or other; one girl is going into the world needing to be directed toward the literature that will help her in improving her home, another into some form of activity in the manufacturing or commercial world requiring knowledge of fabrics. In other words, here are these children, with diversified interests, and what they need now is to be introduced to a large collection of books—but a large collection of books not of the definite type used in the fundamental training in school. In the schools we try to give that kind of training which should be taken in common by all children; and then when they go out into the world, they go into a world where their interests are so diversified that they need a different sort of guidance into a larger world; not so precise, not so definite in character, but nevertheless a type of guidance which will lead them to material which will be useful to them.

It seems to me that the librarian's list of books is the natural outgrowth of supplementary reading in schools. The schools start with the precise reading of the First Reader. That is enlarged into the Second Reader and the Third Reader. Then the school says to the children, "Now begin to find books that are not Readers and read in those." Then it says, "Here is the subject of geography, and you are going to take up one of the countries of Europe, and you will find something in the geography, you will find something more in the school library, where there is a large body of material about that country, if you are interested in it," or "Beyond the school library is the general library; in this larger institution there is a larger group of books. There you will find somebody who is intelligent not in giving you the narrow limited direction that your teacher had been giving you as you first acquired this art of reading, but in giving you a larger list of books which will help you in a more general way."

If this is taken as a working conception of the teaching of reading in the school and the extension of reading as it is found in the libraries, it will be recognized that there are all sorts of intermediate stages. There are first those intermediate stages where the school does not have adequate facilities for supplementary reading. School boards and the world at large have not come to see as clearly as teachers and librarians the necessity of putting books where they will be easily accessible. The result is that books have not come in large numbers into the budgets of school boards. The books are more commonly purchased by the libraries. School superintendents sometimes believe that the superintendent ought always to be a member of the library board in order to help librarians see what books ought to be purchased for school purposes, and in order to purchase books for the school use. That is a reflex of the general attitude of the school that it cannot afford to buy as many books as it ought to have. Books were bought formerly in the schools by the individual patron and not by the school. A few reference books were tolerated in the school and provided by the school board, but in the main the school did not expend its money for books. Now we find in some places the required books demanded for school purposes, and in other places books purchased by the children themselves, but we do not find in most schools, and we shall not for some time to come, a sufficient collection of books to make collateral supplementary reading what it should be. Consequently, the school must depend on the library.

It is the opportunity of the library to see that a collection of children's books, such, for example, as is shown in the Exhibit, is generously provided as an aid to schools. It is the opportunity of the library to come into the school and supply the school with what the school now realizes that it needs; namely, a supplementary collection of books. If there were in the schools librarians or a sufficient collection of books of that sort, then it might be said that the business of the public library is merely to deal with the adults. The schools do not have what they need. The library as a public institution in possession of the material today should supply this material in the first instance to the schools. There ought to be, therefore, in this city very much more material than there now is, and there ought to be more and more done by the library in the direction of carrying over into the school the material that the school realizes that it needs.

In another direction, too, the schools need help. The school claims to teach the children how to read. As a matter of fact, there are many limitations on the efforts in that direction, and the school does not always succeed in making first-class readers of these children. In fact, if one were talking to an educational gathering rather than to a group interested in libraries primarily, that subject might be discussed somewhat more fully. It may be said in general that almost all who deal with the schools are conscious of the difficulty of making people good readers. Many adults do not read properly. They take up some book only as the last possible source of information; they would rather ask somebody, listen to a lecture, do almost anything to escape reading a book for the purpose of collecting information. And there are a good many people who do not know how to collect technical information at all; they do not know how to go to the books on mechanics that might offer them very valuable information in their trades. Adults do not know how to read the things that they ought to, because our school training has not succeeded as fully as it ought. Consequently the schools come to the libraries and say: "Can you not offer to the children some stimulus, some inducement in the library to read the broad material which you have at hand? Can you not show perhaps by pictures or lists that there are opportunities of learning to read books in such a way that the children will come back from the library more eager to do the sort of thing that is done in the school when it is training them to read?" In other words, one looks from the school to the library, not only for the material resources for supplementary reading, but for that sort of impulse toward reading which will make the children more eager to read broadly. In this stimulation of reading the school will try to co-operate in an increasing degree as the years go by. All the library will need to do later will be to post a list of books in order to have an eager rush for books on mechanics and technical arts and various things of that sort, provided help is given at this time to stimulate the children in that direction and to cultivate their minds so that they will make mature readers.

In two or three centers libraries are working along that line very actively. In Washington, for example, they prepare reference collections valuable for people who are looking for vocational information. There are materials collected with reference to the particular crafts and particular subjects. There are monthly bulletins sent out for the training even of teachers. The following statistics show that librarians have a rich field in the training of teachers. In the year 1909, eighty-five normal students in one of our normal schools in the eastern part of the country were examined with regard to their qualifications to direct children toward reading, and the results were as follows: Only sixty-three of the eighty-five had read the "King of the Golden River"; fifty of them had read the "Arabian Nights"; only fifty-seven of them had read "Treasure Island." There are more statistics of that sort, but these are enough to show librarians that they ought to prepare lists of books for the use of teachers as well as for the use of children.

The parents, too, need those lists of books; parents are eager to get lists of books into the hands of their children, and if librarians will co-operate with the teachers in the preparation of lists of books for parents, they will do a very great service. If, for example, there could be had in other fields the sort of admirable list that has been prepared for this Child Welfare Exhibit by the Public Library, then the kind of guidance for which I am asking could be had.

In conclusion, then, the school will go on trying to teach reading. The school has an enlarged conception of its function in teaching reading. It no longer teaches in a merely formal way. The children are induced to read the supplementary material. The library must help by furnishing enough material and by providing the facilities for putting this material into the schools and into various other places where it will be immediately accessible. Librarians must help in classifying that material in such a way that children will have guidance all along their course. The larger and more intelligent the guidance given by the librarians, the more intelligent the children will become in the use of the public collection of books now and also in later life when they come for technical literature and general literature.

The school needs increasingly in this community a place for the training of teacher-librarians. It may be said that some efforts in this direction in our own school are meeting with immediate success. Just as soon as there is somebody who is trained with the interests of both teacher and the librarian in mind, that person can find a very useful position in the community. One young woman, a few months ago, with that sort of double training for teaching and library work, was taken by one of the high schools just outside of the city of Chicago.

This teacher has gone about organizing in that high school in a general way the study of all the children, doing the work of a librarian, doing the work of a teacher, doing it in that hour which happens to be one of the difficult hours to manage in any high school or in any school—the study period. Here is exactly where the librarian-teacher can give that training in independent reading which it seems to me is so natural for the librarian to offer. The experiment to which I refer was a distinguished success. The principal of that school not a great while ago said that it was one of the best pieces of organization that had ever been worked out in that school.

The co-operation of individuals trained with the double interest of teacher and librarian would justify such a gathering as this and would lead to a realization of the plea for better co-ordination of the school and the library.

LIBRARY EXTENSION IN CHICAGO

CARL B. RODEN

Assistant Librarian, The Chicago Public Library

We librarians are fond of declaring that no other human occupation has experienced quite so complete a revolution in its aims and its practices as that of librarianship. Within the space of one generation the very ideals of library management have been completely reversed. The library of the mid-nineteenth century was an institution of calm and dignified aspect, sober, self-contained, and self-possessed. It proceeded quietly and steadily to accumulate, and to add to its stores of the sources of knowledge, which it made accessible, in a tentative sort of way, to those who came well credentialed and who bore evidence of comporting themselves in a manner that should leave inviolate the holy calm and atmosphere of cloistered seclusion in which the library was steeped. The custodians of these libraries were commonly gentlemen—or ladies—of great erudition and with a vague but impressive love for books, which frequently manifested itself in a distinct aversion to letting their treasures pass even temporarily into other hands. Most often they were advanced in years and had passed their most active days in other pursuits; too often they brought with them a record of failure in those other pursuits, which made it necessary for them to earn a modest but dignified livelihood in their later life, and this necessity was not infrequently their chief recommendation for the post.

But in the late eighties it began to dawn upon a few of the bolder and younger spirits among them that the library must have a duty towards the whole community which supports it, and not only to the erudite and to those in search of erudition; that the inspirational and recreative influence of good books might well be brought to the attention of even the least among its constituents, and that thus the patronage of the library might embrace every grade, kind, age, race and condition of citizens.

But here was an idea calling for new methods of management, and so doctrines began to be formulated and to be crystallized into practices, seeking first to simplify the internal economy of the institution, to make it accessible and even inviting to the less favored; and, second, to attract, to educate, to create public sentiment, to the effect that the public library was for all of the people and was not destined to serve only those whose special gifts rendered them specially fit to enjoy its advantages.

After twenty years of debate and conference, of experiment and propaganda, librarians suddenly looked one another in the face and agreed that they had created such a body of doctrines and practices, based upon so high an ideal and springing out of so comprehensive and universal a purpose, that they had every right to call their occupation a profession, closely allied to that of the educator. And so the new profession of librarianship sprang full panoplied into being, with a declaration of principles, as stated in the motto of the American Library Association: "The best reading for the largest number at the least cost."

To carry out to their fullest extent the promises of that declaration may well be considered a worthy life-work for any man. And it is one, the full exposition of which might well occupy many hours and fill many volumes, as the bibliography of our professional literature well sets forth. I wish to deal only with one part of that declaration, that part which names "the largest number" and with that part only as it has been applied in Chicago—that is to say, library extension in Chicago.

One of the first principles laid down, after the iron-bound traditions of library custodianship as against library administration had been shattered, was that in order to reach "the largest number" it was necessary for the public library to penetrate to those regions where the people of the community make their homes, rather than to continue to house itself grandly and exclusively in a stately, monumental building in the central or business portion of the city, and wait for its prospective patrons to make their way to its inhospitable doors. The idea of smaller collections, installed in branch buildings, began to form; and those cities that had the means or were favored with the benefactions of public-spirited citizens quickly developed a system of branch libraries, which showed the most astonishing results in public appreciation and showed also the vastness of the field awaiting the activities of the enterprising and adequately equipped public library. And then came the final development, which was to admit and to care for and to minister to the little children who played around its door and peeped wonderingly in at the strange new place from which for all ages past, they had been driven as from places that it was not good for them to enter and that they could occupy only to the discomfort and disturbance of their betters.

And on the day when librarians admitted the little children, they took their place among the forces making for the advancement of the race through each succeeding generation; and one of the earliest of the agencies making for child welfare had its beginning.

Will you allow me to say a few words in detail about this fascinating new profession to which so many young women are turning—the profession of librarianship for children? It is a specialty, self-contained and most clearly defined, a specialty that boasts a school all its own, endowed by Andrew Carnegie and operated in connection with the great Carnegie Library of Pittsburgh; a school, by the way, which in seven years of its existence has never yet succeeded in sending out enough graduates to answer to the demand for trained assistance in the field. For the daily work of the children's librarian calls for qualities of head and heart all too rarely found in combination, while it is of such variety and attractiveness as must appeal to everyone at all prepared to comprehend the scope of its possibilities and its consequences.

First of all the children's librarian must possess enthusiasm in her work and the conviction of its worth and dignity. She must be able to carry that conviction into the hearts of her charges. She works without the powerful aid of a truancy law, or a system of disciplinary rewards and punishments. Her patrons must all come to her voluntarily; they must accept her ministrations because those ministrations are acceptable. She must know how to attract and, having attracted, how to hold the interest of the children. By means of story hours she must be able to awaken their interest in the great tales of the heroes of folk and fairy lore and so to form a connection with literature through the great elemental world epics, which have come from the very dawn of the world itself. And, having formed that connection, she must know how to proceed in order that the taste built upon so stately a foundation shall not be allowed to fall away for the want of stimulation and development. For the children's librarian is engaged in implanting the germ of one of the most portentious and fruitful tendencies in human nature, the possibilities of whose cultivation and direction toward good or evil are practically limitless; whose results bear upon and modify human character in a way open to no other psychological process short of the systematic and comprehensive work of the schools. I mean the reading habit.

Is it any wonder, then, that with such a conception of their task before them, librarians steadfastly continue, in spite of sprightly comments and facetious criticism, to insist upon scrutinizing the books which they place into the hands of children, and to consider certain elements, the presence or absence of which are conclusive as to whether, for their purposes, a book is good or bad?

I say "for their purposes" advisedly, and let me add that most of the periodical hue and cry raised in newspapers about librarians "barring out" this or that book, adult or juvenile, is mere sensational claptrap. No librarian "excludes," all librarians "select" from the deluge that pours steadily from the modern press. And surely even librarians have the right—not only the right, but the sacred duty—to select out of the welter that which is best for their purposes. And this they must and will continue to do.

The praises of a good book have been sufficiently sung. But the effects of a bad book are only faintly realized by the average man, the "man in the street." Will it be deemed presumptuous to say in this place that the librarian lays claim, by virtue of his training and professional equipment, to the title and functions of an expert?

But what is a "good book" for a child, and what is a "bad book?" A good book for a child is by no means always a book bristling with morals and harping upon the beauties of virtue and the hideousness of vice. Such a book may very often be one for a "Good Child," but rarely is it a good book for a human child. The book for a human child must deal with other human children, in a thoroughly human way. It should deal with their little trials and tribulations, and with the solution of them, without exaggeration or the suggestion of martyrdom in the one, and with neither the exploitation of any special heroism nor the intervention of factitious or superhumanly improbable aid in the other. The natural boy has his natural problems and mishaps, and he gets out of them or faces them in a perfectly natural way. His book companions must do the same in order to be fit companions for him and to earn his lasting respect.

The stage villain does not stalk abroad in our streets, seeking to circumvent the crafty and sophisticated activities of supernaturally endowed small boys. Neither does the banker's daughter fall off the pier at the very moment when "our hero" appears to snatch her from a watery grave, so that she may give her hand to her rescuer while her father endows him with half his fortune.

And the small boy who devours this sort of pabulum with gaping mouth and staring eyes may fare forth in search of similar adventure for a little while; but not for long. Despairing of doing anything so "heroic" because cruel fate denies him the occasion, he begins to lose faith, first in the books of his boyhood and so in the whole unreal world of books, next in himself because he has had no chance to "make good" in such a blazing fashion, and finally in the world he lives in for being such a dull, drab, work-a-day world, so wanting in spirit and high enterprise.

Are we drawing on our imaginations for such a picture? Not at all. The stage villain, the banker's daughter, and the superhumanly crafty small boy are the stock figures of the common run of juvenile fiction—one of the most difficult fields of literature, by the way, in which to win success. And if their vogue is somewhat on the wane, let it be said in justice, that to the watchfulness and the fearless criticism of the children's librarian this improvement must be laid. You would be surprised to learn how many manuscripts of juvenile books, and how many first copies from the press, are laid before the Training School for Children's Librarians at Pittsburgh; how anxiously its judgment is awaited, and how often it seals the fate of some industrious author's hopes.

And the small boy who reads these thrillers with staring eyes and boundless faith; who grows up contemptuous of books because the only books he read were those of his youth, which were untrue to life as he has found it; who loses faith in himself and the world because in his boyhood he lost the opportunity to know either, through the right kind of books—is he imagined? This Child Welfare Exhibit itself, and the conditions here portrayed, supply the answer.

That is the substance of the indictment which librarians bring against the widely known and ravenously devoured writings of the redoubtable Oliver Optic, of Horatio Alger, of the Elsie books and all of that ilk; their transparent tawdriness and falsity of plot, their cheap and paltry "written down" style; their general tone and aspect of insubstantiality; like a stick of chewing gum, tickling the palate for the moment with their fleeting flavor, only to turn into a nubbin of sticky nothingness in the end, to be cast out and forgotten. Why is it that we turn again and again, and always with pleasure, to the books of Louisa Alcott or of Robert Louis Stevenson? Because they deal with human beings in a human way; not with prigs. Because they portray the common incidents of human life in a natural way, instead of setting forth the prearranged jerkings of puppets worked by perfectly apparent strings. Surely there is opportunity here for the application of standards and the exercise of judgment. And if the librarian and the children's librarian have set up such standards and formulated principles for such judgment, let us support them with our confidence and our co-operation. And if occasionally they seem to overshoot the mark, be it remembered that at least their aim was well directed, if perhaps a little too high, and that their bullets are sped by a noble and righteous motive.

Thus far I have said nothing directly germane to the topic assigned to me. But the opportunity to present the case for the librarian in the matter of children's books was too good to be passed over. And in so doing—in a very sketchy way—I have not departed as much as it may seem from my title, for library extension in Chicago has been largely connected with attracting the children, both by penetrating into the home regions and by removing the restrictions and limitations that heretofore served to prevent their close and intimate relations with the library.

And allow me to preface my brief remarks on our own work by the statement that whatever it has been possible to do by way of expansion, in face of discouraging conditions and perennial poverty, has been accomplished through the energy and the organizing genius of the present librarian, Mr. Henry E. Legler.

The methods employed in Chicago for the promotion of library extension do not differ from those in use elsewhere, which is merely to say that Chicago has availed itself of the experience and principles evolved by other communities where this work is somewhat more firmly established and older in point of time. But in the application of those methods Chicago has been obliged to introduce variations and new practices, chiefly by reason of the grievous lack of means to do what the other cities have done, mainly in the way of erecting and maintaining an adequate chain of separate and thoroughly equipped branch buildings in the home districts where, particularly, the children can be reached. On the other hand, our splendid system of small parks, and the whole-hearted co-operation of the park commissions in tendering space in the fieldhouses thereof, has enabled the library to overcome the limitations of its poverty in some measure, and this it has done in a way that has drawn the attention of the library world. But these new conditions—in some respects unusually favorable and happy—have given rise to, or have compelled, new methods and practices. The one-room quarters in the fieldhouses have prevented as complete a segregation of children and adults as librarians deem desirable. A bookcase set through the middle of the room is commonly the only sort of partition possible. Again the small quarters necessitate a closer and severer scrutiny of the books, while the single attendant in charge of such a room must embody qualifications which, under other conditions, would be supplied by a staff of from three to five persons.

It is a strange and unaccountable fact that Chicago, usually so quick to grasp opportunities and to respond with lavish generosity to her common needs, has been so neglectful of her Public Library.

With an annual revenue subject to the idiosyncracies of our municipal taxing system, we are keeping house at the library with $45,000 less this year than we had a year ago, and the prospects are that our income will continue to dwindle as our city grows richer and greater.

Again, during all the forty years of the library's life, for it sprang literally out of the great fire of 1871, but two citizens thought well enough of it to enable it through their help to make a beginning in the direction of library extension by means of branch buildings. Two branches in a city of 2,000,000, divided into thirty-five wards, any one of which is more populous than the next largest city in the state!

So the library has had to accept the hospitality of kindred and more fortunate institutions. It has become the tenant of the great park systems, occupying rooms in the field houses, tendered without charge, even for heat, light and maintenance, by the park boards. And because the South Park Board is the richest and best equipped and the most generous, therefore the South Side has the most library facilities—to say nothing of the two branch buildings, both of which are in the south division. And because the great West Side has not so prosperous a park board, there are only three library branches over there; and the North Side, having the least prosperous park board, has no branches at all.

The old suburban railway station in the former suburb of Lawndale has been converted into one of the busiest and most successful of all our branches. A "store" on West Twenty-sixth Street, formerly occupied by a saloon, attempts to serve the library needs of that vast region. Makeshifts—miserable, pitiful, inadequate; that is what Chicago has had to employ in order to keep somewhere within hailing distance of the march of library extension, in which it should hold the front rank.

I refer you to our exhibit in the Child's Welfare Exhibit for more detail and further information as to our equipment and the want of it. We have tried to show by means of pictures and statistics, both what we are doing with what we have, and how sorely we are in need of means—means, if not adequate, at least a little less than pitiful in the prosecution of one of the greatest missions of civilization.

Let me, in closing, fall for a moment into figures. The library now has: One main building, seventeen circulating centers, ten depositories in business houses, fourteen school depositories, thirty-seven other temporary depositories, eighty delivery stations which are mere places of call for books and return of books on requisition, eight reading-rooms from which books cannot be drawn for use at home, a total of 167; of these only three have more than 10,000 books. From all but eight of these centers, books may be taken home by registered book borrowers, of whom there are now 125,000—in a city of 2,000,000.

So much for statistics, which I have intentionally avoided in this account. If I have introduced them here, it was only in order to hold before you a faint suggestion of what might be done by way of library extension with an equipment measurably adequate; an equipment, say, comprising one separate branch building, with 25,000 volumes and an income to support it, in every ward. Can you imagine what library extension might mean under such conditions? We of the library staff have never dared to follow the possibilities of this dream to a conclusion!

RESOURCES OF EDUCATION

THOMAS C. CHAMBERLIN

Professor of Geology and Director of Museums,
The University of Chicago

The key to modern education may be found in the principle of coming into as close contact as possible with the subject to be studied. If the subject is tangible, it then appeals to those activities of the human mind which are clearest and firmest and most reliable in their workings. It is fortunate that the subjects of this conference lie chiefly in the field of the visible and the tangible. They embrace things that present themselves impressively, things that may be made the basis of visual and tactual scrutiny and of corrective and critical tests. These naturally lead on to clear and sound thinking, and thence to sound and true feeling, and at length find their consummation in right action. In the combination of clear thought, of true feeling, and of righteous action, lies the trinity of good citizenship, as well as the trinity of noble manhood and womanhood.

The subjects of our conference bear on lines of education which concern the actual work of life as well as the general activities and culture of life. We are coming to realize that there is an education—an education of peculiar power—in those things that concern the activities of the whole being, the activities of physical labor, the activities of sight and touch, followed by pondering and reasoning on what is seen and handled, and the activities of feeling aroused by nature and by art followed by reflection on the emotions called into play. We are coming to the conviction that in the industries of life there are resources of education of the highest value. An American citizen who chooses to have no work to do is not entitled to be counted worth while. There are, to be sure, idlers in the lower walks, and idlers in the higher walks, but they are not worthy of a place in the serious concerns of the American people. Every good citizen has his work, whatever be its line, whether of the hand or of the head, whether of the voice or of the touch. And every child who is trained for his own truest happiness and the community's highest welfare, is educated for some form of productive occupation.

Now, we shall hear directly, in the course of the program, respecting several resources of education. Among others we shall learn of the resources for the promotion of child welfare through the ordinary occupations. But education is not confined to this field. Those who are familiar with the field of art tell us that in the training of the artist there is a schooling not only in close observation, but in a peculiar type of observation. To me a footrule here or a footrule there is much the same thing, a mere footrule, but to the artist the measure becomes a dimension and takes on a world of meaning according to its relations. So the artist must see accurately not only the measure itself, but its relations; he must see not only objects but perspectives. If he reproduces in plastic substance, he must see not only the flat form, but the solid, round object as it stands forth in its place. More than that, not only must he see form and position, but, if a true artist, he must feel the soul and the spirit that is in the subject of study and in its activities. So in the child, if he is to have his full measure of happiness, if his whole nature is to be developed, there must be not only the seeing of the thing and the seeing of the relations of the thing, but the feeling of the soul and the spirit that is in it and in its activities.

THE CHICAGO ART INSTITUTE AND THE CHILD

W. M. R. FRENCH

Director of the Chicago Art Institute

The Art Institute has two great departments, the School and the Museum. The School has for many years had a juvenile department. If I remember rightly, it was in the autumn of 1881 that I started a little class of children under Miss Caroline Wade, who was a very young lady then, and is a teacher now in the Art Institute. It was a little group of perhaps not more than five children who desired to take lessons. It was, however, a recognition of what the ministers call "a felt want." Presently more children came; we found new teachers and new space, until at length upon Saturday forenoon there are four or five hundred children studying drawing, painting, modeling, and a few minor arts.

The children are subdivided somewhat in the manner of a Sunday school, into classes of ten to fifteen, by age and sex; and they are taught for the most part by advanced students, young men and young women of the Art Institute. The young teacher remains with the group of students during the whole period of the lesson, the two hours from ten to twelve. The children draw from objects, and from statues, and occasionally from domestic animals such as rabbits and fowl, small creatures that can be brought into the classroom.

The favorite medium perhaps is colored chalk and gray paper. It is surprising how good some of their drawings are. I often remark that the children do about as well as the older people, partly by reason of the naïve courage with which they attack their subjects.

With us, children not only are taught to draw and exercise their faculties, but are occasionally taken by their teachers through the galleries, where explanations are made of the pictures.

There are other juvenile classes, which have grown up on certain afternoons in the week, but which are by no means so large as the Saturday morning class. Of course these are not free classes. We have no free classes. It is rather a matter of pride with us that the hundreds and thousands of students who attend the Art Institute are all willing and are, for the most part, able to pay. We find many ways to help them out with their tuition; moreover, the fees are extremely low. On the whole, we would not have our school free if we could.

The juvenile department has not increased in the last three or four years; and we think that perhaps the automobile, the danger of our streets, has something to do with it. I know of no other reason, for it is an admirable and useful department. It is Goethe, I believe, who says: "Happy is the child who early learns what art is."

We also have a normal department, which again brings us into relation with children, a department in which young men and women—mostly young women—are trained for teachers and supervisors of drawing in the public schools. This is a three-year course, and the graduates are almost sure of appointments. These students study in the regular school one-half their time, and they are very good students of what we call "academic art," the regular drawing and painting. It is one of our theories that a very good qualification for a drawing teacher is to know how to draw. This seems to be somewhat overlooked in some systems of training. I remember one young lady who entered our school, who said she didn't want to learn a great deal; just enough to teach.

Our normal department includes instruction not only in drawing, but in the manual arts that are suitable to the school, that is, small metal-work, pottery, woodwork, and the like, which may be taught to children in the public schools.

Another point at which we come in contact with the public schools is the production of mural paintings for the decoration of public-school buildings. For several years past we have been in the habit of taking in work, as it were, for the decoration of schoolrooms. Our students are trained in decoration, illustration, and mural painting. A school in the city will raise a small sum of money, a hundred dollars or two hundred dollars; this money will pay for the canvas and the paint and the models that are necessary; and our students make decorations, sometimes twenty-five or thirty feet long. It is a matter of great interest to our visitors from other art schools in the East, or in Europe. When they are sufficiently dignified and important, we take them in an automobile around to the different schools of the city to show them the mural paintings that have been produced by our students; scenes, perhaps, from the life of Columbus; or a certain scene of the American Indian, and the like. The sailing from Palos is one of the subjects, I remember; a miracle play is another; and the landing at Jamestown, another. The teachers say that they are of exceeding value in the inculcation of history. They certainly decorate the buildings; and I scarcely know of anything else like this done anywhere in the world.

The young man who executed the best work last year, who surprised us by taking our first honors while still under nineteen years, explained to us that he had been attending the Saturday juvenile class ever since he was twelve years old. So you see that the Saturday juvenile class has its office in the education of an artist.

With regard to the Museum, I noticed a placard in the Exhibition stating that there was no museum for children in Chicago, and I reflected that there was no museum for old gentlemen in Chicago. At the Art Institute we welcome children as well as old people; and we have found no need for such restrictions as are adopted in many museums, namely that children shall be attended by grown persons. We have never had any trouble on that score. It has never occurred to us to keep any account of the number of children who come to the Art Institute. I suppose the number must be considerable, for I often see groups of them going about, frequently with their teachers but sometimes unattended, examining the collections. We always admit groups of children with their teachers free of charge; and when we are asked, we furnish a guide, or, to use the Boston word, a "docent," a person to guide and teach.

We have at times put our galleries at the disposal of the art departments of the public schools. There have been times for weeks and months together when those beautiful galleries have been occupied by the drawings and other works of the public schools. They have excited a great deal of interest, and I hope that these exhibitions have done a great deal of good. Indeed we have gone a great way in this matter, for we have admitted objects produced in manual training, which would scarcely be admitted in any other class of exhibitions.

In the same way, we have exhibited the works that the Public School Art Society has collected for different schools—works suitable to children.

I may say in passing that it is a fortunate thing with regard to the graphic and plastic arts that their productions are comprehensible by old and young alike. It has always seemed to me a wonderful advantage of pictorial art that it is enjoyed not only by old people and middle-aged people but by children as well; it is a universal language.

There are other things that it is conceivable we might easily do, and if they are useful things, we shall scarcely rest until we do them. I may explain that we do not carry out all our plans at the Institute, because the constant activity, growth and extension of the institution tax the small force of officials there, so that we imagine things that we cannot carry into execution.

I believe that in some cities, such as Pittsburgh and Philadelphia, they have offered prizes in the schools for essays on works of art exhibited in the museum. It seems to me that is a very good device and would interest a great many children.

Of course our cult is not especially children, but rather the whole community. As I have said, we make children welcome; we recognize them in the schools; we recognize them in our exhibitions; and we are glad to do all we can to promote this most fundamental matter in the cultivation of children.

A NATURAL HISTORY MUSEUM AND WORKSHOP FOR CHILDREN

WALLACE W. ATWOOD

Professor of Geology, The University of Chicago; and Secretary, Chicago Academy of Sciences

We have thought of our museum, and of our exhibit here, as playing a unique part in child-welfare work, a part quite different from that of any other institution in the city, and I think quite different from that of any other institution in the country. We have arranged our exhibits to illustrate some of the ways in which natural-history material may be displayed so as to hold the attention of children, so as to be of interest to the children; so as to be educationally effective.

We appreciate the fact that many adults come into our section, and with a glance pass on, and, like the "globe trotter," check it off with no more to say than: "There, I have done it." But the children come right into the booth, they remain, they ask questions, they put their faces to the glass and hold them there; their interest is intense, they want to know of the natural objects about them, their minds are open, their wits alert, they want to study and to learn.

A natural-history museum, as we look upon it now, may serve several purposes; the display-exhibits may arouse an interest in the natural-history objects. That is but a beginning. The child who has become interested will ask to join one of the classes. The more advanced student will ask to see the materials in the drawers and the large systematic collections that are stored away.

We know there are museums, perhaps most of us have visited them, where each group of objects is arranged according to the orders, the families, and the species, until we are tired of looking at the abundance of material. Such exhibits are interesting to the specialists in the particular lines, but we are arranging our material so as to arouse an interest in the study of the natural sciences. We are arranging the objects, so far as possible, as they are out of doors; the birds are seen among the branches, the insects upon the bark or leaves or in the flowers.

In addition to the material on exhibition in a museum and the research collections for the specialists, there is an abundance of material which might be used in laboratory courses of instruction. We have started such work and have found a greater demand than we can supply. We offered the courses to the children of the public schools, and they came in such numbers that we had to devise some way of selecting the classes. We now receive one delegate appointed from each class, and these little delegates come as representatives of the classes, as little reporters. They go back to the school and report the lesson which they have attended; the teachers give them an opportunity on the following Monday, or on some day when they have a general exercise. The principals and teachers say that these little reporters bring into the classroom something new and fresh, something which is really a great inspiration to the other children; and the little reporter is ambitious to come again to the Academy and to obtain another story to tell. You realize this if you think back to your school days when everybody knew the same lesson; it was in the textbook and you could recite it as well as anybody else. How tedious it was to sit through such a period! We send the child back to the room with something fresh, something new. He has something to interest his audience and to give to his audience. By this method the work of the Academy reaches about five thousand children each week.

In addition to this work for children at the Academy building, we have prepared nearly one hundred loan collections, which are loaned free of charge to the schools. Any public or private school teacher may secure one of them and hold it at her school for a week. We are carrying on this work as a suggestion to Chicago. It is done on a large scale in New York City, where the Board of Education appropriates thousands of dollars each year for the preparation and distribution of such museum collections. In New York there is an automobile service, and the teacher needs but to telephone in and ask for a certain collection, and it comes to the school when wanted. The St. Louis Board of Education does likewise, and the public museum in Milwaukee is carrying on a similar co-operative work. There is a great opportunity for such work in Chicago. The Academy cannot serve more than the North Side at present. We are trying, however, to demonstrate what might be done. We have demonstrated that there is a great demand from the children for opportunities to study the natural sciences.

Soon after the children's classes were begun at the Academy, we saw that among the children a number of teachers were scattered, and we learned, incidentally, why they came. They said that, when "Johnny" came back on Monday, he had a number of questions to ask which they were not quite ready to answer. They were conscientious teachers. To answer that demand, we offered, free of charge, courses of instruction to the teachers of children, and to do this work, we engaged instructors whom we could vouch for as thorough scientists. Evening lectures were offered at the Academy to which the children delegates from the schools could come. Illustrated talks were given at the schools. Special lessons were offered and field trips planned. The work has developed as rapidly as funds would permit. As we have watched this educational side of the museum work develop, we have been impressed with the great demand for educational opportunities. The teachers and the children want a chance. They will do the work, if they have an opportunity.

As we arranged the exhibits in the museum for the children, the parents became more interested; they, too, could then see something in the exhibits. I think it will be the history of the movement as we go on and rearrange our museum from the instructional point of view that the adults will see more in the exhibits. I should like to point out to you briefly what this work ought to lead to. Chicago has no museum dedicated to children. However we are all welcoming the children; other museums in the city are welcoming them. We are all doing what we can for children, but no institution has adapted a museum to children. There is only one children's museum in the world, and that is in Brooklyn and is conducted by the Brooklyn Institute of Arts and Sciences. There is no doubt from our standpoint that the place to take hold and to do the most effective work in the natural sciences is with the children. The parent does not care very much about the minerals, rocks, wild flowers, butterflies, or the birds, unless he has had that interest aroused when he was young. That is our experience as instructors; it is our experience at this exhibit; and it is our experience at the Academy museum. There is nothing in this city which does for the children what the Children's Museum of the Brooklyn Institute of Arts and Sciences does for the children there. We are doing what we can in Lincoln Park to work out a plan for such an institution. Perhaps it will be our duty to work over our museum almost wholly from this point of view.

We work with strong, healthy children. They are active and alert, both physically and mentally. They are first-class material and we, therefore, get high-class results. We work with strong, ambitious, and conscientious teachers of children, and the returns for the work with them are, therefore, large and unusually satisfactory.

A children's museum with a large auditorium, with laboratories and workrooms for instructional work, with model classrooms for teachers to use who bring their classes to the museum, with a suitable reading-room, with a staff of carefully selected instructors, with loan collections for the schools, and with lecture courses for children and parents, might become a wonderfully attractive and effective museum. The field for such a museum is yet unoccupied in Chicago.

THE HULL-HOUSE LABOR MUSEUM

JANE ADDAMS

I feel that the word "museum" is a very large word to apply to our little experiment at Hull-House, although I was naturally very proud to be asked to represent it, with the other museums, in this conference. We opened it perhaps ten years ago in the desire to bring together the immigrant parents and their Americanized children. No one knows unless he lives in an immigrant district and acquires their point of view, how wide the gulf is apt to be between the experiences of the parents who come from the Old World and the children who are born and brought up in America.

In the first place most of them come from the country to the city. Take the south Italians, nine out of every ten of the families who come to Chicago have lived in the country. That in itself is a very difficult adjustment for a grown-up person to make. Then, of course, they come from their own customs, from their own ways of living, from their own foods, from their own occupations, into those of another country; and are surrounded by a people of quite another language and quite another tradition. They have a hard time, but I think never so hard a time as when they feel that their own children are slipping away from them and more or less perhaps—despising them is too strong a word, but at any rate wishing that they were like Americans and not quite so unlike all the people around them.

The parents tell us sometimes how they feel. More often they do not formulate it, but it is not difficult to guess. This Labor Museum of ours was an attempt to bridge over, as best we might, some of the experiences that the parents had in the old country with the very unlike experiences the children were having in America. We began naturally with industries because they were the things that the people could do most easily; the things that would interpret them most directly to their own children and to other Americans. We have a little textile department; perhaps I may confine my illustration to that because it is the most obvious one, the one which has worked out most easily. The mothers knew how to spin and weave and dye and full and reel and use all the things employed in making textiles when they were in the old country. Here the children were working in sewing factories, in sweat shops many of them, with no notion that the goods which they were handling had any connection with anything except a downtown store. They got the goods in the factory, took it home, and made it up; or went down to the factory and did their work; and that was the end of it. The things that they were handling all day did not seem in the least to touch them or any experience in their parents' lives.

But when we could get the Italian women or the Greek women to spin with the spindle and to put into operation four or five methods of spinning, we began to have a thing that was very interesting to people in the schools and that gradually became interesting to the children of the immigrants. When they saw the University ladies, as they like to call the people from the School of Education, standing up and looking at the women spinning in this way, and when they found out that this was a matter of great interest and admiration, of course they began to look at it a little differently. And when we were able to show the connection of this method of producing textiles, both with some of the experiences the parents had in the old country, and with the very goods the children were handling here, they began to see that there was a vital interest, a real interest between themselves and their parents.

Now we have gone on in other arts; we have done something with pottery, something with metals, something with wood; but nothing has stuck quite so readily as the textiles. The women enjoy it very much; they like the prestige that it gives them but they like perhaps more than anything else the respect that it induces their children to pay to the things they can do. After all, if you have always washed in the stream and not in a tub, if you have always woven your garments and not gone to a ready-made clothing store to buy them, you find yourself very much at sea when you have to change all these habits. And some one who comes in with a little story of understanding, who helps straighten out the tangle for you and makes you feel, not as if you were all alone in a new, strange place, but as if you had some connection with it that goes back to your mother or to your grandmother, does bring some solace to your weary and perturbed soul. We see that the Labor Museum has done that for some of the people; we think it has suggested it to many more people; and we know that it has made the children look upon their parents in a different light.

A curious thing is that some women who have come from South Russia or from parts of Italy have never seen a spinning-wheel. They have always used a straight stick spindle, or distaff. If you go to the Art Institute you will see pictures of it. All the wool that was spun into anything had to be spun by that stick spindle. They never knew any other method until they came to the buying of ready-made clothing. It is a tremendous jump from the stick spindle, which was used by the mother or the daughter, I have no doubt, when David tended his sheep, to the ready-made clothing store; it is leaping over a good many centuries of development. And if it can be bridged, as we are trying somewhat gently to bridge it, I think that something has been done from the human standpoint, if not from the museum standpoint.

Then the children of course are very much interested in different materials. We have a little collection of flags, wool, silk and cotton; and the children who sew or do dressmaking are taught something of the material they are handling. And this again is put back into the experiences of their parents. A little chart we have shows the long years in which the stick spindle was used, up to the fifteenth century in Europe; the very short three hundred years when the spinning-wheel was used in Europe, and then the very short century since steam has been applied to textile manufacturing. And when we look about us and see that great adjustment which the textile industry displays, the tremendous sacrifice and difficulties at Fall River, the tremendous difficulties we have had in our own city this year, in regard to the making of clothing, one can be a little solaced by this point of view, that after all it is new; that we have not yet adjusted ourselves to it, and that after we have used steam in the making of textiles for a thousand years or two thousand years, as they used the stick spindle, perhaps we shall get the same beauty and order. At any rate, until we do get that, there is no use throwing aside all the beauty, order, and charm which the stick spindle preserves. Sometimes we get a little sentimental about this. I remember the other evening that a Greek woman was spinning in the museum, and a young Greek was looking wistfully on. I said, "I suppose this reminds you of your mother." He said, "Yes; I don't like to look at a stick spindle; she always beat me with it." So perhaps there is another side to the whole story. At any rate we think that there is a charm about it to which people very quickly respond.

HISTORY, PATRIOTISM, AND THE CHILD

CAROLINE McILVAINE

Librarian, Chicago Historical Society

I have often thought of something that Miss Addams said to me about five years ago. It was, that she was glad that there was a historical society in Chicago, because she came in contact with a class of people from the old world who were used to surroundings that were old and who hungered for the old when they came to this country where things are crude and new. The Greeks especially, she said, were very contemptuous of the lack of age of our American cities, so that she was glad to tell them that the Chicago Historical Society stood for what is old.

For more than fifty years the Chicago Historical Society has maintained a museum for old things—old manuscripts, old books, old newspapers and directories, old portraits, old furniture from spinning wheels to spinnets, and old clothes all the way from Long John Wentworth's sizable slipper to General Grant's "seedy" straw hat or Abraham Lincoln's ample broadcloth coat.

For some reason in past generations old things were supposed to be interesting only to old people. And all honor is to be given to the men and women who in the midst of the general newness of things realized the delight that would be afforded to those who made Chicago, in looking back through the medium of our little museum upon the trophies of their own time of strenuousness. The society has afforded to such people a "place to put things" and a place for meeting people of their own ilk.

But recently, in the last few years, almost unobserved, there has come a change in the work—not that it has shifted entirely, but that a new element has entered it. We have found that there is an increasing number of children visiting us. At first there were classes from private schools; we would find groups of small boys, for instance, in front of the model of Fort Dearborn, the favorite exhibit with children, taking notes about it. Sometimes small notebooks were accidentally left behind; and we would find the most amusing little comments about it. Occasionally the teachers have shown us essays written by these pupils which showed that they had grasped in a remarkable way the idea of the beginning of Chicago.

And so we have tried to adapt, especially from the history of Chicago—although the field of the society covers the entire Northwest—those things that could be graphically represented to children. We never fail to get their interest in the Stone Age of the Chicago region, which is a field rich in archaeological remains—especially Bowmanville, the largest of the Indian villages, where the makers of weapons were the best workmen in the region. Recently we had a very large exhibit of the weapons and utensils from the Bowmanville region, and in connection with it we exhibited a series of maps showing Indian trails around Chicago. It would be hard for you to imagine the interest the children took in them. Often it was simply impossible to separate the groups of boys from those maps. It would become dark and time to close, and they could not leave them.

The next period, the French régime, the period of the discoveries and explorations of Marquette and Joliet and LaSalle and Tonti, we have also made interesting to the children by our series of reliefs showing various scenes from the lives of the explorers. But most interesting of all are the beginnings of pioneer life, the building of Fort Dearborn, whose protection made possible the settlement of the "pale faces." To illustrate this we have an exact model of the fort, which pleases the children beyond description. From it they can study the type of frontier fort and the conditions under which the first settlement in this locality was made.

As you think it over you will find yourself inevitably wondering what this is going to do for them. And I think the conclusion will be reached that, as the children learn of the beginnings of our Chicago institutions, which are thoroughly typical of America, there cannot fail to be developed in them that local pride which will blossom into love of country.

The lectures of the society are open to children whenever they wish to come; and they do come to the illustrated lectures.

The society publishes very little that is simple enough for children. A great desideratum is that a fund be established for this purpose. So far, the funds of the society have been adequate only for the publication of material interesting to old gentlemen and to very learned historical students, but there is evidently room for publications that will deal with these historical subjects in a way that is suitable for the young students. The patriotic societies are about to publish a "primer of patriotism," and it is surely a great and good aim to help the native-born as well as the foreign-born child to be a good citizen.

PART EIGHT

SOCIAL AND CIVIC PROBLEMS OF CHILDHOOD

"Come forth, oh, ye children of gladness"

THE CHURCH AND THE CHILD

REV. JOHN TIMOTHY STONE
Fourth Presbyterian Church, Chicago

I wish to ask you to consider with me, first, the obligation which we have to the child, so far as the state is concerned, or so far as the child is related to society; second, the obligation or responsibility which we have to our Creator; in following out His method and manner of procedure in the development of that which is highest and best as He relates himself to the child, and relates us to the child; and again, our opportunity, responsibility and privilege with the child himself.

In the consideration of the problem from the standpoint of the state or society, we find that those nations have progressed and been blessed of God and of men which have given first place and first thought to the consideration of their children. In classical times although the religious relationship or the religious consideration did not enter in then as it enters in now, from the standpoint of the highest culture and the highest training, the child had first place, and justly so. They recognized the power and the influence of the child. They realized it, not simply for the child's sake, nor with a sense of responsibility to a person, but they built on the great essential units of society, and realized what great men had been in their boyhood and youth, and what they might become with the proper development.

In fact, today, we can judge of the tenor of a nation, the ability, the insight, and the force of a nation by the treatment that nation gives to its children, by the amount of sacrifice it expends for its children, and by the means it is willing to give in order that they may be trained. That is why the great test of a nation today is not her public buildings, her governmental forms, her constitution, her ecclesiasticism; but her relationship and her recognized obligations to the children that constitute her life.

This truth has not always been recognized by shortsighted men and women. A man recently wrote me a letter of which the purport was: "Why spend your time with the children? Why think of the future of the boys? Why not be a great man in your time and take up the great problems of men and women and deal with them, instead of wasting your time with the problems of the future and the children?"

That man is earnest; but there is a pathos about earnestness sometimes, and the pathos of his earnestness is its lack of foresight and the lack of intelligent consideration given to his subject.

There are three kinds of work which may be considered in aiding humanity: Preventive work, constructive work, and the work we call the work of reclaiming.

The most fascinating work from the standpoint of the exterior is the work of reclaiming, but it is shortsighted. A man comes to you with a tottering form; his clothes are ragged; his face speaks poverty and need: or a mother comes with a crying infant in her arms. We see in that child's face a mingling of poverty and want and hunger, and our hearts immediately respond. We instinctively say: "This is the work which should be done at once; we must reclaim these who have fallen by the wayside and need our help."

This condition does not usually appear from the standpoint of the child, so the second illustration may be a little far drawn. It usually appears with the men or women who have gone beyond childhood and who seem to have little hope or little chance; and our hearts go out to them.

It is very much easier to work in a rescue mission than to work with those who are just entering upon life. It seems easier to extend help to the fallen than to keep the youth from wandering. That is the reason why we find a great deal of our religious activity and our philanthropic activity centered in rescue work; and in a city like our own, there ought to be far more work of this character done than is being done. There is an immense amount of it to be done among both women and men. There is no pastor in this city who does not come into personal contact with this problem, whether he be Romanist or Protestant, Israelite or Gentile. The problem faces him everywhere, for it is the problem of the mothers who do not know to whom else to turn, of the stranger who knowing nowhere else to go turns to one who has named the name of God. It is the problem of reclaiming those who are lost.

There is also another great problem—the constructive problem. The constructive problem is not simply the question of the child; it is the problem of those who are no longer children, but who are just at the turning point of life. Anyone who has ever followed a woods road through the forest will realize the tremendous divergence of a very slight angle. The woodsman will tell you to be careful at a turn of the pathway, especially if that woods road is cut up by a great many paths. The forest in which there is little liability of being lost, if careful, is the primeval forest, not the forest which has been inhabited in previous times. The place where you are going to be lost is the place where the old-time woods roads were made by the wild deer; and, if you do not know the woods very well, you do not distinguish between the paths of men and the paths of the wild deer. You take this old woods road; you think that surely this is the way; it makes only the slightest kind of an angle; it will not make much difference one way or the other; but as night comes on, perhaps twelve or fifteen miles have been traveled and your road has turned unnoticed to a greater angle and you are lost.

We find in the study of mankind that this is the condition facing us all the time; this constructive work is the guiding of the young people in our cities who have got to the point of divergence and are waiting for the right leadership into life. This is a much more difficult problem than that of reaching those who are to be reclaimed. The boy does not care to have anything to do with you if he thinks you are after him and want to help him. The girl will keep as far away from you as possible if she thinks you are going to rob her of her independence; and it takes the wisest sympathy to win her confidence and bring her into a relation of true leadership. This is just where we are losing them.

Let us consider some of the work that our religious societies and Sunday schools are doing in the way of reaching the young. A large percentage of the young men and women are lost so far as any permanent influence is concerned just at the turning point. Moreover, many of them are lost by the very efforts put forth to aid them. A girl has been active in her church at home. She goes away to school or to college. She may have made a great effort so that she may be able to do more in the world. But the church in the old home loses her, and unless we are extremely careful, the church in the new home never finds her. When she comes back home, the girls and boys whom she knew have gone away. She does not feel at home. She has grown above those who have stayed at home; she has gone on in her intellectual life. She has no interest in matters that once interested her, including the church at home. She feels that in her study of philosophy and psychology she has solved many of the problems of life, whereas she is at the very place where she needs help for the practical application of what she has learned, where she should realize her obligation to adjust herself to practical life.

There is only one way of meeting the difficulty; that is by putting those young people to work. I remember a young girl who came home with all the enthusiasm of the leadership that she exercised in college. She had been popular in school; she was womanly, attractive and lovable; she led in the drawing-room as well as on the athletic field; no matter where she was, she always led. She came back but did not go back into the Sunday school in her home town. She drifted out of that activity. One day the superintendent said to her: "I have something for you to do. I have a class of street gamins that no one can handle. Three or four teachers have had them. They worked havoc in our Sunday school. Last Sunday they had a man teacher, and they threw him out of the Sunday school, and then went away and said they would never come back. I want you to take those boys, they have something in them; you gain a hold on them and teach them." She replied: "You may give those boys to me." So she took the class and went two or three Sundays and nobody came. She inquired where they lived. She became interested in some of the things boys are interested in; she got two or three of her young friends who understood and could reach boys to go with her. With them she visited the boys' homes. One boy's mother said: "He don't want to go to

Sunday school, but, Miss, I will see that he does go; if you are willing to look him up, he is going to be there!''

Within two months she had all the boys in school, not punching each other or rapping each other over the head with hymn books, but with their heads together, paying particular attention to the lesson, interested in her and in what she said to them.

What was the result? Inside of three or four months, that girl became so interested in those boys that she had four or five college girls, recently back from school, in the same kind of work. The standard of that particular Sunday school was brought up to a mark it had never known before. The officers had never been able to reach the college girls and boys when they came back. They were away at week-end parties on Sunday. They were not interested; but that girl had such an influence that she brought up the standard of that Sunday school simply by the practical application of her knowledge to the work which was needed there. She never had any trouble after that with her philosophy or her religious interpretations. She saw what life was in the homes of those boys. She saw what sin was and what it was doing, and she went to work in a practical, common-sense way, became interested in her work, and interested others.

A very effective device for interesting those who are leaders is giving them something real to do. The trouble with many in philanthropic work and religious work, is that they talk about the work to be done and then do not show people how to do it, or give them anything to do. What people want, is not to theorize, but to do something.

Take a boy and show him where he is going to make some headway, and that boy will be interested and may become a leader. We can get boys tomorrow if we give them something to do. Let me give you an illustration in this city. Out on the North Side, six or seven years ago, Dr. Notman, who was then the pastor of the church which it is now my privilege to serve, found a certain crowd of boys who lived not far from the church, who were known as the liveliest boys of that entire neighborhood; some men and women even said that that crowd was the worst crowd on the North Side. Dr. Notman saw in these boys splendid material. There was at first no place for them to play, but they went to the school authorities and obtained the use of a school playground on the North Side. They played ball regularly there, and worked along together; and this last winter, five of those boys met with me one night and talked with me about the life of Christian character and of the things pertaining to God. They came into the church, and one of them said: "I am interested in my business; I have a good job, but I want to be as much interested in the cause of Christ as I am in my business, but somehow I don't know Him." In coming into the church they were just as earnest and sincere as they ever were in their whole lives.

The fact is: The time we lose the boys is the very time important constructive work should be done. The boy scouts movement may do good in this direction with the younger boys but it does not reach the class a little older, and in my opinion the time spent in theorizing ought sometimes to be spent in gaining the personal spirit and the personal sympathy of these boys; for to gain them is to hold them for society and for the future.

Boys are organized into all kinds of activities all over our city. They know what it is to be true citizens. They have their idea as to the great problems of life. Fifty or a hundred can be gathered together by an active leader, if he has their sympathy and their confidence, and he can say things to them that their mothers and their fathers cannot say. He can point out the temptations that within a year or two are bound to be theirs. He can control them for a better and nobler citizenship, for a more godly character, if he will take his time and his way to present the truth, by having gained them at the time when they are liable to be lost to society and good government.

The most important phase of the work, however, is the preventive work, which is especially emphasized in this conference and Exhibit. That is the work of giving to the child his own opportunity.

What are we to do in this preventive work? Our eyes have been opened by this Exhibit in a way they have not perhaps been opened before, especially as to that which is being done in our city. This city is doing a wonderful amount for the child; it is in the very thick of the fight for child-welfare, facing it even as those who are in earnest. What does it mean, then? It means we must care for our children, not simply for the sake of the state and its opportunity for that which is highest and best; not simply for the sake of fulfilling our obligations to Almighty God, but for the child himself. We must give him a chance in that which is his. Give him his physical nature with all its splendid capacity, his mental equipment, and his moral responsibility. And especially give him his spiritual insight, without which his life would not be four square. I plead for a spirit of interpretation that will give to men an appreciation of life which is four square and give to the child that which he deserves. Fine physical development is a splendid thing. If, however, children face life with simply a physical development, they will not have that complete equipment which is their due; and they will not be able to face life as they should. They should have a love and affection for one who is infinite and eternal and unchangeable; who watches the sparrow in its fall; who numbers the very hairs of our heads. If he does not have that, the child is growing up without that which he deserves and without that which it is our responsibility to give to him.

Men and women, there is a chance, a greater chance than we have ever had before, to do this today, to realize and live up to our responsibilities. The Sunday school that is satisfied simply with principles, with doing for its children what our fathers did, noble as that work was, satisfied to do simply for its boys and girls that which has been done, is falling short and is responsible for a lack of appreciation of its opportunities. Our Sunday schools ought to be as well equipped, as well taught as any of our public or private schools. We ought to give to our boys and girls such an interesting and inspiring instruction as will give them a wholesome impetus through life. We ought to give to the boy his chance; give to the girl her opportunity; we ought to give to them an interest in that which we call the spiritual forces of life.

I see a great city; it needs light. There is an immense dynamo, and that dynamo with all its tremendous strength can put the wheels of industry in motion, so that the city can do all it desires to do. That dynamo has the power to light its streets and homes, even into its darkest corners. There is the dynamo. There is the city, and here is a great cable. That cable is human agency placed in the lives of children. What must we do to connect the cable with the dynamo? It is not enough that we have mere asceticism that worships God in the wilderness without touching humanity. That cable must be connected with the dynamo at one end, at the other end with the city, and human agency working through boyhood and girlhood will put those lights into motion and will light that city, even going into its darkest places and giving light to all who dwell therein.

WELFARE WORK WITH BOYS

ALLAN HOBEN

Professor of Homiletics, The University of Chicago

The first point that I wish to make is that we should follow the order of nature. The order of nature has brought us a boy out of a very long and intricate process, he being the last product of our human evolution and bringing with him a certain nervous and muscular outfit that has to be satisfied. He comes to us with great motor propensities, which in a formative time were worth more than the reflective habit. This kind of boy is inclined to be ever active, whether he is in the Sunday school, in the day school, in the home or in the club. The first thing to do is to connect, if possible, with the succeeding stages in the boy's life; not that any one of the stages which might be called purely natural is conclusive in itself, but that it is the point of attachment for educative purposes; and that as various inclinations emerge we should be sufficiently familiar with the general course in the boy's life to do the best for him at that particular emergence of interest. I think that some of our failures in dealing with the city boy come principally from inhibition; from the endeavor to turn primitive custom back upon itself and to set about it in a very rigid way the standards that the reflective adult has worked out and recognizes.

Of course, the adventurous spirit by which the boy comes very naturally often dominates him; his inclination to run in groups or gangs, his mania for collecting things, his dim perception of property rights—these and other instincts are natively his and belong to him by right of a long process. He has those powers in him that must be released, and he is unfamiliar with the artificialities of city life. Everything depends upon direction. You cannot deal with him as the superficial mother did with her boy when she regularly said to the maid, "Go and see what Willie is doing and tell him not to." And yet that is the constant thing that the city says. We lack latitude in the home, on the street and everywhere; we live so close to one another that we run the risk of mutual irritation; and we seek our own peace by exercising some form of limitation on this native, spontaneous energy that the boy has. The only way is to follow the order of nature in all the stages in the boy's life, whether they be savage, barbaric, or civilized; whether or not they have in them some glimmer of correct association; whatever they may be, not to stop with them as an ultimate goal but to connect with them for the boy's full development. For it often happens that unless a boy has a just measure of development at one of these inferior stages, he will not become so good a man in the end. There are many things in a boy's life to which he ought to give expression so that he can get them out of his system. When they are out of his system and he has had full satisfaction from them, something else succeeds. Sometimes the coarser ways of boys are very pronounced. A great deal of the mischief into which such boys fall is due to their insistent endeavor to let you know that they are here, by doing a thing that is out of the ordinary; and a thing that is very far out of the ordinary is likely to offend. To take off energy which is often tangential, which does not have a boy's good judgment or control, to take his hunting and marauding instincts, to turn those instincts into channels—channels that may be semi-scientific even quite early in his life—that is what the club exists for

Then I should say as a second point, capture the natural group. It is far better to deal with boys in groups than to try to get a collection of individual boys. The loyalties that exist, the mutual attachments of natural groups, are very strong in boyhood. Between twelve and fifteen years of age the loyalty that the boy has to his group of co-equals outside the home is probably greater than his attachment to the home, and very possibly the group with which he runs shapes his morals far more distinctly during that critical first period of adolescence than the counsel of father, mother or teacher. For with that group it is all action; and no education without action is effective. The gang, the natural group of the boy, stands for this—the achievement, not of the individual, but of the individual enhanced, strengthened, and reinforced by a congenial group.

Everything depends, however, upon the character of the group. Every time that we can transform one of these natural groups into a club—and the transformation merely means that the natural group is given a responsible and particular leader—we are doing fundamental work with boys. As a rule the trailer, the weak-willed boy, the boy with the least possibilities of loyalty, the boy who cannot stick, will break away and forsake his natural group, but the boy who has the best stuff in him will stay with that group right or wrong. Thus the moral leverage exerted ordinarily by any one of these groups is almost beyond comprehension. The last word in the code is simply like this: "The way we do," "the thing we stand for." And the individual moral judgment of a boy of the age of twelve to fifteen is practically never sufficient to stand out against the common judgment of the crowd with which he runs.

These gangs exist, in my opinion, in very great

numbers throughout the city. From a careful study of Hyde Park, I should make an estimate of about one gang in every two blocks. Some of these gangs are most amusing. Some of them indulge in just a sufficient amount of adventure with the police and with organized and orderly society to satisfy their desire for risk. All of them without proper leadership gravitate downward.

I saw an amusing group the other day of perhaps ten or twelve boys. They were running through the alleys in the Hyde Park section and had taken the tops from the garbage cans as they ran along. Each one had a long stick, and as they ran, they smote the tops of the garbage cans with the aforesaid sticks, all shouting together, "Votes, votes, votes for women."

We found a gang over on Lake Avenue in the saloon district that was made up of some forty-eight boys. They have made a cave for themselves. Boys usually prefer a cave even to a shack, for it is a little more mysterious, a little harder to detect; it gives a little more sense of hiding away. But often they do build the shacks when they can get enough old packing-boxes or loose lumber. These boys, however, had a cave, with a subcellar which they used for keeping the things that they stole from the community, and also for the discipline of unruly members. They had benches around the mud wall, with numbers on the wall from one to forty-eight, and when they were in solemn conclave each one sat in his appointed place; they were organized to that extent. There is a voluntary social experiment. There is what the boy says that he wants. "I want to belong to something that is more than just my own, isolated self; I want a club; I want to be bigger than my isolated self." There is not a home in Chicago that is so good or so well managed that it can provide in full for that instinct and desire of the boy in early adolescence. He must have his group. By following the natural order, then, or the natural instincts of the boy, we see that club work promises no small amount of good.

The very next thing, the third point to be cited, is so familiar that I shall discuss it very briefly. It is the organization of boys' play. You should undertake this, anyway, but the moment you have a club, you succeed in getting a little more rational form of organization. And since 80 per cent of their activity, perhaps more than that, will be in the form of play, the only rational thing is to undertake to organize that play. It is a mistake, however, for us to jump at the conclusion that play is always of moral value. I am quite certain that much of the play in the helter-skelter at school dismissal in some of the congested districts is very far from having any moral value whatsoever; for it emphasizes might as against right; it gives the bully a chance but it never gives the timid boy the gratification a boy ought to have in play. When boys try to play in an unorganized way and make up their nines in a vacant lot, notice what profanity and dispute there is as to the positions in which they will play and as to whether this one or that one is out, and so forth. The wise leader of play knows that, human nature being what it is, there must be a court of appeal; he knows that there ought always be an adult player there who, because of his own expert knowledge of the game, commands respect all the time. The boys will then play up to him, so to speak, and get the best possible out of the game, for boys are always looking up, and the authority of a leader who is a little older than themselves is very great.

If the club leader can make leaders out of the rank and file, he is doing the best kind of work. A splendid thing to do is to make leaders of the boys who have about three years' start of those whom they are going to lead, for there is a sort of appreciation, a sort of deference among the boys of any age for boys a little older, which is remarkable. Out of that gang of forty-eight who had made the cave, leaders of play have been developed in the Hyde Park Center. This, I take it, is the right kind of achievement. Get the natural group and organize its play, for its play is the first and great consideration with the group, especially with the group from twelve to fifteen years old.

A few words should be said about the supervision of amusements. When we appreciate the very vivid and powerful suggestions imparted by the various forms of amusement in the city, we know that we must take hold of that series of suggestions and make amusement more wholesome than it is today. It is getting more wholesome all the time, judging by recent investigation of the nickel shows, but it can be made still better in the time to come.

The fourth point to be noticed is this: Diffuse and adapt the opportunities for expression. What I mean by this is, that while I appreciate very greatly the standardization of work for boys in the boys' department of the Young Men's Christian Association, and while I appreciate the advantage of having good, up-to-date equipment, nevertheless, in working in behalf of the delinquent boys of this city in connection with the Juvenile Protective Association, it has dawned upon me more and more that the opportunities must be diffused. The big plant is good for its purposes, but the boys' work required in Chicago cannot be done in any big plant or in any series of big plants. The work must be diffused. The opportunities of swimming should be diffused from one end of the shore to the other, clear down the face of the whole city. That is the natural right of the child throughout the sweltering days of summer, when all the temptations of vacation come upon him. Think of the outlets needed just to guarantee safety and the proper release of the energy. Send out men who are free lances; let them find the boys on the open lots; let them find them as they run wild in the city, make friends among them, and extend their acquaintance to the whole group. Thus for summer work, buildings are less necessary than leaders. If there were more leaders, a good deal of diffused work could be done. I feel that the Young Men's Christian Association and other organizations that are leading in this kind of work are more and more putting this principle into practice. I think when it is felt that we are working from institutions for people rather than with people for institutions we shall accomplish greater good.

In this connection we ought to acknowledge with gratitude the recent work of the Young Men's Christian Association in making a study of the conditions of the wage-earning and foreign boys in our midst. One does not have to be much of a prophet to foresee that they may work out methods that will combine consecration with social wisdom. I look for their doing a fine piece of pioneer work in this field.

The fifth point that I wish to make seems to depart from those already presented, but I feel strongly that, if welfare work with boys is going to be done, their schooling must be more motivated than it is at the present time. It is difficult to work out a curriculum that will satisfy a boy, especially on the constructive side.

Recently I spoke at a high school commencement where the graduating class was composed entirely of girls. I have been told that there are 50 per cent more girl than boy graduates from high schools in New York, Wisconsin and Massachusetts. There may be different reasons for this—reasons that I am not able to ascertain. And yet on the face of it, one feels that somehow we have not put a sufficiently concrete object before the boy in his education. One hesitates to offer criticism, because of the noble character of the work of the public school and because of the magnitude of the task that faces it—for all the problems that come from the congestion of the city are being piled upon the public school. Therefore it seems to me ungracious to turn around and criticize the school because it cannot care for everything all at once. But I should say that in addition to motivating education there is need of an increasing regard for the physical welfare of the boys, and of the girls also, in the school. The present physical examination of children in schools is almost a farce. It cannot be done with the present staff, no matter how faithfully the attempt is made. There is need of a more careful examination that will detect minor defects, for the minor defects are fatal to the school boy's career. A slight defect in vision or in hearing causes him to lose grade and inclines him toward truancy; and from truancy to delinquency is an easy step. Welfare work with boys means that we have to get closer to the actual condition of the boys. We have to increase almost a hundred-fold the provision that is made for actual physical development through the trainer and the director of play. To defer this and to apply it only to the few survivors in high school and college is unjust and sacrifices many lives.

There is a great development, a wonderful development of play in America, and Chicago has field houses that anyone may well admire. But play comes under the head of education and cannot rationally be detached from education. The logical place where it must center finally is the place where the children congregate, that is, at the public schools.

The matter of motivated education passes necessarily, it seems to me, into the next point to be made—that is, that the boy must be connected with the world's work. I mean by that, that the vocational interest must be recognized. It seems almost criminal for society to expend the money it does in the training of the child, say until he is fourteen years old, or if he goes through high school, perhaps until eighteen, and then having made this investment, to withdraw all counsel and direction and let him sink or swim as may happen. Society ought still to feel the responsibility, first of canvassing the actual make-up and capacities of that ward of society in order to know where he can count for most, if it were only for an economic reason; and, secondly, of so knowing the lay-out of possibilities in this trade or that, in this profession or that, as to direct the child to the place where he can have the dignity of doing the kind of work for which he is natively and by training fitted. This is the next thing, and this is of course coming. It has come perhaps more fully in the school system in Boston than in any other city in the United States, and has been worked out with great success in Germany. I have no doubt that it will flower out in our midst, and within a very short time Chicago will have the vocational bureau as an addition to our public-school system—a thing to be welcomed by the manufacturer, who would far rather have the capable than the incapable; a thing to be welcomed by the children, who in this way can find the joy of suitable work and adopt an art attitude toward it, doing it because of love of the thing itself rather than as drudgery imposed upon them. A great deal of healthy interest in life and safety for the boys and young men of the future must come by some such experiment.

And the last point that I should like to make is this: Develop the social conscience. It is conceivable that one may attempt a great deal for boys, and may accomplish a great deal, and yet never quite reach the high ground, the highest ground, of actually developing in them a proper social consciousness, so that they do not remain mere recipients of things provided, so that they do not seek just to get good things for themselves, but graduate finally into citizenship in the Republic. That is the goal, the development of high social consciousness. I think this develops in widening concentric circles. I believe that it goes clear back into that initial gang experience of which I spoke: that that, perhaps, is the first significant development of a social sense beyond the nature and confines of the home. Of course, the home produces an ideal condition for developing mutuality, concern for one another, among the members of the family. Then comes the gang, with its more democratic ways, and then refinements of the gang. For instance, today, our school system in Chicago is wrestling with a type of club, a form of the gang, in the school fraternities. Every one recognizes that they are dangerous, and rather drastic measures are being taken to do away with the danger by wiping out the thing itself. I would not dare, with my limited information, to pass any sweeping judgment, but I should like to raise the question whether or not there might possibly be a compromise here likewise and a direction whereby the group that insists on being a group might, through its school life, have the advice, counsel and presence of a responsible teacher or principal. I do not know that they would welcome this, I do not know that they desire this, and it may be that such a proposition is quite apart from the actual situation. But if I could see my way clear to do it, I should try here as everywhere to direct what seems to be a very profound impulse of young people.

Now the highest development of social consciousness does not, as I have indicated, come first. In the little experimenting that I have had in the actual grouping of boys, I have found that their early groups are rather imitative; that such a thing as the Indian wigwam with, of course, its accompanying paraphernalia, will usually have a pretty strong hold upon boys from ten to thirteen. In the next period, fourteen to sixteen, a very successful appeal may be made to the chivalrous instincts of the youth. In regard to the third period in this expansion of social development, I am quite certain that among the boys between the ages of seventeen and twenty the socialization can be made more easily on a civic and deliberative basis, because that is the age of doubt and debate, that is the time when the youth will discuss anything. No proposition can be made to him that is free from question. That is the time to catch him by his civic and deliberative interests; let it take the form of debate, let it take the form of organization. These are some of the stages. And then religion plays its part. I think one can interpret religion, at least from one point of view, as being the highest reach of the social consciousness. And I would, if I had my way, try to bring in as a result of the whole process of club work this final projection of social consciousness; for taking life just as it is, and the temptations just as they are in the city, I have found that those boys are more secure who have some absolute and vertical standards and who after all are not governed entirely by horizontal and mutable standards.

THE CITY CHILD AT PLAY

CHARLES ZUEBLIN
Editor, Twentieth Century Magazine

It is very impressive in the Welfare Exhibit to see a sign saying "Children checked and cared for here." When I first lived in Chicago, children were checked and not cared for. It certainly is an evidence of great progress during this last generation that they can now be both checked and cared for, because, although it is true that the Lincoln Park Board, which is usually a pioneer in keeping up with the course of events, welcomed children, the tendency was in those early days in Chicago to follow the prevailing American idea that the park was a place to be enjoyed only by those who were in advancing years, that children should be permitted simply to visit the parks. That change of attitude is one of the most significant, most beneficial signs of social life. The other side of city life is coming to be realized and recognized, that children should have rights and prerogatives in these things. But we do not have to go very far back to find the time that neither the houses nor the streets nor the parks were planned with any recognition of the children. In fact, the progress of the last ten years has been so speedy that the people who are engaged in making these changes deserve a great deal of credit for the transformation that has been made.

It was as late as 1857, when against the protests of the inhabitants, the park commissioners of New York City had the audacity to establish Central Park. They had a fine perception of the needs of a progressive community when they selected that rocky waste beyond human habitation, as the objectors thought. Now that famous park is located where a million people are within easy walking distance, and Central Park is, indeed, the most appropriately named park in the world.

In Philadelphia we have Fairmont Park. I remember as a boy playing ball there, and I remember the boon it was to the boys who played there, coming from all parts of the city, perhaps three or four miles, to play in the only park in Philadelphia. Located as it was in the northwest corner of the city, a great majority of the inhabitants never used it because they never discovered its location and never knew about it. It is only in these later years that parks have been located and distributed where the people are.

It was in 1866 that the first effort was made in this country to provide public bathing facilities. It was at that time that Boston lifted the embargo on the Atlantic Ocean, which before that time the inhabitants had not been allowed to use for bathing. With that as a beginning other cities located on water fronts have developed public bathing to a greater or less extent. And yet I note by a map of Chicago that in all these years there are only three little places on the twenty-seven miles of lake frontage where it is not indecent to bathe. It is a grave reflection on Chicago that after so many years there has not been more adequate provision made for public bathing.

The city of Milwaukee in 1889, twenty-three years after Boston took that pioneer step, established the first free natatorium in the United States. And it was more than ten years after that, before anything was done in Chicago toward providing such amusement, even in summer.

In 1872, the little town of Brookline, Massachusetts, established a playground. Brookline is a part of Boston, just as Hyde Park is a part of Chicago,

COUNTRY VACATIONS

All Aboard.

The Water's Fine.

From A Wise Man's Will.

"And I devise to children the banks of the brooks, and the golden sands beneath the waters thereof, and the odors of the willows that dip therein, and the white clouds that float high over the giant trees."

From A Real Boy's Letter.

"The country is a good place for baseball if a boy hits a ball it will not break a window or the police will not stop you in the city if you play ball youre going to break a window and if you hit it too hard it might hit someone and you have to pay the doctor bill and besides be put in jail or somewhere else."

but it is divided off into a separate municipality by the curious artificial sort of political institution called the town. It took ten years after this playground was established in Brookline for the news to reach Boston.

It was not until 1893 that a playground was established in Chicago. Before the playground system was begun, it could be said that there were 800,000 people in Chicago living more than a mile from any park. It seems like an incredible situation with a park system inaugurated in 1872, that after twenty years there should be so many people who were not living within a mile of any park. With all the additions of today and with these incomparable playgrounds that have materially changed the conditions, there are still 400,000 people who are beyond the usual radius of these playgrounds.

There are a great many Chicago people who have been resting complacently in satisfaction with their wonderful park system. Is it conceivable that with all these playgrounds that have been established there are still many people who are beyond their reach? Is it conceivable that Chicago should have to be humiliated in discovering these conditions; in seeing that the park system, so beautiful on the map, is yet so inadequate; in realizing that after Chicago has been leading all the cities of the world in the provision of playgrounds, it still occupies such a position? After all these years of agitation we come also to realize that of the several hundred schoolhouses in the city, ten, perhaps, have playgrounds in connection with them. Are we not just beginning to understand the meaning of democracy and just beginning to learn the meaning of play?

In Los Angeles there is a little playground where the responsibility of maintenance is placed upon the shoulders of a husband and wife, who are the physical, social and spiritual parents of the playground. They are paid by the public; they live at the playground and care for the children and are constantly present as the foster-father and foster-mother of the playground; because it is the belief in Los Angeles that while the children are acquiring healthy bodies they must also play under that spirit of democracy that will be beneficial to their spiritual needs. It is of great significance that Chicago should have the foster-father of the playground movement; it was the superintendent of the South Parks, with his associates on the park commission, who introduced into Chicago the fieldhouse, the greatest step that has been taken in twentieth century play and one of the greatest steps ever taken in the provision of public recreation.

In Seattle the playgrounds are established next to the schoolhouses; they are not so ample and not so beautiful as those in Chicago. Yet I am told that there are some very large schoolhouses in Chicago that have sidewalk and yard room sufficient only for the children to stand up comfortably if they do not all happen to be there at the same time.

But playgrounds are being established within reach the children, and I find this true throughout the country, particularly in the smaller cities. There is much interest being shown in the smaller towns from the little village of Winchester, Massachusetts, to Boise, Idaho, and beyond. In the latter city before they have established playgrounds they have secured a human agent to guide the children in their play and in the use of the proposed grounds. They have plenty of ground about Boise, but they have begun to see the need of organized play in definite spots.

Chicago has introduced the playgrounds and the fieldhouses first and is following them by the social center. Therefore, it is coming to be understood what is meant by the true and proper training of children and adults in recreation; we are supplying those who can guide and direct play, and teach people how best to use their leisure.

That leads to one other point I wish to discuss, and that is, how these people may be taught best to use their leisure. There is the training of these children in more than mere play, and in that you will see a necessity for the democracy of the future; you will see in the wise use of leisure a contribution to the whole growth of democracy that will appear in the very fibre of the history-makers of the future. You will see in it the welding of the new generation of American citizens, the many interesting people that compose this homogeneous country, made up to a greater or less extent from all the people of the world. How shall we teach them to use their leisure?

In the institution of these playgrounds and the equipping of the fieldhouses there is needed not only athletics—and that word athletics is used to suggest the ramifications of recreation already recognized—but there should be a moving-picture machine to afford a different kind of recreation. It is said to be an injury to the eyes to look very long at moving-pictures, but one does not have to look at them very long. Moving-pictures should be used in both playgrounds and schoolhouses.

When we come to understand the remote possibilities of recreation, how diversified it can be and should be in all this social work, we will have fully equipped playhouses. We will have a place for the production of the drama, we will certainly have the opera, we will have the finest music, the best that can be provided for the public. After we have learned to provide the people or to allow the people to provide themselves with play in these playhouses and fieldhouses, surely we are not going to lose sight of the drama or of the opera; they will be in every fieldhouse in the Chicago of the future. Because if we are going to learn anything whatever from these new playgrounds except that they were a wonderful inspiration, it must be of what other uses may be made of our leisure.

We must also direct the children in regard to the development of the normal mind. We must give the children an opportunity to come into the world normally and from infancy to have a prolonged education of their physical as well as mental natures; we should develop their constructive as well as recreative sensibilities by training them in such a way as shall produce a normal population that will be capable of evolving the highest type of democracy. In the branch libraries of the fieldhouses, which so happily supplement the public library, we should have a trained public librarian who will be able to direct these children in their reading in the way that will be of the highest benefit to the public service of America, to the best development of democracy. Those librarians should not only administer the libraries for the benefit of the children and adults, but should introduce all sorts of devices to make the libraries interesting and to stimulate the natural instincts of the child, guided by the foster-mother or father of our great institution. If the public is not interested, then we should go out into the byways and hedges and compel it to come in. In the city of Pittsburgh the public library sends out into the private houses at regular intervals, the books, in that way bringing the library into the homes of the people.

The playgrounds in our cities are doing a great work in another direction, that of overcoming the prejudice of nationalities and races. In every neighborhood there is a certain discrimination against the Negro, which is particularly true in the South. But we all know that there are parts of northern cities where the discrimination as to nationality is very strong, and we find in this work that these prejudices are disappearing. We have learned that snobbishness knows no bounds. It is one of the most wonderful things that has been done by the playground, the breaking down of these ridiculous, historical racial distinctions. We are welding the people together as in a great melting pot on the playgrounds of Chicago.

As the patronage of these public playgrounds increases the standards of our children and our school teachers will increase, and we are thereby meeting one of the greatest needs of the time. We should not relax in our compulsory education laws or in seeing to it that the children get these advantages, because they are in demand for the revenues of industrial concerns. The State also needs its dividends, and the greatest of these is the human dividend.

In Boston they established in 1893 a park system of 17,000 acres, which the people rightly thought was a wonderful accomplishment for a metropolitan district of nearly a million and a half, comprising forty different municipalities. Nothing more has been done because they have sat around admiring it ever since. When there was established this comprehensive park system in Chicago in 1872, the same hypnotic effect was felt. The addition of these unique fieldhouses and playgrounds is one of the most wonderful steps of the century, due to the discovery of the inadequacy of the boasted park system. I feel perfectly sure that Chicago is not going to repeat this stupid self-satisfaction; that

Chicago is going to wake up again so that it cannot be said that there are 800,000 people who are beyond the reach of any park, that is to say, outside of the natural radius. The opportunity in Chicago is just as great as it ever was to provide playgrounds wherever needed, and today there is in addition to the recognized need of physical culture on the one hand and social culture on the other, the moral welfare of the young people. This can be cared for only by demanding that these facilities may be available every day of the year. In order that in every community there may be developed the only true kind of democracy, namely, the intelligent co-operation of all the people of a given geographical area, there must be places for the expression of this faith. There are certain geographical divisions within which people will logically co-operate. We shall never have that true democracy until every person in the neighborhood has abolished racial, religious and class prejudice. Then every municipality may be organized for conscious co-operation in satisfying the great functions that other cities have met, for borrowing from each other those facilities which enlarge social life. Chicago lacks nothing now in principle to go ahead and make each one of these centers a real germinating spot of the best type of democracy that we have in this country in the twentieth century.

THE CITY STREET

ALLAN HOBEN

Professor of Homiletics, The University of Chicago

Etymologists are divided as to the derivation of the word "street," but it probably comes from the root that we find in the words "stray" and "strew." If we walk through some of the congested parts of the city, we shall probably see the fitness of "strew"; while, if we are trying to find our way in an unfamiliar neighborhood, the utter lack of street signs will favor "stray." At any rate we are not satisfied, I am sure, with any definition of the street as a merely physical factor in our midst. The street is the real commons and it is psychic. By it every home is extended and in it all homes meet. Especially in those portions of the city where the home is somewhat restricted, does the street become an extension of the home. It is alike the parlor and the playground of the poor. Look at it from the point of view of physical danger, and it is one of the most patent arguments for life insurance; look at it with the hopeful eyes of youth, and it is "Youth's Happy Hunting Ground," as it has been pictured by Jane Addams; look at it from the point of view of amusement, and it is the common theater in which we are both audience and actors. It affects alike the bearing, the manners, the health and the morality of our boys and girls.

In Chicago there is a street and alley mileage of 4,315 miles; the streets proper have a mileage of 2,880 miles. Of this mileage only 1,674 miles are paved; and the unpaved remainder would make a street from here to the city of Boston.

In this wonderful area, which falls to the care of the city, there is necessarily some danger of accidents. Consider, however, these figures taken from the report of the General Superintendent of Police for the year 1910: Street-car accidents caused by alighting from or boarding cars improperly, 1,036, with six fatalities; caused by collisions of cars with wagons, 1,088, with eleven fatalities. These collisions with wagons should not always be charged against the motorman. My own observation of motormen in Chicago is that they are exceedingly patient. We often find, owing to the lack of pavement, that teamsters stick to the street-car tracks to the last possible second and even where the streets are well paved the "track hog" impedes traffic and endangers life and limb. Those run over or struck by street cars numbered 1,074, with 81 fatalities; those knocked off the cars, flipping cars and caught between cars, 771, with 21 fatalities. All street-car accidents for the year 1910 totaled 3,969 and resulted in 119 fatalities.

In railway accidents within the city that have to do with the streets particularly, 237 people were run over, resulting in 114 fatalities; collisions with street cars, wagons, and so forth numbered 123, with 12 fatalities. Accidents on elevated railways numbered 88, with 12 fatalities. The total number of railway accidents was 448, with fatalities of 138.

Accidents due to teams and vehicles were: Persons struck by teams, 1,417, killed 59; struck by automobiles, 998, killed, 52.

Falls on the street and sidewalks numbered 1,254; fatalities, 16. The total number of street accidents during the year 1910 in Chicago amounted to 8,086, total fatalities, 384; the average number of accidents per day was a little over 22; the average number of deaths a little over one for every day of the year.

These figures suggest to some extent the problem of safety for life and limb in the public street; they indicate the toll that we are taking. Undoubtedly those persons who are familiar with the devices and methods used for safety, especially in European cities, would be able to help us out of this deplorable condition.

One is almost disposed, at the risk of seeming to cherish class prejudice, to interpose a remark as to the rights of pedestrians as opposed to the aggressions of automobilists. I am well aware that there are very many considerate people who own automobiles, and I am sincerely impressed also with the fact that there are a great many others who operate "machines" to the very great danger of children and aged people, and who testify with noxious fumes and noise and dust clouds that they practice the might-makes-right policy. The engineers of our railroads are made to go through a long training, and yet the locomotive is restricted in its course; we know where the train will go. But it is not so with an automobile in the hands of raw and unbalanced youth that delights in keeping the muffler "cut out" and in careering around our city streets and corners at terrific speed. The children who are so often on the curb and whose play impulse simply forces them into the street are not safe so long as the reckless driving is permitted. And it is to the credit of our police that they are more and more restraining the "joy rider."

Passing from these obvious dangers to the more general dangers to health, we are glad that no longer the sidewalk is the public cuspidor, and the street the public dustpan, as they used to be. Still, one frequently sees the sweepings going across the sidewalks into the streets. And sad to say, there is a great deal of dry cleaning, which is not cleaning but redistribution of dust in the name of cleaning.

When we see the peddlers going through the streets with their wares exposed to all sorts of germs, when we consider the vast number of unsuccessful provision stores and the constantly rising cost of living, the complexity, expense and waste practiced in getting the food from the fields to the people, we should raise our voices for a series of district markets where the people may buy their supplies in a more convenient, safe and inexpensive way.

One might also say that streets would be made better by a great reduction in street vending among the children, if a law could be enacted that would put into the hands of the board of education, and so virtually into the hands of the teachers of the public schools, the licensing of those who should sell papers, gum and confections in the streets. A great deal of good could be accomplished in this way, and many a physical and moral breakdown could be prevented. Probably it is not fully appreciated how detrimental to health and morality is the work of the newsboy on the street. Out of 200 newsboys of New York who had been in the business for eighteen months and over, 148 had one or more diseases; 73, chronic indigestion; 48, stunted growth; 46, throat trouble. Newsboys, especially those who work at night, are subject to great fatigue, exposure and irregularity. I realize that the newsboy's life has often been painted in glowing colors as a real entrance to the business world; the place where a boy can give proof of his ability. But usually those who are distinctly the newsies of the city have paid the price of precocity and vice and are without qualification to make further progress in life. To be perfectly specific, it is a shocking thing that boys of tender age should be selling the Sunday morning papers in our streets and on our street cars from ten o'clock Saturday night on through the small hours of the morning.

We could also wish that in all our streets we were free from the flying nuisance of smoke. If a man takes a stone and throws it at you and does you any considerable damage so that you can show a black-and-blue spot in the courtroom, or so you can have a doctor come and give you treatment, you seem to have sufficient cause for a damage suit. But a man or a group of men can do you more damage and inflict more pain by the gentle spreading of cinders and soot throughout the city than this other person could by hitting you with a stone, and yet you have, so far as I know, no redress.

Then there is the noise nuisance, which, I think, is dangerous to health and sound nerves. At any rate Chicago is not calculated to improve the American voice. On the down-town streets one needs the sign language or a megaphone to carry on any conversation. How pleased we are just now to learn that the elevated roads are being merged, but we shall be more pleased when they are submerged.

Now as to the danger to morals arising from street conditions: In 1910 there were 1,619 arrests of street walkers in Chicago. Perhaps it will seem to be a bit of hypercriticism for one to suggest, looking at it from the point of view of the street boy, that probably three-fourths of the women on our streets today are doing the boys no good by their general appearance. These women do not deliberately wish to do harm by their present make-up, but at the same time, taking human nature just as it is, to be noticeably stylish right now is to be measurably harmful.

Take another thing upon the city streets: Not only this sex appeal which is unconsciously made by the dress of many of our women, but the endeavor to sell goods is often the undoing of the street boy. The merchant makes a thing look just as you wanted it; he will put it right out in front so you can almost pick it up; he tempts the boy to steal it and the boy does steal it. The crimes of the boys in Chicago are found to be 80 per cent stealing of some kind or another. We throw temptation in the path of the boy who is not yet trained to that right standard of personal property that has been cultivated in our breasts by force of law and custom of long standing, and the boy has to fight against the temptation thus unwittingly placed in his way. The merchant's attempt to sell is often the boy's temptation to steal.

Another matter that enters into the morality of the street is the utter lack in Chicago of public comfort stations. Chicago has imposed upon the downtown stores and public buildings to provide the public with the necessary comforts. The city is absolutely negligent in this respect. The result is that the saloons get probably double and treble the patronage that they would otherwise get. Through the city's neglect the saloon patronage is increased.

I hardly dare speak of the billboards, for there has been so much talk and so much trouble about them in the city of Chicago. Traveling along our streets, instead of viewing green vistas, we have a vast source of information at our command, great splashes of color thrown upon us in every part of the city. Many of the billboards are such as to create wrong impressions in the minds of the young. They are more than the merchandise they advertise and worse than the shows they depict. They are an offense, a scandal, an imposition, a wrong educational device, and a covert for mischief.

Then there is the constant demoralization of dirt. In Chicago the child's hands can never be clean; he always has streaks of dust over his face; he must make an everlasting struggle to be self-respecting. And a child cannot be brought up in the midst of what is ugly and dirty and grimy and be the best kind of a child. It is impossible. Aesthetics lie close to education and morality. The general smudge in which we live is worse for the little girls than for the boys.

The street gang must not be forgotten. The street gang will be found in every neighborhood, running free through the streets and alleys, the boys together encouraged to do without hesitancy things that they would not otherwise contemplate. The influence and spur of the pack is very manifest and often gets the boy into trouble. But like every other power, if it can be given into the hands of a competent leader, it may be made a power for good in moral development and in civic service.

A word or two about the improvements: One thing is that the street must be made to serve the people—all the people. And the street that must serve the most people and that must most serve the people, must have the most care. The street, because it is the extension of our homes, must today serve the life that is forced upon it. If we are true to the principle of the welfare of the children of Chicago, we will see to the adoption of a principle like that, and we must begin in the most needy districts. An attempt to lift must be an attempt to lift by taking hold of the bottom of things. Our streets are nearly all stem and no blossom; they ought to flower out here and there into open spaces. I would have a street that would run along for a little while and then seem to take it into its own hands to branch out into a circle or a semicircle, throwing the buildings back and making an open space. What a different kind of view that would be. If we had only been given the wisdom to have done that when we were making Halsted Street and indeed all the rest of this industrial checkerboard!

In connection with that, it might be noted that we should set aside and properly guard and supervise children's play zones in certain streets. That would be quite possible at certain times in the day, say in the late afternoon after the dismissal of school. Quarantine or set aside by police patrol, chains, or in any way you like, a certain space in the congested districts, and put up signs at the end of the street, "Play Zone, Turn Out." The street is indeed the door-yard of the poor.

I have a few figures, recently compiled, that may be of some interest. Within the past week officers of the Juvenile Protective Association took occasion to travel through certain sections of the city at a certain time in the afternoon for the purpose of observing the number of children playing in the streets. It was found that in seven blocks there were 2,249 children playing in the streets in the afternoon, and in the evening 3,687. The total observation covered eighteen or nineteen blocks with a grand total of 5,936 children. Some of these blocks were exceedingly crowded. For instance, in the three blocks along Halsted Street between Taylor Street and Twelfth Street about four o'clock in the afternoon, 418 children were playing in the street, and in the evening at half-past seven in those same three blocks 744 children. In the district at the corner of Ewing and Desplaines streets the playground was crowded to its full capacity, but there were on the street outside in the afternoon 236 children and in the evening 327. In another section, the block bounded by Division, Dixon, Blackhawk and Holt, in the afternoon after school was out, 386 children of school age were playing in the street. In the evening between half-past seven and eight there were 1,174 children playing with old boards, piles of stone, and anything else they could get hold of. In the evening it was noticed that there were five games of cards on the street, three games of ball, a number of games of craps, and that the boys were grouped around the saloon on the corner listening to the music that came through the open door, and that a great many adults also were grouped around in the street drinking beer. We can take these people in the streets and organize their fun with a little supervision.

One of the things we can do is to teach the children of Chicago to respect the good will of the officers of the law. Since Satan has ceased to figure very largely and since witches are no longer believed in, most families are making use of the policeman for the purpose of frightening their children; and if Johnny does anything that is not right or indicates that he is likely to do anything that is not right he is told that the policeman will come and get him. This is entirely wrong. Through the entire city there is remarkably little done in the way of teaching the children that they should trust the officers implicitly, that the officer is their friend, that he is the one they should go to if in any danger or trouble. These policemen ought to have a good word said for them. During 1910, 639 of them were injured and four were killed in the actual discharge of duty. The police department during the past year cut out of the moving picture films of this city 54,000 feet of bad films.

At the Cripples' School in this city, one of the schools conducted by the Department of Compulsory Education, who is it who carries, day by day, 135 little cripples? It is the blue coats.

At the school, who is it who stands on guard at the corner to see that the children are free from danger? Who is it who sees that they are safely on their way home? It is the blue coat. He is "Daddy" for the whole crowd. That is the spirit that the police will in general show. When we quit lampooning and misrepresenting them, they will respond to the public estimate; and we shall have more of civility upon our streets and a more human interest taken in our boys and girls.

Let us work for a greater and especially for a better Chicago; let us dedicate our streets to the children; let us make the child's welfare the touchstone of our civic life. The wonderful vision which appeared to the Apostle when he was in exile on Patmos was a perfect city coming down from Heaven—a city with streets of pure gold, as it were transparent glass. And that is the place to put your wealth; let humanity walk on it; let it rise on it; and let your wealth be pure from taint, pure as transparent glass. One of the Hebrew prophets saw Jerusalem restored, the old men and the old women sitting in the streets of Jerusalem, every man with his staff in his hand for very old age—"and the streets of the city shall be full of boys and girls playing in the streets thereof."

THE CITY PLAN

CHARLES H. WACKER
President, The United Charities of Chicago

The work of making a comprehensive plan of building the Chicago of the future was formally undertaken by the Merchants' Club of Chicago in 1906, and was continued by the united Commercial and Merchants' Club.

Over four years have been devoted to the preparation of the plan of Chicago. No money has been stinted; the best expert talent obtainable has been at work upon it; and behind this plan, giving their money, time and thought to it liberally, stood, and still stand, not dreamers, but many of our foremost business men.

The result of these efforts is presented in the book called the "Plan of Chicago," known the world over as the most complete, comprehensive and most beautiful book ever published anywhere on city-planning.

This book was presented to the mayor of the city with a suggestion that the council be requested to authorize the appointment of a commission whose purpose as set forth by the mayor was to take up this question so that the whole city might be fully informed regarding the plan and so that an official plan of Chicago might be produced having the endorsement and support of the entire municipality.

This duty, therefore, was imposed upon the Chicago Plan Commission, which was created as a result of this suggestion.

The platform upon which the commission stands then and the task that our fellow citizens will expect us to accomplish is the elaboration of a plan that will have the endorsement and support of the entire municipality.

"To make cities—that is what we are here for. For the city is strategic. It makes the towns; the towns make the villages; the villages make the country. He who makes the city makes the world. After all, though men make life, it is cities which make men. Whether our national life is great or mean, whether our social virtues are mature or stunted, whether our sons are moral or vicious, whether religion is possible or impossible, depends upon the city." So said Henry Drummond.

Senator Burton of Ohio well said:

"The marvelous growth of our cities, the almost instantaneous transition of small villages into flourishing centers of trade and population has intensified these problems.

"Important as is the artistic improvement in itself, it involves, I believe, also in logical sequences, the material development of the city. In all conservatism, I regard this national sentiment for civic betterment as one of the most encouraging and hopeful signs of the time. It predicates the birth of civic patriotism."

What is the object of the Chicago Plan? The object is to direct the future growth of our city in an orderly, symmetrical and systematic way, so that Chicago may attain a metropolitan character and retain her position among the great cities of the world.

The Chicago Plan, aside from its hygienic and aesthetic value in enabling us to develop our city symmetrically and along well planned lines, will produce an actual commercial asset of incalculable value to every citizen, rich or poor.

I was advised not to dwell upon the material side of this project, not to say too much to an audience such as I would meet here about commercial assets of incalculable value, about industrial development, about the fact that the men behind the gun and the power behind the throne are hard-headed business men, although their interests are bound up with the industrial and commercial growth of this city; but I have chosen to disregard that advice, because, as president of the United Charities, I have learned to know, respect and appreciate social and charity workers; because I know history has taught us that a demand for better surroundings, better utilities, better public improvements, better hygienic conditions and more comfort will always follow in the footsteps of increased commercial activity and wealth, and because I know too well that nothing of a substantial and far-reaching nature can be accomplished without means and without money, and that the necessary means will not be forthcoming until we have succeeded in educating the people up to the importance of city-planning and have demonstrated to them that city-planning is basic and co-related with better conditions, both hygienic and aesthetic, and because I know that you are not only willing to teach but also willing to be taught.

What are the main recommendations of the Chicago Plan?

The first step in the work was a study of existing conditions, the general tendency or direction of the growth of the city, and the rate of increase of population. The line of growth was found to be towards the southwest from the site of the original Fort Dearborn, at the mouth of the Chicago River; that is to say, the centers of business and of density of population have been steadily displaced in this general direction, and the center of population today is a little north of the intersection of Halsted and Twelfth Streets.

In regard to the streets, the intention has been, first, to connect in a systematic manner the heart of the city with the surrounding districts, business and residential—and the basis for this is found in the existing diagonal streets, radiating from the city center; second, to free the most densely populated districts of the city from congestion.

It is proposed, therefore, first of all, to widen and develop existing rectangular streets, and secondly, to cut diagonal streets in order to bring the different parts of the city closer together, to shorten the distances and to facilitate the movement of traffic.

The circuit of first importance for immediate relief of the congestion, and one that will be typical of all others to be executed as the city's growth demands, is Twelfth Street, Halsted Street, Chicago Avenue and Michigan Avenue.

(1) Michigan Avenue: This may be called the base line of traffic of the city, and a great development of this avenue is proposed.

(2) Twelfth Street: It is proposed to widen this street from Ashland Avenue to Michigan Avenue in order to bring the West Side people down to the shore of Lake Michigan and to Grant Park. This artery would be supplied with the best possible surface car lines.

(3) Halsted Street: This great business thoroughfare is so situated that its usefulness, already great, might be very much increased. It must inevitably carry an enormous traffic, and is selected as the north and south axial line of circulation.

(4) Chicago Avenue: This avenue, already 100 feet wide, will, if well maintained, serve for a long time for the traffic which it will be made to carry. Connecting as it does with the proposed North and South Boulevard at Pine Street, it will form the fourth side of the rectangle, constituting the first circuit of improvement.

A great park system already exists, encircling

the city on three sides, and along parts of the shore. This system it is proposed to extend and complete by the addition of park lands and parkways on all sides, including a complete development of the shore line, in order to provide adequately for the needs of the growing population, to give the teeming multitude a touch of God's nature, as it were, "within walking distance."

Numerous small parks also are proposed. While the smaller parks require to be artificially created, the larger forest areas proposed already exist and need only be acquired and connected with the city to become at once a part of its life. On the north and west they run along the banks of rivers and through lovely meadows, and on the southwest through beautiful and hilly forest lands.

Let the people of the West Side consider what it will mean to them to have an avenue with the best transportation facilities, running from the forest preserves south of Elmhurst and in part bordering on Salt Creek, comprising between four and five thousand acres of the most beautiful lands near Chicago, to the Lake Front and Grant Park on the east, a distance of about sixteen miles, reclaiming for the people, as it were, beautiful Lake Michigan with its health and pleasure-giving lake front.

There is no doubt in the minds of those who have given the matter thorough study, that it is a practical proposition and if carried out would be an incomparable boon to the entire city of Chicago, particularly to the people who now live in these congested districts and who are in so great need of pure air and sunshine.

In addition to this general scheme, the plan proposes to create a center of administrative buildings, or civic center, on the West Side of the city. A civic center should represent the intellectual and moral quality of the city. A civic center on a proper scale and artistically planned would exert a daily influence, not only upon its citizens, but also upon strangers. As has been well said: "This grouping of the city's buildings forms a rallying place for the city's life. Here the best impulses may crystallize, inspired by the noble character of the edifice, into devoted action for the public good."

The shore of Lake Michigan is regarded as of first importance and has been studied in detail. Already the north shore is being developed in order to secure a complete line of public occupancy of the shore in the near future. Similar steps will be taken by the South Side, as the great need of the population of our city demands that the ownership of, and access to, the shore of the lake be restored to the people.

The plan, of course, proposes that the whole lake front should be converted into a public park. The lake is the chief adornment of Chicago, and its shore is the only place from which Chicago people can get an unobstructed view of it. The Plan says eloquently:

"The lake is living water, ever in motion and ever changing in color and in the form of its waves.

"Across its surface comes the broad pathway of light made by the rising sun; it mirrors the ever-changing forms of the clouds, and it is illumined by the glow of the evening sky.

"Its colors vary with the shadows that play upon it. In its every aspect it is a living thing, delighting man's eye and refreshing his spirit. Not a foot of its shores should be appropriated to individuals, to the exclusion of the people.

"On the contrary, everything possible should be done to enhance its attractiveness and to develop its natural beauties, thus fitting it for the part it has to play in the life of the whole city."

SHOWING THE
CHICAGO LAKE SHORE
AND LOCATION OF
EXISTING
BATHING BEACHES
27 MILES SHORE LINE
ONLY 4 BATHING BEACHES
CHICAGO
PROTECTING
HER LAKE FRONT
FROM THE
CHILDREN

Why should not these recommendations be acted upon without any further procrastination or delay? "Because there are," as Dr. Charles E. Eliot says, "three obstacles which prevent the prompt execution of the needed public works":

(1) "The absence of a well-informed, benevolent and urgent public opinion on the subject.

(2) "The prevailing distrust of existing municipal governments, a distrust founded on their demonstrated business incapacity.

(3) "The failure of the common methods of local taxation to produce an adequate revenue for municipal purposes.

"It appears, then, that reform in the laying out of American cities must, in general, wait for the coming of two other great reforms: First, for municipal reform; second, for the reform of the existing methods of local taxation.

"Every successful effort in favor of municipal, or tax-law reform, will tell towards the physical and moral improvement of American cities; but in the meantime the men and women who appreciate what immense losses of life, health, happiness and industrial effectiveness are due to the bad planning, or not planning, of American cities, must do their best to enlighten the public on the whole subject.

"One good way is to study and publish a good plan for an actual city, as public-spirited people have already done in the case of Chicago, San Francisco and Boston.

"Another way is to lay before the American public the facts about the provisions for the public health and happiness made in Paris, Naples, Rome, Budapest, Berlin, London, Edinburgh, Glasgow and many smaller European cities, which already possess sound municipal administrations, rational taxation methods and just powers of eminent domain.

"Democratic America is far behind Europe in providing effectively for the health and happiness of the urban part of its population."

We have published—so we consider—a good plan for our city, and we now propose to lay the facts before the people in an honest, broad and comprehensive way, whereby we hope to secure for our project, not only a benevolent, but an aggressively urgent public opinion, without which we can never hope to succeed in a country governed like ours.

It has been stated at different times that the plan is not a practical one and is not democratic enough; that it is a "visionary plan" and a "dream." All progressive men have, however, at some time or other, been dubbed dreamers and all monumental undertakings have been called dreams.

Have the pessimists ever accomplished any great constructive work? Is it a sign of strength to doubt your own power and your own possibilities?

The optimist is the man who pushes ahead himself, his business, his community.

Is the World's Columbian exposition of 1893 now thought of merely as an artist's dream? All realize that the world's fair of 1893 was the greatest reality ever achieved by any American city, and that the benefits derived from it and the fame thus won for our city was the best and most permanent investment the city of Chicago has ever made, intellectually, morally and financially.

But it is a "picture plan," they say. Yes, it is a picture plan. Just such a picture as our splendid new hotels present in comparison with the old Tremont House—which was good and sufficient in its day—as the new City and County buildings appear compared with the former ones, as the new Northwestern Railroad Station compares with the old one, and as the modern bank and office buildings compare with those of former years. Such a picture is the Plan of Chicago, a picture of progress, convenience, symmetry and good order.

We cannot afford longer to grow in haphazard fashion. A distinguished and competent foreign visitor to Chicago said recently: "Chicago appears to be an overgrown collection of villages, and its arrangement is worse than the antiquated cities of Spain."

We cannot afford to leave it to a few wealthy land owners and speculators to decide for us how our city is to grow; we cannot afford any longer to waste wantonly huge sums of money for ill-considered improvements.

In the twenty-five years ending in 1906, there has been spent of the taxpayers' money for extraordinary betterments and improvements over $222,000,000, and what have you to show for it, except an ill-planned, haphazard and disjointed city?

Do you, as citizens, believe that this will do for the future? Do you believe that the success of a Marshall Field's or of a Hull-House was attained without the minutest planning? Is there any big, live business, philanthropic, or charitable institution today which has not a plan for future growth and expansion? Why not also this city, the biggest organization of all?

Even though no plan has yet been adopted, the good effect of this work is already evident. There is a tacit understanding that no important public work of any kind shall be undertaken without reference to the Chicago Plan Commission.

Already the Sanitary District of Chicago, the Board of Local Improvements, the Chicago Harbor Commission, the South Park Board, the City Council Committee on Pleasure-Piers and Bathing-Beaches are working in perfect harmony with the Chicago

Plan Commission. Can the value to the city of Chicago of such co-operation be overestimated?

We want to economize in our expenditures; we want to obtain the greatest and best results at the least possible cost; the only way to do it is by the adoption of a plan making each improvement, each new step forward under that plan a component part of the whole.

Now is the time to consider and adopt such a plan. I am glad that it was not done before, because, if we are dubbed "dreamers" today, what would have happened to any man, twenty or thirty years ago, who dared to predict that Chicago would, within a measurable time, become a city of many millions of inhabitants, and what would they have done to a man who had the temerity to propose at that time such a plan for the future?

A plan is a paying investment; it will bring you two dollars for every dollar invested. In this connection let me tell you this: In the sixty days of June and July of the year 1909, 17,343 Americans registered at the twenty-five leading hotels in Paris. Let us assume that the hundreds of other hotels in Paris housed only 10,000 more. Supposing that each one of these spent only 300 francs, this makes $1,640,000 spent by Americans in Paris in two months, for hotels alone, and add to this, expenses in restaurants, cab and amusements, and the total expenditure by Americans in two months in Paris will exceed $2,000,000. In this estimate no account is taken of the purchase of clothing, jewelry, objects of art and other things, which our countrymen buy in abundance every year. These figures were collected and published by a French newspaper in Paris on August 1, 1909.

We want some of this business; we want to be put in shape to attract visitors; we want to make our city healthy and comfortable, and no other city in the world has a better chance to do it, if only we adopt a plan. It cannot be done in a day; it will take years, but there must be a beginning.

It took the city of Paris fifty-seven years to develop fully the plans of Baron Haussmann, which made Paris the most beautiful city in the world. Was that a paying investment? It must have been, for on December 26, 1909, the Paris Chamber of Deputies ordered a municipal bond issue of $180,-000,000 to carry out a new scheme of improvements for the city, which it will take fifteen years to complete. The Frenchman is not a spendthrift. After paying to Germany, since 1870, a war tax of 1,000,-000,000 francs, France is today one of the wealthiest countries of the world.

It is surely well for us to look around and see what others are doing. The business man who will not follow the march of progress and who thinks that what was good enough yesterday will also be good enough tomorrow, will soon be left behind and crowded out.

Germany has in the last forty years achieved a leading position in the world, in science, industry, commerce and wealth, and nobody realizes better than the business and professional man, the world over, that this position has been attained only by far-sighted planning and conscious development to attain ends deliberately aimed at.

Berlin, a city of the same size as Chicago today, has, since 1872, grown even faster than the city of Chicago, and is now considering the adoption of plans based upon an estimated population of ten million people; and the time for realizing this project is set at sixty to seventy years.

We have not, since the fire of 1871, grown any faster than the beautiful, well-regulated and well-ordered city of Berlin has grown since the Franco-Prussian war of 1870-1871, but we have grown aimlessly and without a plan, in strong contrast to the symmetric and carefully laid out development of the city of Berlin.

The following quotation is of interest in this connection: "The amount of money spent in the city of New York by visitors every year has now reached a point where it surpasses the estimated cost of the Panama Canal."

In the month of November alone New York entertained nearly two million visitors, which is double the figures of last year. Calculating that the average visitor spends at least $50, the income to the city from this source accordingly amounted to $100,000,000 in one month. Money spent in that way benefits the entire city, rich and poor.

The Palisades Park Commission of the state of New York was created in the year 1900 for the purpose of developing a great park system along the shores of the Hudson River, easily accessible to those who lived in congested quarters in New York City. Mrs. Harriman has given ten thousand acres of land in Orange and Sullivan counties, New York, to be used for playgrounds and parks, and also $1,000,000 for their proper maintenance; and the Governor of New York has recommended the enlargement of the functions of the Palisades Park Commission so as to include the management of the land donated by Mrs. Harriman.

Our aim is to secure the forest preserves and develop the lake front for exactly the same purposes.

The city of Cleveland, Ohio, with its 600,000 inhabitants, is expending about $19,000,000 for a new civic center with an esplanade leading down to the lake front. St. Louis recently issued $11,200,000, with its primary object to supply the city with a plan that will, to some extent, direct its future development along right lines.

Can Chicago afford to do nothing? Fifteen cities in the United States, such as Pittsburgh, St. Louis, St. Paul, Buffalo, Washington, San Francisco, Denver, Columbus and Indianapolis, are preparing city plans, and propose to make radical rearrangements in order to create civic centers, while forty-eight more are working on general schemes of improvement.

Chicago has surely no disposition to ignore the example, based upon the experience of ages, set by foreign cities in this respect. Nor can she afford to disregard the examples set by her more enterprising, more up-to-date sister cities of the United States.

The city of London is today paying dearly for its refusal to carry out, although they had been adopted by the municipality, the far-sighted plans of Sir Christopher Wren, after the destructive fire in 1666. The men of 1666 in London were not big enough to see the advantages of a city plan, and lost the golden opportunity then at hand. It will now cost the city of London millions where it would have cost them only hundreds, if the mistake then made can ever be rectified at any cost.

Is Chicago to make the same error, or has she misgivings as to her future?

We have today an area of 191 square miles within the city limits; we have 4,200 miles of streets; 1,500 miles of sewers and fifty miles of boulevards; we have 22,000 manufacturing plants in Chicago, with an invested capital of $700,000,000. With these figures in mind, is it not probable that it will pay to plan for future growth and expansion?

This is not a plan for the rich and aristocratic; they can get beauty and comfort and health without a city plan, in their homes in the city as well as in the country. This plan is primarily for the benefit of those who cannot afford to leave the city and who cannot afford to get privately that which this plan proposes to give to every inhabitant of the city of Chicago, rich or poor.

Mr. H. Inigo Triggs, in his book on "Town Planning," says:

"Everybody desires to live in a clean and beautiful town, and if the authorities can provide such surroundings, they not only benefit the inhabitants, but also attract new residents from other places.

"The efforts of municipalities should not be confined to matters of hygiene alone, but should be directed toward providing everything possible to relieve the dull monotony of the town by creating and preserving the spots of beauty, by providing not only wider streets, but better open squares and places.

"In a word, the more agreeable the town is made, the greater is the probability of its becoming a self-contained borough possessing every means of satisfying the moral, intellectual and physical demands of its inhabitants."

In making our plan and in executing it, we must have regard for the feelings of the taxpayer; in other words, for our own feelings.

The greatest stumbling-block in the way of carrying out great plans for the future in a community like ours is the financial question; but I have such faith in my fellow-citizens of Chicago that I believe if we can but educate them and show them the advantages of this plan, they will not only permit us to put it through, but they will arise and demand that it be done with the least possible delay. They will understand that conditions of today in city life are not what they were thirty or forty years ago, and that new and serious problems have arisen.

At the time of the Civil War only three per cent of the population of the United States lived in cities, while at present forty-two per cent are living in cities, and twelve per cent in three cities—Chicago, New York and Philadelphia. In the past the problem confronting the people in rapidly growing cities was to provide pure water, adequate schools, and public institutions for both the sick and the improvident. The problem of our great cities today, and for generations to come, is to provide light, air, ample means for healthful recreation, relief from congestion, better transportation to the multitudes congregating in our cities, better facilities for housing the poor, and more attractive surroundings.

The industrial development of the age, the expansion and perfection of means of communication, the invention of farm machinery, which upon the farm, in a marked degree, has replaced manual labor—these developments are among the underlying natural causes for the concentration of the population in cities.

The same growth of the cities also obtains in Europe. And it is a matter of government record in those countries where conscription to army service is compulsory, that the physique of the city dwellers is degenerating, so that only a relatively small percentage of those living in congested cities are found to conform to the strict requirements for military service.

During the Spanish-American War, our War Department became truly alarmed at the number of young men who could not pass muster. The same fact has alarmed Germany, and there is now on foot in that country a country-wide movement, intelligently and systematically directed, to work out proper city plans for betterment of present conditions and for future growth.

At the time of the Boer War, England also found that only a small percentage of recruits to the army offering themselves from the large cities were physically fit for service.

Nature has been good to Chicago in laying at our door that vast reservoir of pure air, pure water and health—Lake Michigan—and in giving us a territory for expansion without natural limits.

These two factors alone, without the aid of intelligent human planning, have given this city next to Milwaukee the lowest average death-rate of all large cities in the United States, and one of the lowest of all cities in the world.

Nature has richly endowed us with possibilities for making our city the best, healthiest and most beautiful of all cities, if only we get together and adopt a plan for the development of the existing natural conditions and possibilities surrounding us.

There is no doubt that with a better understanding of the project, it will be realized that there is absolute necessity for planning for the future growth and expansion of a city which has grown in seventy-five years from a village of ten houses to a metropolitan city of nearly 2,250,000 people—an increase of 2,000,000 since the great fire of 1871.

Now, why should those who have made it their life task to extend a helping hand to the unfortunate ones, to elevate the downtrodden and to take sunshine into the homes of those whose lives are dark and dreary, why should they fall in line behind this plan and assist in every way possible to crystallize in its favor a public opinion so strong as to force the authorities to act?

Because they, of all others—and I feel justified in modestly including myself in the number—know fully the value of expert educational and systematic work.

In order to show how closely interwoven and how related are the efforts of the Chicago Plan Commission in bringing about a clearer understanding of its aims and policy and the efforts in the field of charity to educate the people to a better understanding, I may be permitted to diverge a little from my topic.

We must teach our citizens to realize the truth of what Mr. Harry A. Wheeler recently said at a meeting of the Citizens' Committee in favor of the United Charities of Chicago:

"Now, logically, is this money being gathered as an undeserved sum begged from the business community, or as an amount due from the business community as a legitimate tax? Human life is the price paid for industrial progress, and it is more exacting and terrible in its consequences than war itself.

"In this country alone 35,000 human beings sacrifice their lives on the altar of business, and additional to those, 2,000,000 annually suffer permanent or temporary disability for the same cause.

"Trailing in the wake of this great army are the innocent women, children and aged, robbed of support and thrown upon a merciless public, not of their own volition, but because industry has taken away the bread winner or deprived him of his ability to provide.

"These appalling figures form the unanswerable contention that if through industrial advancement great suffering is caused, then out of the surplus of industrial earnings may rightly be demanded an amount sufficient to relieve in some measure this suffering."

The minds of our American fellow citizens should be impressed with the truth of the statement made by Professor Charles R. Henderson:

"It is also difficult in American cities to secure a sufficient number of friendly visitors to render the most effective service. In Berlin the municipal authorities can secure over three thousand men to visit the indigent families, because it is a civic duty and men lose certain political rights who refuse to act.

"If our men and women knew the value of this kind of service many hundreds would volunteer."

The community should realize that if the poor among our citizens did not help each other to a very remarkable extent, chaotic conditions would exist.

The rich must be made to understand that signing checks for the poor is not enough; that they have not performed their full duty by sending a check; that money alone will not accomplish their ends, nor will work without money; but that brains, work and money are the requisites necessary to produce the results which we are striving so hard to accomplish.

It is a pity that our laws do not, like the German laws, make it an unshirkable duty, punishable by disfranchisement, to neglect or to refuse to perform such duties to the unfortunate and deserving poor in their respective communities.

We must teach the people that promiscuous giving does more harm than good, that the essential features of modern charity are investigation, co-operation, and registration of relief for guidance, in order to prevent duplications and impositions, and that these principles must be strictly adhered to.

We must teach them, also, that there is much more work to do; that there are many problems, hitherto touched upon but superficially, such as infant welfare, wife desertion, vagrancy, regulation of bakeries and tenement houses, the establishment of municipal lodging houses for women, and problems of a similar nature, which need exhaustive study and thorough treatment.

We must make it clear that it is the duty of organized charity, by careful investigation, to ascertain the causes of distress, suffering and misfortune, to spread broadcast the information so obtained, to suggest remedies that indicate to what extent the government may justly be called upon to make private charity unnecessary, to demand the necessary legislation for relief. And let us hope the day is not far distant when every good citizen will consider it his or her duty to agitate until this is brought about.

Now what must the Chicago Plan Commission do?

We must demonstrate that the Chicago Plan is basic; that it is an indispensable permanent foundation for an orderly arrangement of the future growth of our city along lines dictated by the natural conditions surrounding us. A scientifically and carefully worked out plan should not be changed in its essentials, but hygienic measures must of necessity keep pace with advanced knowledge resulting from scientific research.

Upon this foundation then, can we build further by the adoption of such hygienic and philanthropic measures as our changing conditions may demand from time to time, and as scientific research along these lines and our constantly advancing knowledge of human nature and human needs may prescribe.

The Plan Commission must educate the people up to the conviction that it is not a Plan for the rich, that it is a Plan for the whole people and particularly for those who cannot afford to go elsewhere in search of recreation; that the Plan, first of all, will reclaim for the people the shores of Lake

Michigan, will give them more convenient and more direct transportation, and will, in short, make our city more healthy, more comfortable and more attractive.

The Plan Commission must show that this Plan will concern itself with the rearrangement of streets and arteries of traffic, where that is demanded by intolerable conditions of congestion or inconvenience, for congested districts are the hot-beds of vice, sickness and misery; it must further lay down a plan for the growth of the city, its park areas, small parks, playgrounds, bathing-beaches, recreation piers and boulevards along proper lines; but, as I have already stated, it cannot enter into administrative functions such as the inauguration of hygienic measures or measures for the amelioration of living conditions of our people, which should be left to the experts for study and recommendation and to the proper authorities for execution.

It seems to me that such meritorious questions as the proper regulation of tenements and the housing of the poor are in themselves important enough to demand special consideration as separate and distinct measures, and no one has yet said that the adoption of a plan for the city of Chicago, as here outlined, will in any way conflict with such worthy measures of relief. On the contrary, the execution of this Plan will mean better air, better light and more breathing places for the poor.

Let us, therefore, work and agitate for the adoption of the Plan now being considered by the Chicago Plan Commission.

Let us, also, join hands and work for the betterment of our city in every other way—and I believe that we can do it much better when that great fundamental Plan is ours. Let us join forces with those who predict that Chicago's future will be even greater than her past; that this city, the capital of the Middle West with its 60,000,000 people, will ere long step forward into the place for which nature has destined her, and become the most convenient, the most healthful, and the most beautiful city on the American continent.

PART NINE

THE UNCOMPLETED TASK

"Thither our path lies"

THE VISION SPLENDID

HARRIET H. McCORMICK

You must, I am sure, sympathize with me in my embarrassment because of Miss Addams' very, very kind words. In spite of the fact that my name is written in such large characters outside the Coliseum, I do not consider myself the chief speaker this evening, and I will only detain you for a very few moments.

Madam Chairman: Fine as are our agencies seeking to meet the wants of children, this Exhibit impresses our minds with the fact that they are pitiably inadequate. The idea to be kept ever prominent before the public has been that the sum total of child welfare work *being done* in Chicago, when set over against the tremendous total of *need for it,* presents such a disparity in size that every person seeing it goes away with a sense of humiliation and shame, and not of complacency. The idea of emphasizing the lack of welfare service for children by showing what is *being* done, and comparing it with what is *not being* done, has been prominently brought out in the exhibits in the several sections.

Now that we know the evils, now that we know what is undone for children, we cannot stand still. We are caught in the rushing stream of awakened public opinion. Our civic conscience is stirred as never before. Justice and common-sense must now direct our energies, and we must concentrate our efforts upon our youngest citizens. What avail our plans for the new Chicago if we have forgotten to plan for the children? What avails Chicago's boastful "I will" if we shut our eyes and our ears to the cry of the children? Let us fling wide our banners, let us never pull down our colors, never lower our standards of citizenship: until then, and not until then, shall come the vision of that real City Beautiful, when young and old may say: "I am a citizen of no mean city."

As to how the efforts in this Exhibit may be most effectively connected with the future program for child welfare in Chicago and the country as a whole, I leave it for others to discuss who are better qualified than I am to speak on the subject. And one word about those others. Miss Addams—and what is not Chicago's debt to Miss Addams?—Mr. Kingsley, Mr. Allinson, Mr. Burchard, Miss Breckinridge, Mrs. Jerome, who has marshaled twenty-seven thousand children in and out of that court during this past two weeks, Mrs. Blaine, who has been the Chairman of the Administrative Committee; and so on, and so on. May I remind you that this undertaking would not have been possible if they had not put their minds and bodies and souls into the gigantic task of preparing, inside of two months and ten days, this Child Welfare Exhibit and of making it such a splendid step forward?

And before I take my seat I want to call your attention to the leaflets which have been prepared under Mrs. Blaine's direction with the co-operation of the chairmen of the various departments. If you have not already secured a set of these leaflets, I hope you will take the time when you leave Grace Church to step into the Coliseum and get copies of them. They are a most wonderful, a most remarkable contribution towards the needs of our city.

UNTO THE LAST

ANITA McCORMICK BLAINE

"I was an hungered, and ye gave me meat: I was thirsty, and ye gave me drink: I was a stranger, and ye took me in; naked, and ye clothed me: I was sick, and ye visited me: I was in prison, and ye came unto me."

"Inasmuch as ye have done it unto one of the least of these my brethren, ye have done it unto me."

You have done it unto the whole world.

We all belong to each other—the children belong to us—every one—and we to them. There is not one that is not ours—not one that may not look to us for care and love. We have been caring for them all, and loving them all, in these last days. We have been walking with them through the valley of the shadow of death.

We have been trying to prepare the table in the presence of their enemies.

The oil has been poured—their cup we have been trying to fill. May goodness and mercy follow them that they may dwell in the house of the Lord!

How has this been? By the munificent gift of one, and by the lavish, prodigal outlay of time and strength and thought, and also of means, of two thousand—aye, of many more—we of Chicago have found ourselves possessed by the great opportunity of the great exhibit whose slaves we have been.

Originally in New York, someone thought of a child and wished to show one good thing that might be his —planning to make a Sunday School exhibit. Another laid hold on this thread and found it leading to every good that a child might have. All of New York was aroused, and the result was the Exhibit which chained the attention of the whole country to what it was showing. Its waves reached Chicago and the offer of New York to send it to us—which seemed too much to hope to accept—till the word came from Mrs. Cyrus McCormick of her purpose to carry the whole. The load of the burden of means lifted, the work set off apace to find the ways. It needed to set off apace for there was not a moment to lose.

The story of its accomplishment from then till now is the story of one concerted effort and achievement, of knowledge, skill, energy, strength and time—not forgetting patience—all buoyed up by the one great purpose of heart and brain.

Falling heir to the stimulating opportunity of what New York had achieved, Chicago set herself to add in like kind for the instruction of her own sons and daughters. She bounded forward like a steed let loose, in the lines laid out by New York so ably, and carried her part as far along the track as she could, in the short time at her command.

The great whole that Chicago has been able to present in adding her own to New York's will make a standard for the whole world that will never be lowered, for thought on children and their care. The achievement of this purpose has given to Chicago an illustration of the power of highly concentrated and entirely concerted effort, which must react in the conduct of all of the affairs of our city.

Why has this been done? Just for one reason. Everyone has loved a child and everyone expands to the extreme of his powers in the thought of a child's maltreatment or neglect by malice or by ignorance.

There is nothing that we would not do to save the children.

This great moment in the history of our city records our love of them forever.

All have poured of their nectar into this great fountain and all have drunk of its inspiration, each in his own kind.

To know all that this moment has meant would be to see a gem with as many faces as the one thousand and one Arabian Nights.

We have given to the children. Is that aught compared with what we have gotten from them as they have surged in and out of the Coliseum—transformed as it has been by them in its lovely setting?

Can anything we have given, compare with the inspiration we have drunk deep of, as they have opened their throats and their hearts in song—thousands together?

We can give to them, but not so much as they can give to us—for that is—Heaven.

"Except ye become as a little child" has rung through and through us, as we have gone in and out amongst them, uplifted by them.

And while we have been asking questions for them and their welfare, we have had questions from them asked of us.

Wherein have we too greatly left them in the development we call our civilization?

Is there not between us and them a chasm which is wholly false?

In our adult development, do we not break with them at some point wrongly?—and instead of going over in a broader, greater road, do we not go off the track into a mistaken path?—and then lure them in turn from their divinities?

Heaven grant, if this be so, we may return and become again of them and in one growth go forward together.

For them, in the questions we have been asking, we have found a wealth of misery and mistake and waste. For them we have been unearthing the conditions of their lives as they are found in the city—in their homes—on the streets—in their schools and libraries—in their play hours—as deadly disease may strike them and hold them—and how, when they go to their work, they may be ground between the wheels of industry—and how, when their natural protectors fail them, they are wisps on the surface of conflicting and confusing currents, swept hither and thither we hardly know how or where.

We have asked what our laws are doing to protect them.

And we have seen where the smiling and sweet face of philanthropy appears between all these bars to shed the ray of light and hope.

The deep question that confronts us, in all of this view, is the deepest question for our country. Wherein have we departed from the fundamental idea of our democracy that all are born to equal opportunity?

It is in the thought of the children that this questions presses home most deeply. We do not surmise. We *know* that it cannot be right nor necessary that human beings brought into this world should, for their beginnings and growth and development, exist under the two extremes of every benefit, and of none. We have cherished a fond belief in our country that these extremes were not so extreme as in other countries—and in comparison with some others this is surely so. We may take heart and courage and cling to the thought of our public schools, free to all. But have we not rested too long in this pride and satisfaction? We must see all the facts and we must realize the dire needs for the children that have been shown us in this Exhibit.

The settlement of the economic question, as to how much more one parent should be able to do for his child than another, is a difficult thing. Even if the question could be surely answered, the bringing about a solution is a more difficult thing.

The right care of our children here and now will not wait for such far-off solution of intricate problems. We know that they are being daily ground between the wheels—caught in the meshes—hurt—stunted—injured irreparably—killed. We know that they are helpless to save themselves—and, under the conditions, their parents are helpless to save them. It is upon us who see, and all who govern our communities, to act for them.

We must take such agencies as we have and must make effective the means of saving our children's lives and minds and souls,—of making it true that a free chance is offered to all—in securing to all the prime common needs.

And in the doing of that plain duty—by infusing imagination, we may do more and make life beautiful as well as possible for them, and let them not only grow, but grow in a garden.

Is it hopeless? It cannot seem so after this Child's Welfare Exhibit. If this means anything to Chicago, it means that the unexpected can be attained by the right effort.

And that brings out the question of the evening—what next?

The power, the vision, the attainment of this Child Welfare Exhibit must not be lost—cannot be lost.

We cannot jump at once at how they will focus—in just what directions they will proceed—it would be perhaps a mistake to do so too quickly.

We know that good has gone into the life of our city and that out of it will come corresponding and beautiful results.

From our dwelling in the thought of Chicago's 640,000 children and Chicago's care of them, we know that the first need is to attain a high standard of doing the public business. The public must reach the actual result of seeing that the only legal building in which children may be housed is a sanitary one and that the conditions about the home are sanitary, too—

That there is space enough left free to enable the children to play safely;

And we must reach the point in our educational thought of holding this play, in organized play places, as a part of our educational system and a part as important as any other;

That libraries belong to the children, as well as to adults, and since they cannot come to the one center, centers must go in sufficient numbers to them;

That the schools are manned with the ablest possible people to do the highest work in our republic—build citizens for the future!

That in the menace to health in the aggregation of people in vast numbers in a great city, public health measures are fully carried out;

That in the exigencies of life, leaving children in the hands of the public, the public is equal to the responsibility and is ably equipped to conserve those children, many of whom have in them the making of the best citizens;

And that the laws are equal to all these situations—to fortify them by their provisions and their enforcement.

We know, too, from our study, that until the city shall do all of its part ably, philanthropy must step in and e'en do the public business. But when the city is equal to its noble task, then may philanthropy take the gentler part of holding up the feeble hands and cheering the downcast and strewing flowers in a thousand ways in the lives of people.

Cannot the city of the future—and is that not, for one, Chicago?—place these works for children as high ideals and so lift the public service all to the plane on which it should be?

Can we not co-operate with the city to that end?

If so, we shall indeed have the City Beautiful which we have been working forward to. And in its streets and in its playgrounds will stream happy, cared-for children—all looking forward to making cities beautiful and homes beautiful of their own.

And in those streets we shall remember and ever more remember the streets of our Child Welfare Exhibit, where our children sang us into a higher sense of our responsibilities and opportunities.

INDEX

(Wherever a reference runs over more than one page, the first page only is indicated.)